The Wounded River

The Civil War Letters of
John Vance Lauderdale, M.D.

John Vance Lauderdale c. 1861

The Wounded River

The Civil War Letters of
John Vance Lauderdale, M.D.

Edited by Peter Josyph

Michigan State University Press
East Lansing
1993

All Michigan State University Press books are produced on paper which meets the requirements of American National Standard of Information Sciences— Permanence of paper for printed materials. ANSI Z39.48-1984

Michigan State University Press
East Lansing, MI 48823-5202

Printed in the United States of America

00 99 98 97 96 95 94 93   2 3 4 5 6 7 8 9 10

Library of Congress Cataloging-in-Publication Data
Lauderdale, John Vance.
   The Wounded River: The Civil War Letters of John Vance Lauderdale, M.D./ edited by Peter Josyph.
      p.   cm.
   Includes bibliological references and index.
   ISBN 0-87013-3328-4(alk. paper)
   1. Lauderdale, John Vance—Correspondence. 2. United States—History— Civil War, 1861-1865—Medical care. 3. United States—History—Civil War, 1861-1865—Personal narratives. 4. Physicians—United States— Correspondence. I. Josyph, Peter. II. Title.
E621.L38 1993
973.7'75'092—dc20
                                                            92-56859
                                                                CIP

All photographs and drawings are reprinted with permission of Yale University, Beinecke Rare Books and Manuscripts Library, Yale Collection of Western Americana.

To Mom,
the best there is.

We mustn't speak hit or miss about affairs of olden days.

— Layman P'ang

Contents

Acknowledgements   ix

Textual Note   xi

Part I: The Seat of War

Introduction   3

The Letters   41

Part II: Bellevue

Introduction   143

The Letters   147

Part III: The Devil and Mr. Lincoln

Introduction   177

The Letters   181

Appendix A

Walter Lauderdale on the Draft   191

Appendix B

The Plantation Letters of Willis and
   Samuel Lauderdale   193

Notes   207

Bibliography   229

Index   235

Acknowledgments

Organizations which have been helpful during the preparation of this book include Yaddo; the Millay Colony for the Arts; the Virginia Center for Creative Arts; the Alden B. Dow Creativity Center; the New York State Council on the Arts; the Huntington Township Arts Council; the Suffolk County Medical Academy; the Smithtown Township Arts Council; Imaginarts; and the Pollock-Krasner Foundation. Individuals whose support and assistance are greatly appreciated include Ferenc and Clara Gyorgyey; Rick and Rowena Wallach; Nancy and Gus Gerstman; Nick and Rita Lenn; Ron D'Alessandro; Norman Marin; Richard Soden; Mel Bartholomew; Myra Sklarew; Charlie Bergman; Janet Selzer; Dr. Donald Kitzis; Dr. Martin Fausold; Lorinda Klein; David W. Parish; Alan Hawke; Bruce Kersten; Lori Misura; Earle Hyman; Justina Laniauskas; Philly and Joe Viola; Michele Brangwen; and Kevin Larkin.

Special thanks to Vance Lauderdale Jr. for his kind permission to publish his grandfather's letters; to George Miles, curator of the Western Americana Division of the Beinecke Rare Books and Manuscripts Library, Yale University; to Norma Cohen, executive director of the Smithtown Township Arts Council, the organization which, above all others, has been instrumental in obtaining invaluable assistance; to Ed and Lisa Scott, whose kind hearts and Imaginarts enabled me to see what I was doing; to Fred Bohm and Julie Loehr, for editorial patience and expertise; to all those who encouraged, inspired, and assisted me throughout; and most of all to Barbara Mann, for helping to keep me alive.

Textual Note

Most of the correspondence is written in brown or black ink, sometimes in pencil, on sturdy paper, generally around 16" x 10" folded in half to make four 8" x 10" sides, or around 10" x 8" folded to four 5" x 8" sides. If a sheet is ruled, it is generally a faint blue line on only one side. JVL's experiment with onion skin, which a stationer had advised him would bear writing on both sides, proved a disaster that was, at least, mercifully brief. At some point, probably as late as the 1920s, when he indexed his vast store of letters and collected them together with other printed memorabilia, JVL appears to have bound the correspondence by taping the letters to larger sheets of paper and taping the sheets into the stubs of a series of thick letterbooks. Although the letters have been disassembled, some remain inseparable from their sheets or from each other, and the tape (or its imprint) has left a legacy of unwanted margins obscuring the final half-inch of countless lines which can only be read by shining a light through the page and decoding the word in reverse from the opposite side.

I have, as well as I could determine it, retained practically all of JVL's spelling and capitalization, although some questions of capitals call for guesswork, and others more suggest a quirk in penmanship than a conscious choice for the sake of form or expression. There is also ambiguity with respect to marks which may be periods, commas, dashes, or space-saving indications of paragraphs. In deciding these cases, I have tried to remain conservative. Occasionally, for clarity and/or convenience of reading, I have made minor modifications in JVL's punctuation, chiefly in cases where sentences lack periods or initial caps to set them apart from the next sentence. I have italicized the names of boats, books, and journals, even when the names given by JVL may not be strictly accurate. My own guesses at dubious words are bracketed with a question mark preceeding them, and guesses at meanings of words (or abbreviations) follow in brackets with a question mark after the guess. Missing or indecipherable words are so indicated.

In a few rare instances, JVL added a clarifying word or phrase at a
later date, either by writing it over the text in question, or by noting it
on another part of the page. Whenever it has been useful and not disruptive to do so, I have silently added these, and have added a few others with or within qualifying notes. All of my own additions or
comments are in brackets.

Part I presents a selection from nearly all available letters written by
JVL aboard the *January*, with most of the letters appearing complete.
Deletions from the sum of a text—in Part I, mostly brief sections of gos-
sip on family and friends—are denoted by points of ellipsis. The letters
in Parts II and III are only a sampling of the many which were written
in those periods, and the majority of these selections are only excerpts
from much longer letters.

The John Vance Lauderdale Papers are in the Yale University Western
American Collection at the Beinecke Rare Books and Manuscripts
Library. The interior of the Beinecke is a delightful, welcoming place, the
staff there is congenial and efficient, and for the task of handcopying
hundreds of pages in pencil, one could not have wished for a more conducive environment.

Part I
The Seat of War

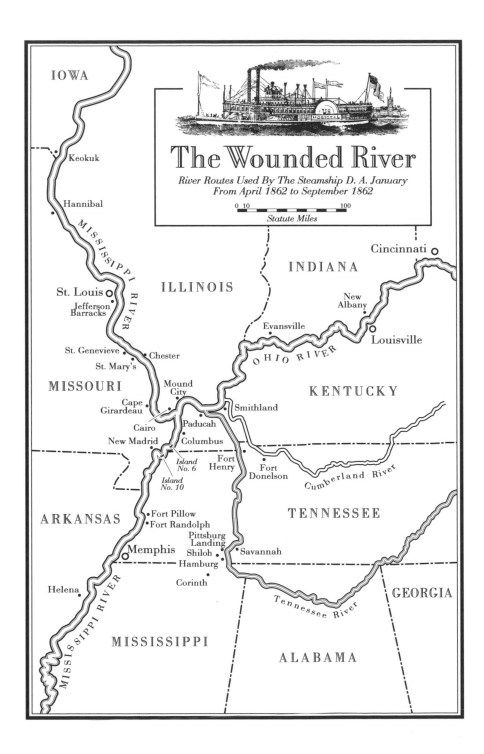

The Wounded River

*River Routes Used By The Steamship D. A. January
From April 1862 to September 1862*

0 10   100
Statute Miles

IOWA

Keokuk

Hannibal

MISSISSIPPI RIVER

St. Louis

Jefferson
Barracks

ILLINOIS

INDIANA

Cincinnati

New
Albany

Evansville

Louisville

St. Genevieve

Chester

St. Mary's

MISSOURI

Mound
City

Cape
Girardeau

Cairo

New Madrid

Columbus

Island
No. 6

Island
No. 10

Paducah

Smithland

KENTUCKY

OHIO RIVER

Fort
Henry

Fort
Donelson

Cumberland River

ARKANSAS

Fort Pillow
Fort Randolph

Pittsburg
Landing
Shiloh

Savannah

TENNESSEE

Memphis

Hamburg

Corinth

Helena

MISSISSIPPI RIVER

MISSISSIPPI

Tennessee River

GEORGIA

ALABAMA

Introduction

The American Civil War was young John Vance Lauderdale's first major appointment as a physician. Fresh from the Medical College at the University of New York, he had just passed his exam for Junior Assistant at Bellevue Hospital in New York City when the offer arrived from St. Louis, Missouri to take one more exam in order to qualify as a surgeon in the Federal Army. His brother Willis, working as a telegrapher in St. Louis, had connected with a fellow New Yorker, Brigade Surgeon Dr. Alexander H. Hoff, who was willing to try the young doctor as his assistant on a commission from the governor of Missouri. Willis was exuberant. "It is my opinion," he wrote to his brother, "and also that of all the Doctors I have conversed with that you would learn more of surgery in one year in the Army than in a life time of private practice or in the hospitals in New York." Equally to the point, Willis added: "Besides, you receive a good salary." According to Dr. Hoff, the Western theatre of the war was just the place for the young novice. "You would probably be ordered into the field at once," Willis continued. "There will be a big fight at Corinth and Memphis soon." In a follow-up letter a week later, unaware of the magnitude of the events which had transpired in the interim, Willis wrote that General Henry W. Halleck, the Federal commander in the West, had left St. Louis for Corinth, Mississippi just that morning, and he concluded his case by saying: "There will be lots of work for surgeons now."

Just how much work there was going to be for surgeons in that region could not have been imagined by either brother or by anyone else on either side of the war. Between Willis's two letters, the Army's view of the war, and of war itself, had been drastically altered. The first letter, dated April 2, 1862, preceded by four days the Battle of Shiloh, which was fought at Pittsburg Landing, Tennessee, and at first news of the battle Dr. Hoff was hurrying there aboard the hospital steamer *D.A. January*, sorry not to have had the young Lauderdale with him. Three

3

weeks later, the completely inexperienced Dr. Lauderdale would arrive on that same ship to commence his career in the aftermath of the bloodiest battle yet fought in the history of American warfare, its casualties exceeding all three previous American wars together.

Although he opposed secession and condemned the extension of slavery, Lauderdale had questioned the necessity of the war, suspecting opportunistic motives amongst its promoters in the North. He had no desire to see it continue and showed no interest in joining its ranks. While preparing his thesis in December of 1861, he had written to Willis: "I begin to think that it is no use fighting any longer and wish the finale of this great family quarrel would come." A month later, he wrote to his sister Frances: "I am getting quite disgusted with the war, as well as the generals, and would give more for a picture of the individuals who would put a stop to this miserable capital consuming quarrel than for photographs of all the Union generals." Given such photographs, there would be few whom Lauderdale could identify, his medical studies having prevented him from keeping properly posted. He wrote to Frances: "I must confess (with regret) that I am very ignorant of war news. If I hear of a Generals army defeated, I always have to ask a friend of mine here whether he was Fedr'el or Rebel. Since this war has begun, I do not know who Gen Pope is."

With significant modifications—he did not join the Army, but signed on as a contract surgeon—Lauderdale accepted the offer to enter the war for sound practical reasons. Having secured a leave of absence from Bellevue Hospital until October, he could store up a wealth of experience in his profession while earning the highest pay he had ever received, one hundred dollars per month, which was a hundred per month more than a Junior Assistant at Bellevue was getting, Junior Assistants being paid only in board. As an extra bonus, he would be seeing his brother Willis in St. Louis. It was the best prospect ever to come his way, and it solved, for a time, the great problem of gainful employment which had grieved him since he struck out on his own ten years earlier.

ざ ざ ざ

Lauderdale's father, Dr. Walter E. Lauderdale, was not at all happy as a physician in the rural, northern New York village of Geneseo, and he did not encourage the eldest of his five sons to pursue a medical future. In 1852, at the age of nineteen, John Vance left his family and moved to New York City, aiming at a hopefully more satisfying career in the lucrative business of pharmaceuticals. He rented a shared room in the Chambers Street boarding house of family friends, the Watsons, and a little further along Chambers, opposite City Hall Park at lower Broadway, he was hired as a druggist's clerk with Rushton, Clark & Co., expecting there to learn all of the aspects of the business to which he would not have had access in the country.[1]

What he learned, quickly, was that his employers would teach him nothing which would warrant increasing his salary, not permitting even senior clerks to dispense drugs until they had worked in the store for a full four years.[2] Lauderdale considered this "all humbug," and already, in only his second month, he declared to his father: "My future prospects are not at all flattering. The Drug business is a very good business for the employer, but not for the clerk." Working sixteen and seventeen hour days of putting up medicines, running errands, and attending the soda counter, he was earning barely enough for his room and board. If, as his father insisted, the rural physician's life was "slavish" and "thankless," the son's life as a clerk in New York City was little better.

The senior Lauderdale's letters of this period, typifying a timeless parental duality, were at once sympathetic toward his son's disaffections and concerned that his reputation as an employee should remain beyond reproach and that his material situation would be secure. Reminding his son to "be faithful to their interests," he advised him to stay with his current employers until he learned the profession thoroughly, perhaps even augmenting the job with courses in pharmacology. By turns, the younger Lauderdale appealed first to one of his father's ears and then the other, and the shifts and stretches by which he attempted this were sometimes less than subtle. After one particular recitation of grievances, he suddenly checked himself and hastened to add: "You must not think from what I just said that I am sick of the Drug Business. Oh no, that is not the case because I like the business as well as ever, but I *do* think that to[o] much work and no play makes Jack a dull boy." How well Jack ever liked the exactions of working at Rushton, Clark & Co. can be inferred from the following passages:

> Mr. Rushton... is one of the most particular sort of man I ever saw. He wants everything kept in the strictest order. If he sees the least thing out of place, a little dust on the counter scales or anything, he is sure to speak of it, and scold the boys for being so careless, so that when we see the "old man" (as they call him) we have to rush around, and get things to rights....
> I do not think that I shall ever regrett leaving. There are several regulations and rules which we must obey. For instance, we are not allowed to sit when we are in the store. We are not permitted to take a look at any paper or book during business hours. If King [the senior clerk] sees a newspaper any wheres about the store, he makes inquiries about it,

Francis (Frank) Lauderdale (top left); Willis Lauderdale (top right); Robert Lauderdale (bottom left); and Nettie Lauderdale (bottom right), in 1866. In the 2nd row is Willis's wife Nellie, and a friend, Charles Gohien. The photo is affixed to the back of one of Willis's business cards.

who left it in such a place, and if he finds the one, he gives him a scold-
ing. I have had to use the greatest caution to avoid being caught with
anything of the kind. We are not allowed to converse with one another,
except it is about our business. I do not believe in being so strict.

It is not surprising that during his few free hours, Lauderdale did not
attend pharmaceutical courses. But much of his spare time was solitary.
His roommate, Hiram Fonda, a grocery clerk, was easy to get along
with; the Watson house was frequently full of boarders; and his life was
not without its share of personal calls by and to acquaintances or members of his very large circle of relations who were visiting New York
City. But in his desire to find a constant close companion in whom to
confide, Lauderdale was ruefully disappointed. Social relations in the
metropolis were not remotely as simple or as easy as they were in
Geneseo. He wrote to Frances:

> To be sure, there is enough going on all the time, but I am not
> acquainted with the people, so I dont take much interest in their
> affairs. Society here in New York seems to be divided into social strata,
> if I may use that geological term, one layer overlying the other in regu-
> lar gradation, and it seems almost impossible to commingle them, and
> there are only a few who, like veins of granite, are found associated
> with every strata alike. The amount of ones property assigns him his
> rank in society.

Lacking entree into Manhattan social circles, Lauderdale recruited
himself by devouring the sights of the city and as much of its culture as
he could afford, and by chronicling his experience for his favorite correspondent, his sister Frances, who was two years his junior and whom
he liked to call Frank. After exchanging letters with her for several
years, he told her: "I have some correspondents who are cash cus-
tomers, and others who write me on a long credit. You are one of the
cash ones." A decade older than their kid sister Nettie, Frank was a
gentle, loving sister, the only relation who wrote to him frequently, and
despite their being seldom in the same city together, she was, in a sense,
his closest companion for many years. He described to Frank his view of
the Hudson River Palisades from an observation tower on 31st Street;
the construction of the spectacular Crystal Palace on the site of what is
now Bryant Park on 42nd Street;[3] and the awesome crowds that gath-
ered to hear the wildly popular songstress—the Swedish
Nightingale—Jenny Lind. Reports of the store, however, continued
bleak. He performed his duties assiduously, but clearly, like Melville's
Bartleby who was a scrivner on nearby Wall Street, Lauderdale would

have preferred not to. He was even glad for a minor injury to his hand, as it was "very agreeable to have a day once in a while to stay away from the store." He endured the situation until July, when he finally quit.

Anticipating his father's concern for the terms under which he was leaving, Lauderdale assured him that the firm was pleased with his work, and in reiterating the logic behind his departure, he offered as a conclusive factor something with which his father, a pious Old School Presbyterian, could not have taken issue. One may suspect perhaps a trace of filial strategy in his emphasis, but it is nonetheless characteristic of Lauderdale's religious sensibility at the time:

> Just as soon as I get another place I shall leave for someplace where they have more respect for the sabbath than they have here. What I refer to is that of selling soda water on Sunday. Last sabbath I had to sell soda most all the time. The call for soda was twice as great as that for medicines. I do not feel as though I was doing exactly right, in selling soda on Sunday, and I will not work for a firm who requires it.

Having found a suitable situation at Boyd & Paul, a pharmaceutical wholesaler on Courtland Street who agreed to start him in August, Lauderdale treated himself to a much needed vacation. Although he lived for nearly a century, as a young man Lauderdale did not have the sturdiest constitution and he welcomed the opportunity to strengthen his health, restore his spirits, and "rusticate" in the country, visiting first with an uncle in Greenbush, New York, then staying with other relations in Dorset, Vermont, where he assisted in getting the hay in and was glad to be joined for a few days by his mother. In writing to Frank of how deeply he missed the country in his small room on Chambers Street, he had quoted a song: "Oh give me a cot in the vally I love/A tent in the wildwood, a home in the grove." It was, in a sense, a song he continued to sing throughout his life.

❦ ❦ ❦

Compared to Rushton, Clark & Co., Boyd & Paul was a liberation. In repetitious menial labor, the bracing high spirits of even a superficial camaraderie can be helpful in surviving the dull day, and at Boyd & Paul, which wholesaled to retail druggists and was not open to the public, the boys wore blue shirts and overalls and could "talk and sing and carry on as they please, only they must tend to their business." With few exceptions, however, Lauderdale found his coworkers a rough class of fellows and formed no lasting friendships within their company. "I never felt the need of acquaintance as much as I do now," he told Frank. Nor was he contented with his earnings or his prospects. He was obliged to send his socks home for mending, and his shoes were "most wore out." He was happy to have a dollar sent for extra spending money. But the shorter hours were certainly less of a strain, leaving more time for his favorite recreations, which now included reading and frequenting free lectures. He discovered the Mercantile Society Library, where he borrowed books and enjoyed the extensive selection of newspapers and journals in the quiet of its capacious reading room in the Clinton Hall building, located at the corner of Nassau and Beekman streets. He was impressed at reading Shakespeare and Milton for the first time, and he finally got around to reading the current sensational bestseller, *Uncle Tom's Cabin*:

> It is a very extraordinary story. I liked it very much. What a pity poor old Tom was never permitted to go back to old Kintuck, and see his wife & chillen once more. Mas'r George served him, Legree, right when he lam[e]d him over his head. He ought to have been punished in a more severe manner for his cruelty to his poor slaves. Was not little Eva a lovely little thing?[4]

When one spate of reading delayed his characteristically regular letters to Frank, he explained that he was correcting for having formerly read so little that he was pretending to others' opinions about books he had not read.

Another opportunity for improvement at the Mercantile Library, the winter lecture season in the Clinton Hall auditorium, found him in constant attendance, sometimes nightly, for talks on a wide range of topics, including the American Indian, life in great Britain, "The Discoveries of Science as Applied to the History of Creation," success, India, phrenology, physiology, and psychology. "This last subject is something that appeared strange to me," Lauderdale wrote about psychology, "but I am convinced that there is something in it." The talk on phrenology was given by Orson S. Fowler, of the popular Fowler and Wells Phrenological Cabinet, also housed in Clinton Hall, where a curious Walt Whitman had submitted his head to Orson's brother Lorenzo for a craniological survey—known as having one's bumps read—and where the first edition of *Leaves of Grass* was displayed for sale in 1855. The speaker on Great Britain was Horace Mann, whom Lauderdale admired both as a lecturer and as a man, his talk having addressed both the pleasing and the dark side of his subject, concluding with a warning lest America should abuse its poorer classes in the manner of Great Britain. Lauderdale told Frank: "I thought that our slaves at the south are much better off than the people there."

Apart from life at the store, where daily routine among the stocks of patent medicine seldom varied, it was generally an expansive time for Lauderdale. He visited New Providence, New Jersey, the birthplace of his maternal grandfather.[5] He went for a "sea bath" at Coney Island. He ferried out of the city for fresh air in Hoboken, Staten Island, and Brooklyn, or to attend Sunday services in the quieter, less bustling Brooklyn churches, although he also attended Henry Ward Beecher's Plymouth Church, which was so well attended that Sunday ferries from New York became known as Beecher's Boats.[6] During a visit to Williamsburg, Lauderdale was enthralled to witness the maiden launch of a steamship, the *Yankee Blade*. At the foot of Warren Street in lower Manhattan, he watched another steamer, the *Cherokee*, being destroyed by a fire, which he confessed to Frank was "truly a grand sight," albeit a tragic one. In the Brooklyn Navy Yard, he was walking the decks of the warship *Carolina* when it thundered its naval salute to the late Daniel Webster, whose funeral pageant he later encountered on Broadway, where "all the principal buildings were festooned with black drapery, & all places of business were closed during the passing of the procession." A demonstration of acrobatics at a gymnasium ranked as high for him as anything at the circus, and he was equally pleased with a convention of the American Canary Birds Fancier Association.

Some of Lauderdale's choices for recreation scarcely seem credible to our modern sense of enjoyment, such as observing a sewing society or, during a visit home, auditing the oral examinations at his old school, the Geneseo Academy at Temple Hill. Clearly, Lauderdale's taste in entertainment did not extend to the prurient or the excessive. He was happy simply to see new things and to learn as much as he could. He especially enjoyed the aquarium and the assortment of curiosities on display at P.T. Barnum's American Museum, which was located on Broadway only two blocks down from Boyd & Paul's new location on Chambers Street.[7] He enrolled in a weekly singing course, and he underwent his own initiation as a teacher when he accepted an invitation to lead a class at a sabbath school for wayward, homeless boys, "the rudest, roughest, [most] saucy set" he had ever seen. At the school's anniversary celebration, Horace Greeley gave the address, after which the boys succeeded in bringing off several rehearsed hymns and were dismissed each with a book and a piece of cake. Considering Lauderdale's reports of their behavior, one need not wonder whether the prospect of the book—or the presence of the distinguished Mr. Greeley—was somewhat less of an inspiration for this singular performance than the cake.

In the spring of 1853, Lauderdale formally aligned himself to a church, the Brick Presbyterian on Beekman Street, an aptly named old brick structure built before the Revolution, now seating a somewhat fashionable congregation under the conservative pastorship of the aging Reverend Gardiner Spring.[8] It was a serious step for Lauderdale. In a letter to his mother, even the style of his writing reflects his votive mood about the occasion. "To morrow," he wrote on April 9, "is the day set for the celebration of the Lords Supper, when I shall come forth for the first time to seal the covenant now which I have made with my God. I hope that through his strength given me, I may be enabled to live a Christian life, and be a true disciple of his." With the missionary ardor of one newly sanctified, he hoped that Frances, his brothers, and all of his friends would come to a like conclusion. He wrote to Frank: "I hope that you have given the subject some attention and have decided whom you will serve, whether God or Mammon. If not, do so without any longer delay."

In fact, none of the Lauderdales were at all close to Mammon at this time. His father, newly elected postmaster, a position he needed to supplement his meager medical practice, deputed two of his younger sons, Willis and Samuel, to work the telegraph, and he tendered a standing invitation for John Vance to come and work for him as well. However, when Lauderdale wrote of a possible situation in Chicago, his father strongly encouraged it. Success stories of ventures Westward had lately stirred him to contemplate a move there of his own. "The prospect for young men of small means is much better in the West than in N. York," he wrote to his son in March of 1854. "I believe that we might better our situation if the whole family would go West." Walter Lauderdale had caught a touch of Western fever, and now, in a reversal of father-son relations, Lauderdale became the voice of caution in the face of his father's eagerness to transplant the family to a place of opportunity. Not that he too did not long for a brighter horizon. "It has been all hopes and disappointments with me thus far," he wrote to his mother. "I have not been able to realize anything yet…. I know something of what it is to have the 'blues'." But the wealth of culture in Manhattan was too vital for him to trade for speculation, and his father at least agreed that he should secure a firm offer before leaving.

Until such an offer arrived, Lauderdale, by his own admission, did not know quite what to do with himself, likening his situation to that of a boy who goes fishing by too briefly casting his line in one location after another. Where and when would he find challenging work that enabled him to be solvent and to do a bit of good? After a summer of intense heat and a cholera epidemic throughout the city, he was no closer to finding an answer. He contemplated teaching; his father discouraged it. He considered medicine; his father discouraged that. A gap in the correspondence between December of 1854 and August of 1855 suggests that he resigned from Boyd & Paul and returned to Geneseo, where his father had offered him higher pay and where he appears to have taken Willis's place at the telegraph while Willis attended commercial college in Manchester, Vermont. The correspondence resumes with an attractive invitation to stay in Cleveland, Ohio, with his Uncle Robert and Aunt Miranda. Uncle Robert, a successful dealer in the fish trade, was optimistically looking to buy a house, and he assured his nephew assistance in finding employment, perhaps in his own office. He even urged Lauderdale to bring Willis with him. This was not exactly a firm offer, but Uncle Robert's confidence was too much to resist. Lauderdale took the bait and left for Ohio almost immediately.[9]

Shortly after arriving in Cleveland on the steamer *Crescent City,* he discovered, as many Easterners were to discover, that to dream a Westward future was a much easier business than to make one. Uncle Robert's fish trade was foundering, leaving Lauderdale in Cleveland unemployed and sharing quarters with his relations in a boarding house that buzzed with gossipy socializing and small talk. An uncommonly vitriolic report to Frank berated the "perfectly nauseating" bores who were driving him to distraction and driving his uncle to move to a nearby hotel, but, typically, Lauderdale refrained from faulting his uncle for building up and disappointing his great expectations. In November he took a clerk's job at Fiske's, another pharmacy, and by December he was living on his own in a hotel, the Bennett House. It was not in Fiske's, however, but in the course of a day's excursion into a coal mine in April of 1856 that Lauderdale made a connection which would lead him to the profession of his father.

❦ ❦ ❦

With a boyish naiveté which endured throughout his twenties, Lauderdale enjoyed being an amateur natural scientist. It was an age in which being an amateur could mean almost anything; there was not the long, requisite distance of academic training between playing at being a scientist and becoming one. But Lauderdale was completely without pretense or ambition as he read, collected specimens, prowled museums, and heard lectures in pursuit of his various scientific interests, which were especially keen in marine biology, geology, and American Indian archeology. His books were catalogued with cards that read "Scientific Library." His letters of travel are always attentive to descriptions of terrain; he sometimes discusses modest additions to his cabinet; and often—especially during the war—his letters have a journal-like inclusiveness of detail, augmented by diagrams and sketches, and are referred to as reports or rough notes, suggesting that Lauderdale was, in a sense, practicing science in the only forum he had: his correspondence. Ironically, it was social science to which he would come to make a lasting contribution by recording and collecting his own experience. Toward the end of his life, he chronicled, indexed, and bound the many letters and journals he had saved, along with clippings from periodicals and other memorabilia which would help complete the picture of his life, an indication that he knew there was something of value in what he preserved. At twenty-three, however, his excitement was more for the fossil record than his own.

Living in Cleveland, Lauderdale was interested in the area's rich deposits of fossil remains, and his sights were set on collecting some prize samples. After a disappointing trip to a coal mine in nearby Tallmadge, he made inquiries which by the spring of 1856 had united him with John Strong Newberry, a physician and seasoned geologist who had explored northern California with the U.S. Army under Colonel Richardson and who was currently preparing an exhibition for the Smithsonian Institution. Dr. Newberry brought the amateur from New York on an excursion which marked a turning point in Lauderdale's life, more for the friendship it ignited than for the specimens which were taken, although Lauderdale was highly pleased with both. "I found him to be a very interesting companion," he told his father. "His tastes and mine are congenial. I learned from him a good many things in regard to our favorite science.... I had a delightful time down there splitting open the coal, and revealing the relics of a former world." In fact, one finding of special interest proved to be a hitherto unidentified prehistoric reptile, a discovery which the following year was added to the scientific literature.[10]

At a meeting of the American Association for the Advancement of Science held in Albany, New York in August of 1856, Newberry proposed Lauderdale for membership, and he was notified of his election in September. In November, he was invited to join, on a subscription basis, an expedition sponsored by the Lyceum of Natural History of Williams College, Massachusetts, which was leaving in early spring for the Florida Keys. When, on February 19, the schooner *Dew-Drop* sailed down the East River and made its way past the cakes of ice floating in New York Harbor, Lauderdale, thanks to a loan from his father, was standing on deck. Shivering in the February frost, Lauderdale watched the Battery of Manhattan recede in the distance, the first of many sights on a southward voyage that proved to be far smoother sailing for him than the previous year had been.

Around the time that he met Dr. Newberry, Lauderdale's employer, Fiske, had laid him off. He mismanaged and lost a good prospect in Detroit, Michigan, and applications to run a ship's store on a riverboat and to work in a railroad office were also unavailing. When he ran into debt with his hotel, its owner, Bennett, allowed him to work it off in his office. "It is not to tend bar," he assured his father, "for I have not gotten to that yet & our house is a temperance one." His father's practice was still poor and, feeling the strain of tuition for Willis's second year in Manchester, he needed better news from Cleveland than of fossils. "Allow me to inquire," he wrote to his son, "whether too much of your attention is not taken up with your favorite studies of Natural Sciences, Indian relics, etc., & that the practical duties of life are omitted." As for his son's being in debt, his views were clear: "It would be better to act as porter than to depend too much upon your friends." His father suggested several options in Geneseo, including teaching at the academy. Although for the moment he was forced into another store for the summer, and in November he was working again for his father, Lauderdale's views on teaching reveal an important—if belated—understanding about himself.

A situation teaching science, he wrote to his father, "would be just the place I should like and would give me a chance to exercise those peculiar tastes that I have for those studies. I sometimes think that I have spent too much time in studying and reading to make much of a commercial business man." Casting about for a surveying or engineering position, he most of all longed for a place on a research expedition, doubtless inspired by the example of Dr. Newberry. Newberry did his best to help usher him into the professional world of science, and from Newberry came a crucial piece of advice which he resolved to follow as soon as he could afford it. His best chance for joining an expedition, Newberry told him, was to apply as an M.D. "Make a doctor of yourself then first, and a thoroughly good one," he later wrote to Lauderdale in a long and powerful discourse on the travails and the rewards of doing science, "and if you continue to feel the fire of scientific enthusiasm burning in your breast, keep it alive & glowing, feed it with good hard-wood fuel—no light-flashy 'kindling stuff'—until you have a furnace which reduces the most refractory substance, and brings the fine metal out of the hottest oven."

In the Florida Keys, Lauderdale did not want for enthusiasm. He sprang at every occasion for collecting like a starved man at a banquet.

> I started off after shells along the beach. The weather looked squally, and before we had gone far it commenced raining quite hard, but I did not let this stop me.... I followed the beach to the east of the island a distance of five miles picking up every thing in the way of shells & sea weeds.

It rained about all the time, and I having no shelter got thoroughly drenched as wet as a rat, but the excitement of picking up shells was too great to leave till I had explored the whole coast on the south side.

At Key West Harbor, the return of a different sort of expedition presented a sobering sight, recounted by H.M. Lyman in the Lyceum's official report in the *Williams Quarterly*:

The *Tennessee* had a large number of Gen. Walkers soldiers on board, returning home from the wars in Nicaragua. They were a sorry looking set of men, pale, emaciated, suffering, many of them, from wounds and disease, and destitute of anything but the clothes on their backs. The *Tennessee* was a new and splendid steamer, but the wretchedness and misery that we witnessed between her decks was sufficient to extinguish all feelings of pleasure as we examined her beautiful proportions.[11]

It was a spectacle of a kind which for Lauderdale would soon become familiar. Events were brewing which would thrust him into the midst of even sorrier sets of men, men who would be destitute of everything but the small, fleeting comfort he could give them. There is novelistic irony in the ship having been named the *Tennessee*, for that was the state in which Lauderdale received his initiation into the war.

❦ ❦ ❦

In Cleveland in May of 1856, Lauderdale received a letter from his former New York roommate, Hiram Fonda, posting him on the latest news in Manhattan. "The City is in great excitement nowadays," he wrote, "with the Sumner outrage, Kansas affair, and our difficulties with England. A dark day is approaching—fearful things are apprehended."

The "Kansas affair" arose out of Stephen Douglas' Kansas-Nebraska Act, which nullified the Missouri Compromise and promised new states popular sovereignty in deciding the issue of slavery, inevitably provoking a swiftly escalating battle in the new Kansas Territory. When Reverend Henry Ward Beecher first began to appear publicly in favor of abolition, he sent, on behalf of the Plymouth Church, 25 Sharp's rifles for use in the Kansas struggle, and thereafter rifles shipped to Kansas from New England became known as Beecher's Bibles and were loaded with more than rhetorical ammunition. In Congress, Senator Charles Sumner, an obdurate Massachusetts abolitionist, bombarded the Senate Chamber with such a vociferous peroration that a few days later, Preston Brooks, a South Carolina representative who was related to Senator Andrew Butler—a target of Sumner's verbal attack—retaliated by taking his cane to Sumner, beating him nearly to death at his desk in the Senate. That Brooks's action, which incapacitated Sumner for several years, was openly applauded by certain Southern members of Congress showed that the war of secession was, in some respects, already opened among the nation's powers. With physical violence in the Capitol, the rest of the country could not be far behind, and before the month was out, Missouri Border Ruffians attacked Kansas Free-Soilers in the town of Lawrence and killed a man; then John Brown's men countered by killing five Southern pro-slavery men near Pottawatomie Creek.

As the November presidential elections approached, the choice between the Democrat James Buchanan and the Republican John Frémont became a choice between extending or curtailing the growth of slavery, but many Northerners who opposed the creation of new slave states feared encroaching federal authority and the consequences of total emancipation. They therefore leaned toward Buchanan, the choice of Lauderdale's father and of Frances. "On the subject of Politics," Lauderdale wrote to Frank in September, "I can hardly say that I am on your side. I would like to talk with Father to find out what his reasons are for supporting a presidential candidate who pledges himself to support and extend the slave power. I am partly for Filmore and part for Fremont. The prevailing sentiment in this town is for Fremont."

On October 22, still wrestling with indecision as to where to cast his vote, Lauderdale appealed to his father for just cause to support what appeared to him an immoral policy. He found the question, "which must be settled before Nov 4th's sun goes down," extremely confusing, as he was poorly versed in politics and did not have the right shaped head for it. "It all seems to me to be a complete muddle and what the politicians say (and they are the only ones who do the talking) only serves to make the subject still darker. It is like throwing sand in our eyes to prevent us seeing for ourselves." The real issue, he felt, was state equality. "By state equality I mean of course the right of each state to have slavery or not, just as its citizens may agree upon. I am in favor of this right being given to each new state except that part of it which admits of its holding slaves. I am opposed to slave extension *entirely*."

Although he agreed with Republican principles, he regarded Buchanan as far more qualified for the presidency than Frémont. His dilemma was that he could not in good conscience vote for Buchanan. "It is hard to tell among so many conflicting theories which to believe. Just now I incline towards the Fremont party. If I am in error please set me right."

His father's response, furiously scribbled on several pages before the mail left town on November 1, is the angriest in their entire correspondence. His father's customary reserve dropped completely as he fired off an arsenal of invective, a telling sign of the volatile passions being ignited on the question throughout the country. He even implied that his son should refrain from voting if he was going to be misled, nor did he doubt that it was the powerful Horace Greeley's Republican press that was the source of the misguidance.

> I have frequent regretts that you devote so much time to the perusal of *The Tribune*.[12] I regard that paper politically as dangerous & heretical & treasonable in its doctrines as I do the writings of Tom Paine in a religious point of view.
>
> Have you carefully perused the Constitution of the United States, particularly the articles relating to the subject of Slavery—the Fugitive Slave clause also? Have you read the Farewell addresses of Washington with due consideration? Do you distinctly remember his counsels in reference to sectional & geographical divisions of parties, of the importance of cultivating a conciliatory feeling between the citizens of the North & South? Do you wish to preserve inviolate that sound Legacy & to hand it down to posterity unsullied? Do you approve of the course of those Republican lunatics who scant at the Constitution & farewell counsels of Washington & Jefferson & trample them under their feet & who wish to ride into power on the ruins of those sacred relics?

A contemporary of Jefferson, his father viewed the current crop of Republicans as descendants of those who fought Jefferson's candidacy by branding him an infidel who would close down their churches, "but Jefferson was elected notwithstanding all their cant & fanaticism [and] their Bibles were not destroyed & the spires of their Churches still continued to point toward Heaven." Barely pausing to lift the pen from the page, his father continued heatedly:

> These same political croakers now tell you that if Buchanan is elected Slavery will be extended indefinately & that the North will be subservient to the South—do you believe they are sincere? What has Fremont done to merit your Vote for that high responsible office? What confidence have you in his ability to restrict the extension of Slavery? Has not Congress placed the disposal of that matter with the Territories? It is not prepared to repeal that power.

As for the cry to admit Kansas as a free state, "the Democracy say No let the people decide and when they do decide we have the confidence to believe they will decide right." Although he was too rushed to advance a tenth of the reasons for choosing Buchanan, his father closed by saying:

John Vance Lauderdale (2nd row, center) with students from the Geneseo Academy at Temple Hill, c. 1859.

"I hope you will not infer from the above remarks that I would want to influence your judgement in the least."

We have no record of how Lauderdale voted, or of his response to the Dred Scott decision, the Lincoln-Douglas debates, or John Brown's raid on Harper's Ferry. But a passage in a letter after two years of Buchanan's tumultuous presidency suggests that his opposition to slave extension had not abated. After a year in the Geneseo post office, Lauderdale had saved enough to move back to the Watsons' in Manhattan and commence his medical studies. When his friend Fonda left to conduct some business in Georgia, Lauderdale wrote to his mother that it was a fine chance for Fonda to "become acquainted with the people of the South & catch a glimpse of their sacred institutions," but he hoped Fonda would "not have his slavery sentiments changed by his near view of the master, as did a friend, a drug clerk who spent the best part of two years at the south."[13]

It is not until the intensely heated presidential campaign of 1860 that a letter to Lauderdale, who had to interrupt his studies in order to teach natural science at the Geneseo Academy, offers a clue to the next stage in his political evolution, which appears to have made a radical shift to the Democrats and Douglas, the result, perhaps, of his father's daily persuasion. The letter, from Charles McLaren, a Manhattan grocer, draws a vivid picture of Lincoln-Douglas electioneering in the city.

> Well so you attended a political meeting in your village and went home fully convinced that the little Giant was the man that would get your vote, and here you have the advantage of a New Yorker, in this way, viz.
>
> There will be a large political meeting... in Cooper Institute this evening at 8 o'clock, and the advertisement will read thus: Every man that is an admirer of Henry Clay and of our glorious Constitution as handed down by our patriotic father will attend the meeting this evening, without fail. Well we go to the meeting this evening and come home fully convinced like your self that we will vote for Douglas. So far so good.
>
> To morrow night there will be another meeting, and the notice will be like this: Friends of Freedom rally, Wide Awake on deck, [14] we expect to see at the meeting to night, every man that believes in freedom, free territories, free trade, and that every man is born free and equal. Well we go to the meeting, and go home fully convinced that old honest Abe is the man. Although it appears to me that the only requisite [for a] candidate for the Presidency is for a man to be a Rail Splitter.[15]

Despite all the clamoring, McLaren insists that "they could never make anything out of me but a rank Democrat," and he hopes that "Abe Wide Awake may on 6th Nov be found *fast Asleep*, and all rail splitters *split*, and that the remnant may never be put together again, for they are bad eggs."[16]

Ten days after Lincoln's inauguration, the Commencement Program for the winter term at the Geneseo Academy featured Lauderdale as one of the readers of essays from the school's two literary societies. Amid such ponderous topics as "Character and Destiny," "Progress of Civilization," "Mind and Its Effects," and "The Model Man," there was an essay entitled "Our Union," and another, by John Young of Geneseo, entitled, simply, "Secession." The political earthquake was being felt everywhere.

Lauderdale had one more term of teaching before he could return to New York City and complete his medical course. On Friday morning, April 12, 1861, Lauderdale took his seat for breakfast before beginning his day of classes at the academy. He would not know it until later that day, but just a few hours earlier, at 4:29 AM, Confederate troops, under Captain George S. James, stood expectantly at a battery in Fort Johnson on the northeast edge of Charleston Harbor, South Carolina. A minute later, James ordered his assistant, Lieutenant Henry S. Farley, to pull the lanyard on a ten-inch mortar that sent a shell soaring high

over the harbor before exploding just above Fort Sumter, a signal to all
surrounding batteries to commence their bombardment, and a signal to
the world that the war had begun.

❦ ❦ ❦

"War! War! War!" The war which was declared by the Charleston
Harbor ordnance and by headlines such as this one in *The Philadelphia
Inquirer* was soon made official by Lincoln's April 15 "Proclamation
Calling Militia and Convening Congress." But this was only one of two
wars that ravaged the nation between 1861 and 1865. The second of
these, which was fought undeclared because the strongest of its belliger-
ents remained undisclosed during its sanguinary progress through the
enlisted population, killed more American men than all the bullets fired
during the 10,000 military engagements of the war. As they marched
against each other, North and South alike fought blindly and were
defeated by the same intractable enemy: disease.

Disease accounted for approximately two-thirds of all casualties during the Civil War, a total of over 400,000 deaths out of some 10,000,000
cases of illness. For every thousand Union troops which were active
during the first year of the war, there were 4,000 cases of sickness. In
four years, there were nearly 128,000 Union cases of typhoid, typhus,
or typho-malarial fever, resulting in roughly 33,000 Union deaths.
Twenty thousand Union soldiers died of pneumonia, and over 44,000
Union soldiers died of diarrhea or dysentery, of which there were more
than 1.6 million reported cases. Statistics for the Confederacy show a
comparable mortality rate from a similar list of diseases. In addition,
perhaps more than with any other war, the deaths of countless veterans
are attributable to diseases which were contracted, or conditions which
were suffered, during the time they were in the service. How greatly
they would add to the sum of casualties can never be determined.

The true causes of most diseases prevalent during the war were not
known, and most remedies—when there was any treatment at all—fell
far short of a cure. On neither side was anything known of bacteria as a
possible cause of dysentery or any other illness or infection; nor was
anything known about the relation between malaria and the mosquito.
When Lauderdale joked to his sister Frank about his battles against
mosquitoes, he had not long ceased taking quinine in an effort to check
the malaria ("the ague") which he had doubtless contracted from them.
In fact, malaria was the only major disease for which there was any
treatment at all, and smallpox was the only disease against which pre-
ventative measures were taken. There was no antisepsis before Lister's

use of carbolic acid in 1865—far too late to have any influence on the war—and there was no aseptic surgery before 1882. In the life of the average soldier, conditions were perfect for the rampant spread of a long list of afflictions which could decimate a regiment even before it tasted the smoke of its first battle. Between disease and the Civil War soldier, there was not a fair fight.

When Lauderdale was on his way to the seat of war in the West, his train stopped at Crestline, Ohio, to take on troops who were going to Cairo, Illinois. Late that afternoon, while the train stopped briefly for repairs, the men left the train to refresh themselves in a nearby brook. If these troops were new recruits, some of them may have been sick or infirm at the time they entered the service, for enlistment standards, nonexistent at first, were still either poorly enforced or completely disregarded. Men from rural areas, who comprised a high percentage of all recruits, had not developed immunities to a number of the diseases which the men from urban communities carried with them, and from the moment they interacted, in close quarters on trains and transports, they could easily have contracted a fatal illness. In fact, carriers of a contagious disease could create an epidemic. After Grant's victory at Fort Donelson, for example, many of his men died of a typhoid epidemic which broke out on the crowded steamers taking them down the river to Savannah. As for the seemingly innocent visit to the brook, a single sip of it could have created that incontinence of the bowels which by the end of the war had plagued—and in many instances ended—the life of 995 out of every 1,000 Union soldiers. What is often omitted from accounts of the Battle of Shiloh is the debilitating, demoralizing effect of the persistent diarrhea, ascribed to the ill-reputed waters of the Tennessee River and nicknamed the Tennessee Quickstep, which attacked Grant's army weeks before the Confederates did and, according to Dr. John H. Brinton, medical director for the Army of the Tennessee, "contributed to weaken the most robust."[17]

Also, in Crestline, in Cairo, in and around practically every city, town, and camp where there were troops, prostitution spread 82 cases of venereal disease to every 1,000 soldiers. Malnutrition was common everywhere, even when food supplies were ample, for there was so much wrong with so much of the food that whatever was deemed edible had to be cooked for so long that most or all of its nutritive value was destroyed. When troops had to subsist on local forage, their diet might have been nothing more than parched or green corn, or grass and weeds, and in extremes of deprivation such as armies under siege, disease-carrying horses, mules, dogs, cats, and even rats were made as palatable as possible. Pure water was almost nonexistent, water being commonly tainted by garbage, insects, decomposing animals, human waste, and other detritus of the squalid conditions obtaining in most camps. In addition, often grossly inadequate clothing, tenting, and bedding made frostbite, sunstroke, and respiratory diseases a constant hazard.

When Lauderdale arrived in St. Louis to receive his orders from Dr. Hoff, he discovered that the doctor had left St. Louis and would be joining him in Cairo. Lauderdale sailed down the Mississippi River on the *Crescent City*, the same boat on which he had first arrived in Cleveland and which was now moving a large, noisome artillery company, seven cannons, horses, cattle, and supplies to Pittsburg Landing, Tennessee. The soldiers, required to sleep on the cabin deck, had only their blankets for beds and their knapsacks for pillows, but despite the crowded, makeshift conditions of transport, these troops could be thankful that they had not been bound for the same location twelve days earlier. Then, they would have awakened to a savage surprise attack that began the two days of fierce fighting which, in his *Memoirs*, General Ulysses S. Grant called "the severest battle fought at the West during the war,"[18] the Battle of Shiloh. A brutal clash between 100,000 men, there had never been anything like it. Shiloh was a surprise attack on everyone both in and out of the military, a great enlightener that forcibly opening all eyes to what the war was going to cost in human suffering. And in the cries of thousands of unattended wounded was an inarguable indictment against all previous systems of army medical organization.

The "big fight at Corinth," which Willis Lauderdale had forecast, had been planned by General Halleck as a joint attack by Grant's Army of the Tennessee and General Don Carlos Buell's Army of the Ohio, which was moving down from Nashville to converge with Grant at Pittsburg Landing. Corinth, a major military objective, was one of the lifelines of the Confederacy, being the junction of its two major railroads. Situated about twenty miles northeast of Corinth, where the Confederates were recovering after major defeats at Forts Henry and Donelson, Pittsburg Landing was chiefly an old 15' x 30' warehouse on a red clay bluff beside the Tennessee River, at the terminus of the main road from Corinth. At the top of the steep rise, a hundred feet above the water, was an intermittently wooded plateau, bordered by two creeks, which General William T. Sherman, the camp commander, judged to be perfect ground for drilling the army's raw recruits, and he established his own headquarters a few miles southwest of the river near a log-built Methodist chapel named Shiloh.

The encampment was, in fact, serviceable as a junction of two armies about to launch a major offensive, but defensively it was perilous, perhaps even reckless, it being predicated—as was the entire strategy—on the assumption that the enemy planned to be fighting from the security of its entrenched position at Corinth. So confident was Grant in his safety from general attack that he left his army with its back to the river, a creek at either side, unprotected by entrenchments, fortifications, or any tightly drawn defensive line, the greenest troops closest to the enemy, the most experienced in the rear, with one entire division four miles away at Crump's Landing, and Buell's reinforcements moving with no great urgency, while Grant himself spent the night nine miles away across the river at Savannah, where he could greet General Buell upon his arrival. Stung by the journalistic criticism which followed news of the battle, Grant wrote to his father and to a friend that his army could not have been better prepared if the enemy had provided them with particulars of the attack, and in later assessing the controversial opening of the battle, Grant claimed to have taken every precaution. But on the previous evening, enemy troops were two miles away, and even the fundamental precaution of having intelligence personnel or a troop of cavalry on reconnaissance would have discovered them.[19]

Under the command of General Albert Sidney Johnston, Confederate forces were moving to strike Grant's army before Buell's arrival doubled the Federal numbers. Johnston's army was even greener than Grant's, and the march from Corinth was so fraught with delays and audible signals of their advance that it was impossible not to believe they had been detected. General G.T. Beauregard, second in command under Johnston, later called the attack "one of the most surprising surprises ever achieved."[20] Even after Confederate troops had skirmished with Federal pickets and a number of Confederate prisoners had been taken, Sherman and Grant persisted in the delusion that they were secure from a major assault. Grant suggested that Sherman's advance guard should keep watch for reconnaissance forces, but while Johnston was mounting his horse, vowing: "Tonight we will water our horses in the Tennessee River," Grant was reading his mail and awaiting breakfast in Savannah, and as a consequence he did not arrive on the field until his army had been pounced upon and thrust back by four hours of hard, close fighting. Like Grant himself, Grant's awakening army expected Sunday breakfast, not a battle.[21]

In mid-afternoon, while his staff surgeon-in-chief attended captured Federal wounded, Johnston bled to death from a shot received behind his right knee, a minor wound that could have been checked with the field tourniquet which he kept in his own pocket. Sherman was wounded twice. After twelve hours of constant fighting that drove the Federals nearly back to the river, Beauregard, now in command, withdrew his exhausted troops and spent the night in Sherman's evacuated

headquarters at Shiloh Chapel. Grant, whose headquarters—the log
warehouse at the landing—now doubled as a hospital, found his proximity to the suffering men "more unendurable than encountering the
enemy's fire,"[22] and he spent most of the night in the rain under a tree,
wincing in pain from a swollen ankle that hindered his movements for
several days. Under Grant's potent leadership, with strong artillery
coverage both from batteries on the landing and from two wooden gunboats, the *A.O. Tyler* and the *Lexington*, Grant's last remaining lines
had managed to hold. Although the belated arrival of fresh Federal
troops was not a factor behind Beauregard's withdrawal, it certainly
would have halted him had he continued, and Grant was now sure he
could "lick em" the following day. Beginning at dawn on Monday morning, with more men than he started with, Grant drove the Confederates
into a general retreat to Corinth.

Behind the melodramatic sentiment that the South never smiled after
Shiloh, there is the deeper truth that in losing Shiloh, the South began
losing the Western Confederacy. But the loss of life on both sides was
nearly equal—the total casualties approached one quarter of the number of troops engaged—and that evening, with neither army having
gained an inch of ground, there were roughly 20,000 dead and wounded
soldiers on the field. Many wounded lay untreated where they had
fallen the previous day. Some of the dead and dying were reportedly
eaten by hogs, and some wounded were roasted alive in fires which were
spread after retreating Confederates burned camps as they left them.
Grant described one open field as being "so covered with dead that it
would have been possible to walk across the clearing, in any direction,
stepping on dead bodies, without a foot touching the ground."[23] Over a
month later, stationed aboard the hospital steamer *D.A. January*,
Lauderdale was still evacuating and treating the Shiloh casualties, still
burying the Shiloh dead.

❦ ❦ ❦

In the face of such unprecedented bloodshed, it is doubtful that even
the most efficient medical planning could have been equal to the emer-
gency. But in fact, like Sherman and Grant before the battle, leaders in
the Army Medical Department resisted stubbornly the notion of such a
contingency, preferring to alter the facts to suit their views until forced
to alter their views to suit the facts.

A conflict that was supposed to have ended quickly in a single great
Napoleonic battle, did not, on either side, have a Napoleon in command,
and was spreading across the geography of the nation both physically

and emotionally, swallowing up men by the tens of thousands, calling upon developments in technology which did not so much antiquate the tactics of its generals as amplify their ineffectual organization and leadership.[24] The proportion of casualties to numbers of troops engaged was greater than ever before in history. In the first year of the war, inexperienced medical personnel were taxed with crises of desperate need that called for sudden authority far beyond their qualifications. The situation demanded inspired, resourceful leadership at the top, but the war's first two surgeons general were backward old men whose chronic ineptitude more hindered than advanced the Medical Department's rate of adaptability to the demands of modern warfare, and at all levels the department showed symptoms of the retrograde thinking, the indifference, the intrigue, and the profiteering which retarded progress in all branches of Army administration.

Over time, as the scale and scope of the war became clearer, some of the Medical Department's directors and medical officers, along with civilian organizations such as the U.S. Sanitary Commission, began to examine and correct many lapses and abuses, and by the end of the war the Army could boast of a vast system of medical organization featuring countless innovations that served as models for other armies throughout the world. But in the first days of the war, there were only 98 doctors in the Department, which, far from keeping abreast of recent developments in research, did not possess a single microscope. There was not one general hospital, no major field hospitals, no regulatory bodies or inspectors, no standard examinations for hospital stewards or volunteers, no regular hospital corps, no trained ambulance corps. The army owned a total of 20 thermometers. Stretchers were commonly carried by regimental bands and convalescents, each regiment being responsible for only its own wounded. Ambulances, predominantly of the two-wheel variety, called "avalanches"—small, fragile vehicles that were notorious for the damage they did to the wounded and the ease with which they collapsed—were often driven by hired hands who, if they did not bolt at first fire, performed with callous indifference to the suffering of their charges. Incredibly, there were some regiments—even entire brigades—which did not have one stretcher or one ambulance. In November of 1861, Grant's troops at Cairo were supplied with two stretchers and two ambulances per regiment, and frequently only a single tent. When Grant's men were first stricken with typhoid as they steamed down the river from Fort Donelson, only one deck of a single ship was free for treating and transporting the sick, and until supplied with additional hospital ships from St. Louis, Grant was forced to leave men at every stop along the river, where they lay on bare floors, uncovered and unattended.

At least Grant was responsive to medical issues and tried to follow his medical directors' advice. By contrast, General Buell was so contemptuous of the sick that he undersupplied his medical staff, freely abandoned ill troops without aid, bedding, or shelter, and insisted that the sick should take care of the sick. In an astonishing letter of April 1, 1862, to General J.S. Negley, Acting Commander at the Army of the Ohio's headquarters in Columbia, Tennessee, Buell ordered that, excepting those "not likely to be fit for duty soon," all convalescents should be drilled from one to three hours per day and should be detailed to regular guard duty.[25] In the official correspondence of this period, Halleck, for his part, exhibits far more interest in dimming the light of Grant's rising reputation than in looking after the medical needs of his army. Emergencies such as awaited the *D.A. January* focused increased attention to adequate medical preparation simply for military if not humanitarian reasons, but the changes were painfully slow, too slow to save the men at Shiloh. "It is probable," wrote Brinton, "that no battle of equal magnitude, where the numbers of wounded were so great, has ever occurred, in which the medical department was so destitute as on the bloody field at Shiloh."[26]

In the hours before the end of the first day's fighting, Union medical personnel, under the supervision of Grant's acting medical director, Henry S. Hewitt, found themselves in a chaos of emergencies, with practically no means of alleviation. Food, medicine, stretchers, tents, bedding, ambulances, and other vital equipment had been abandoned to the Confederates when the camps were overrun during the attack. Troops were falling in such numbers that most of the men detailed to assist the medical corps had been ordered back to the lines, and the constant rush of the enemy broke down whatever stratagems of cooperative organization had existed. It was more or less, as at the start of the war, every regiment for itself, or, worse, every man for himself. Surgeons were forced to recruit assistance from the swarms of stragglers—estimated by Buell at 15,000—who had deserted the lines and were gathering at the landing as close to the river as they could get, a group that Buell's medical director, Dr. Robert Murray, contemptuously derided as a completely useless mob.

Every available tent was pressed into service as a hospital. One hospital transport, the *City of Memphis*, carried a share of the wounded to Savannah, but nothing could be done to prevent enemy shot from falling amidst the majority of the wounded awaiting treatment at the landing. According to Brinton, the worst cases were rested upon a thin layer of hay, but "all others lay on the soaked ground.... The weather was terrible, the rain incessant, and the mud almost knee deep."[27]

Murray, who arrived in the afternoon of the second day, found "literally, no accommodations or comforts, not even the necessaries of life, no bedding, no cooking utensils, or table furniture, not even cups, spoons, or plates, or knives and forks, no vegetables, not even fresh beef for the first day."[28] Dressings were so scarce that female nurses were tearing their skirts to shreds for wrapping wounds. Countless wounded bled to death trying to drag themselves off the field, or waiting and pleading for help, for water, or for the mercy of being put out of their agony. Some were so thirsty they drank from a pond which had turned red with their own blood. Wounded from both armies, trying to help each other, died side by side, their blackened, bloated bodies intermingled with those of hundreds of dying horses and bestrewn with fragments of wagons, trees, and men. Experienced officers, despite previous battle experience, were shocked and dismayed at the sight of so much pitiful suffering. "The situation of a hale man, stricken down by violence," wrote Brinton, "is at times pitiful in the extreme, even when surrounded by those who sympathize and render all the aid they can. But the circumstances attending the battle of Shiloh were fearful, and the agonies of the wounded were beyond description."[29] An order of dubious wisdom protracted the nightmare on both sides by having the *Lexington* and the *Tyler* rain shells on Confederate positions at fifteen-minute intervals all night.

For those who did make it into a surgeon's care, one of the chief offenders was the Minié ball, which was designed by a French Army officer, Captain C.E. Minié, although the men quickly Americanized its pronunciation to *minnie*. In fact, it was not even a ball, but a cylindrical-conical or bullet-shaped projectile about an inch in length, fashioned out of soft lead with a hollow base which expanded under firing so as to spin the lead fast against the weapon's rifled barrel. Breech loaded into an Enfield .577 or a Springfield musket, the Minié ball empowered the troops with faster, farther, more accurate firing than most of the ammunition in the wild assortment of weaponry that made the distribution and exchange of ammunition so chaotic in early battles such as Shiloh. Unlike ball-shaped ammunition, the Minié's conical shape bored through rather than bounced off tissue. As the lead further expanded upon striking its target, there was much internal damage and the consequent loss of velocity caused a larger exit wound, if it exited at all. On impact, it often slowed to a halt and remained in the body, shards of filthy clothing having been carried into the wound, spreading infection so quickly that some doctors wondered whether the enemy hadn't perhaps poisoned its bullets. Murray remarked that practically every Minié ball extracted from either a Union or a Confederate wounded was bent, twisted, and sometimes even split, suggesting that the American version was even more malleable—and insidious—than its French prototype.

A Minié ball in the abdomen augured small chance of survival, the mortality rate being 87 percent; or, if the small intestine was hit, 100 percent. To be wounded in an extremity generally meant losing it, the bone being too severely shattered for surgeons to safely attempt to save it. The likelihood of surviving an amputation was roughly proportional to the distance of the wound from the trunk. Three-quarters of all operations during the war were amputations, the number exceeding that in any American war before or since. The staggering high statistics stirred up a controversy which placed Army surgeons under sharp critical fire, and even menaced some with threats of real fire from behind their own lines. But the more complicated surgical alternatives, such as excision or resection in which portions of bone were removed demanded more time, skill, and equipment than was available in most situations, and the Federal mortality rate for amputees, 26 percent, was two percent lower than for subjects of allegedly more conservative treatments. The great likelihood of surgical infection and the extremely weakened condition in which surgeons received their patients were major factors behind the two percent difference, and they help to explain the comparatively low 18 percent mortality rate for wounds to the bone that were treated with no operation at all.

The supreme irony of Civil War medicine is that its most precious instruments, the hands of the surgeon, were also its most destructive. Manifestations of killer infections were commonly thought to be quite the opposite, a view epitomized by the term *laudable pus*. The lack of clean water or any water at all for surgeons to wash with; the widespread practice of reusing old dressings, sponges, and unwashed instruments; the foul, crowded conditions of most hospitals; and the wide divergence of training, talent, and experience among surgeons, were all factors that mitigated and sometimes outweighed the benefits of submitting to medical treatment. But neither the art nor the science of surgery in the United States had passed much beyond its primitive stages at the outbreak of the war, and given that they were laboring under the worst conditions imaginable, the overall achievement of Army surgeons was truly remarkable. The history of war, however, is chiefly about the killing and not the saving of men, and historians tend to turn to a new scene the moment the generals withdraw and the surgeon enters the picture. The tactical ingenuity, courage, and stamina shown in life-and-death struggles within the bloody, malodorous confines of a tent at the edge of the field, or on the deck of a hospital steamer, have gone largely unexamined and unextolled. The are no memorials to commemorate surgical battles.

An unrelieved nightmare of amputations consumed the surgeons during the first night at Shiloh, bloody lost limbs being piled higher and higher in full view of those who were soon to add their own to the ghastly collection. Despite the hazards of chloroform, it was used as an anesthetic—sometimes in combination with ether—with a surprisingly high frequency of success, as were opium and morphine for pain. When, as at Shiloh, supplies of such medicaments were scarce, a few gulps of any available spirits, or nothing at all, had to suffice, and the hearts of some were too weak to withstand the paroxysms of pain and the shock of unanesthetized amputation.

On the morning of April 6, as soon as Murray heard the news in Savannah, he prepared tents for as many wounded as he could accommodate, and as Buell's troops arrived, he sent Buell's surgeons ahead on horseback with whatever supplies they could cram into their knapsacks. The following day, some of the lost equipment and supplies were recovered, but there were still shortages of every kind. Murray wrote: "From the sad experience of this battle, and the recollections of the sufferings of thousands of poor wounded soldiers crowded into tents on the wet ground, their wants partially attended to by an unwilling and forced detail of panic-stricken deserters from the battle-field, I am confirmed in the belief of the absolute necessity for a class of hospital attendants, enlisted as such, whose duties are distinct and exclusive as nurses and attendants for the sick, and also of a corps of medical purveyors, to act not only in shipping medicine, but as quartermasters for the medical department." In a single sentence, Murray had summarized the medical crisis in the West.[30]

On the evening of April 7, one of Buell's surgeons, Dr. B.J.D. Irwin, imposed an ingenious order on the confusion by bringing together hundreds of infantry tents to construct the first recorded all-canvas field hospital, which he then artfully organized to shelter scores of patients from a cold, windswept hailstorm that pelted exposed wounds for three hours. As supply trains and hospital boats began to converge on the landing, a desperate plea for 10,000 mattresses went out over the telegraph. The call was answered with uncommon alacrity, but Murray lost no time waiting. After having the first of the ships "fitted up with such bed-sacks as were on hand and with straw and hay for the wounded to lie upon, and filled to their utmost capacity,"[31] he started evacuating the worst cases to general hospitals along the Ohio River. Some of the boats from individual states were under orders to carry only their own men, and this naturally caused confusion and resentment, especially when further instructions to take only the wounded resulted in boats pulling away with plenty of room on board for the sick they were leaving behind. But Murray commended boats that were sent by civilian agencies such as the U.S. Sanitary Commission, which "were ready to receive all sick and wounded without regard to States or even to politics, taking the wounded Confederates as willingly as our own."[32] Although both Murray and Hewitt saw that each boat left with a senior surgeon who was qualified to perform operations en route, considerable distances often delayed proper treatment for several days. Since most of the boats were initially loaded with dire cases judged beyond hope of rejoining the ranks, they were also the least likely to survive the hardships of travel. As the war progressed, the injudicious procedure of subjecting critical cases to an exhausting and sometimes fatal conveyance away from the scene of the battle was replaced by taking the hospitals to the troops. But during Lauderdale's term, throughout the spring and summer of 1862, the old system was fully operative, and all of his principal duties, as one of a small team of surgeons under the command of Dr. Hoff, were attendant upon the transportation of wounded and sick troops aboard the *D.A. January*, from whose decks he wrote the majority of the letters in this volume.

ё ё ё

During Lauderdale's tour of less than five months in the Western theatre, the U.S. Army steamer *D.A. January* carried more than 3,000 patients from both sides of the conflict, traversing over 8,000 miles on the Mississippi, Ohio, and Tennessee rivers. Lauderdale was still in New York when the *January* picked up its first load of more than 400 men from the crowded bluffs of Pittsburg Landing and brought them to St. Louis, and by the time he arrived in that city the boat had returned to the landing to pick up its second load of 284, but a few days later the boat found him in Cairo, and when it steamed away toward Keokuk, Lauderdale was one of its team of physicians.

For a hospital transport, the *January* was a tolerably handsome vessel, seaworthy in function *and* in appearance, which was certainly not true of some of the makeshift creations in the bizarre assortment of steamboats and ironclads that were rushed onto the river during the early years of the war. Built in Cincinnati in 1857 and purchased by the U.S. Army on April 1 of 1862, it was referred to by Woodward and Otis, editors of the Army's monumental *Medical and Surgical History of the War of the Rebellion*, as "perhaps the most perfect of the western hospital boats." [33] It was a two-engine sidewheeler, 230 feet long, 65 feet wide, with a 35-foot beam. Directly after Lauderdale left it at the end of August in 1862, it was taken out of service and completely remodeled

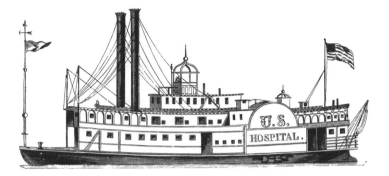

Illustration of the U.S. Army hospital steamer D. A. January *from* The Medical and Surgical History of the War of the Rebellion.

under Dr. Hoff's direction, but by September 29 it was loading troops again. "This boat," wrote Dr. Hoff, "on account of her light draught and airy cabin, was well suited for the purpose."[34] By August of 1865, it had carried a total of 23,738 patients.

The sick rooms of the *January* were located on the middle (or side) deck, with beds also installed on the lower (or boiler) deck beneath it. The nurses' quarters were farther aft on the middle deck, and Lauderdale's stateroom was directly above them on the cabin deck, just behind the larboard wheelhouse, where he often sat by the guardrail in front of his door penning his faithful reports to sister Frank of all that he passed along the river. The kitchen, the pharmacy, and the nurses' dining quarters were also on the cabin deck, at the rear of which was located the surgery. On the upper (or hurricane) deck in the enclosure known as the Texas, there were staterooms for the captain and his officers, and a Texas dining room, where Lauderdale took his meals. The boat flew a yellow flag from the foredeck to betoken its hospital status, there was a U.S. flag in the rear, and in large, bold letters, the wheelhouse bore the inscription: U.S. HOSPITAL.

The combined *corps du hospital* and ship's crew of the *January* numbered from forty to sixty men, with some female nurses—a new phenomenon in the field—whom Dr. Hoff found disruptive and referred to as "our Nightingales." That Lauderdale was not without affection for individuals on the boat can be inferred from his expressions of regret upon their departure, but with the exception of Dr. Hoff, practically no one is ever referred to by name, and there is no hint of any deeply rewarding camaraderie amongst his fellow physicians.[35] As ever, his best friend is Frank, and he is always eager to visit his brother Willis in St. Louis and to receive letters from home. His letters express a yearning for friendly society, but with consistently good grace he bore the isolation, along with illness, punishing heat, insect assaults, and tiring stretches of inactivity while the boat awaited orders. Along with writing to Frank, he enjoyed making small pen and pencil sketches, sometimes using them to augment his verbal descriptions, believing, as he later told his sister, that "there is no way so good to fix the form of any object upon your memory as to draw it."[36] One of his favorite amusements was to go up to the Pilot House, where he relished the fine view—the best on the boat—and where the pilot, a large, jovial Kentuckean, entertained him with colorful yarns and turns of phrase that put him in mind of Davy Crockett.

As a contracted civilian, Lauderdale did not wear a uniform or stripes, although he seems to have taken to wearing an army cap.[37] He is bearded in pictures taken while he was teaching at the Geneseo Academy, and beards were sufficiently common during the war that there is no need to suppose he would have removed it, but we have no portrait during his time aboard the *January*. He was tall and fairly lean, and during his tour in the West—partly due to illness—he became even leaner. It can be risky to read character from photography, especially at a time when slow exposures demanded a long, patient stare into the lens, but we need not read far into the eager, serious, somewhat insecure gaze we find in the Geneseo photos to know that Lauderdale's eyes were the prominent feature in his appearance. And it is fitting that the eyes should be so arresting in a man whose unquenchable appetite for seeing something of everything that was around him makes the letters such a rich fund of experience. Ironically, though, Lauderdale's letters are perhaps most significant not for what he describes, but for who he becomes, the disposition of his views on the subject of slavery and the politics of the war deriving, at times, less from what he observes than from what he does not.

Lauderdale's long, slender hand wrote in a smooth and steady script which was not elegant but which remained fairly legible, despite his familiar complaint that the ship's vibrating engines distorted his penmanship. Lauderdale published a few articles during his subsequent career on the Western frontier, but he was not a professional writer, and his war letters were written only for private consultation. He made this clear when he vetoed Frank's proposal to publish some of them locally, probably in the *Livingston Republican*, a common practice for soldiers but one for which Lauderdale did not feel his correspondence was suitable. It was important to him for Frank to understand that these were impromptu reports of private, completely unnewsworthy excursions and were never intended as polished writings. The letters are, indeed, rough, but their being very much of the moment, written directly after and frequently *during* the event, gives them a vitality and a compelling believability, a combination clearly lacking in some memoirs written for publication years after the war. There are few Great Stories among the letters, but the reader is amply rewarded by a wealth of observation and the knowledge that what Lauderdale owns to be experience can be trusted. "I can only give you the facts as they are transpiring this minute," he told Frank. The letters betray the diarist's obsession with making the dream of one's life real by getting it all down on paper before it vanishes, and fortunately there was ample time for Lauderdale to do so aboard the *January*.[38]

As it happened, Lauderdale served his term without encountering anything like the extensive medical practice which his brother Willis had promised with such assurance. By his own estimate, Lauderdale spent no more than a total of forty days treating patients. There were a number of amputations en route, but he himself performed no surgery, and although at times he was responsible for more than a hundred soldiers, few of his patients remained in his care—because they did not remain on the boat—for longer than two or three days. This floating hospital functioned, in fact, more like a capacious floating ambulance. "We hardly see our patients," Lauderdale told his father, "and make a poor diagnosis before they are off our hands. We cant see the effect of remedies, and the most we try to do is to render our patients as comfortable as possible, and promise them more thorough treatment at the hospitals." As for the question of whether Lauderdale would have been qualified to undertake more complex procedures had he been called upon to do so, a fair answer depends on one's point of view.

The main body of about 1,000 medical practitioners treating the troops during the war consisted of volunteer regimental surgeons, who worked principally on the battlefield, and noncommissioned contract surgeons, who, like Lauderdale, were paid as first lieutenants and were working mostly in hospitals. Being a doctor was not a requirement for volunteering to act as one in a regiment, and frequently states were no more stringent in examining new recruits for the medical corps than they were in supplying the rest of the Army. Physicians under contract may have been trained, highly responsible doctors holding degrees, or they may have been untutored, self-certified quacks pursuing the prospect of regular pay or drunken sawbones with a mania to be hacking away at the steady supply of subjects. Qualifications varied enormously, depending upon individual background, talent, and integrity.

Lauderdale could not compare with experienced Regular Army doctors, or even with newer Regulars or volunteers and contract surgeons who came to the Army after substantial civilian practice. But he had, at least, completed a medical course and was a certified M.D. Letters written upon his return to Bellevue reveal an especially eager and able apprentice surgeon, and if he was not fervidly passionate on the subject of his profession, he was certainly a serious-minded, hardworking practitioner. Although he had passed an exam to graduate, and one to become a resident, there was no qualifying exam for him to be working aboard the *January*. However, examinations or the lack of them did not necessarily raise or lower the level of practice during the war. Nevertheless, even a glance at Lauderdale's course at the Medical College of the University of New York reveals the inadequacy of the training which was typical of the time and how far from any modern sense of reliable were the hands into whose care the war delivered so many thousands of sick and wounded.

When Lauderdale commenced his two-year course in October of 1858, American medical training was still in the stone age as compared with what was available then in Europe. In fact, it was generally education *without* training. Established initially as a corrective against the deficiencies of the preceptor system, by which a student chiefly absorbed the wisdom—and the prejudice—of the physician with whom he apprenticed, the American system basically offered a brief but comprehensive term of lectures which was repeated every year by the same faculty. Now that the preceptor system had fallen out of favor, a medical education was mainly this single series of lectures attended twice. When Lauderdale returned to Manhattan for his second year of studies after a two-year hiatus as an assistant census marshal and a teacher in Geneseo, he wrote to Frank: "Things at the College are just the same, perhaps some improvements have been made." What he meant was that on his second time around, his professors were better at teaching the same courses.

The principal session, in winter, ran from October 20 to March 1. There were also spring, summer, and autumn lectures, but they were optional. It was thus possible for a student to take a degree and become a doctor after twice attending four months of lectures, interspersed with attendance at hospital clinics and rounds, without once touching a single living body.

Fortunately, the course at the Medical College of the University of New York (now New York University) had the advantage of access to several major hospitals, such as Bellevue Hospital and the New York Hospital, where Lauderdale's professors were staff physicians and he could attend interesting rounds and witness a variety of operations. "New York offers facilities to medical students that surpass anything I had any idea of," he wrote to his father at the start of his first term. "Bellevue Hospital has 2 or 3 hundred patients and I saw some operations there this afternoon which were quite interesting and which made me wonder at the skill of our surgeons. And the ease too with which they manipulate is truly marvelous." But Lauderdale himself did not assist or even dress at any surgery during his whole course of study, and his only hands-on task was assisting his father to set a fracture during his time between terms at Geneseo.

In his first term, two weekdays were filled with lectures in general areas such as Materia Medica, Obstetrics, Descriptive Anatomy, and the Principles and Practice of Surgery. The day lasted from 9 AM to 5:30 PM, with an hour and a half for dinner. During the evening, he read texts or wrote out notes from his lectures. On the remaining days there were clinics in the morning, leaving the afternoons free. The course cost Lauderdale a little over a hundred dollars per term, and the difficulty of meeting this expense, along with that of his room and board, caused his delay in beginning the course and the two-year postponement of its completion. At additional cost, extra instruction was available, such as a course in practical chemistry for $25, or one on the use of the microscope for $12, but both were beyond his means. There were also tutors for hire, at $30 per term, to conduct quizzes and answer questions, which were not encouraged during lectures. Memorization did not come easily for Lauderdale—"I am a little troubled in this way like my Mother," he told his father—but the cost for assistance was prohibitive and, following the advice of a helpful friend of his father, Dr. Leaming, he worked to strengthen his memory by relying on fewer notes.

Dissection of human subjects and their procurement having been recently made legal in New York, Lauderdale could at least probe the mysteries of the body within the once-living tissue of cadavers. With a trace of unconscious black humor, the '62-'63 college prospectus (which Lauderdale kept among his papers) boasts that "the supply of material, now no longer obstructed by legal penalties, is ample and constant." It also announces improvements in gas lamps and ventilation, and promises free use of soap and towels; but Lauderdale provides a few details not discussed in the catalogue:

> When we get some subjects we will form classes in dissection and then I will have to pay $2.00 for my fifth of the body. These divisions are distributed by lot to the members of each class of five. We will engage in this kind of business when it gets a little cooler.

By mid-November, he was performing his first dissections:

> I was fortunate enough to get an upper extremity & a lower one for one dollar, the price for fresh subjects being $2 a piece for each. This I have studied the muscles of, and I made a ligamentous preparation of the arm leaving nothing but the ligaments which hold the bones together. I am going to make a muscular arterial preparation as soon as I can get a fresh arm or leg.

Suspecting that these tactile encounters with human anatomy lay "at the base of all medical knowledge," Lauderdale determined to give dissection his fullest attention, although the study for him was not without discomfort:

> The worst part of this business for me is the offensive odor, but this we can get used to after being in the room a short time. When I get home I make pretty free use of cologne upon my hands, & at the table, by not bringing my hands any nearer to my mouth than the length of my fork handle, I can endure it.

His second term was busier than the first, for he was able to join a quiz group in the evenings, and the ever solicitous Dr. Leaming welcomed him into his clinic on chest diseases, one of the two areas—the other being obstetrics—that his father advised would be important for a practice in Geneseo. He spent a good deal of time at Bellevue, "where congregate medical students in great numbers to find out what the latest fashion is for cutting off limbs, and other surgical information." Lauderdale was not being facetious, for ever since the opening of hostilities, conflicting views on methods of amputation had been an issue, and Lauderdale's teachers, some of whom were eminent men in their fields, had added their voices to the controversy. At the same time, advertisements for artificial limbs became conspicuous in daily papers and weekly journals.

Lauderdale also attended lectures and demonstrations at the Pathological Society, the New York Eye and Ear Infirmary, and, "for recreation" on his way home at night he would call at the Cooper Institute to hear talks on chemistry and philosophy and to avail himself of the free use of laboratory equipment, diversions which he hoped would be of assistance to him as a teacher or lecturer. In the same spirit he "took the cars" uptown to Columbia College to audit the senior exams in chemistry, astronomy, and electricity, generally finding himself the only person in New York City who cared enough to attend them. In his spare time he read medical books at the nearby Astor Library. His excitement at all this constant study is summed up in a rare, exuberant outburst of delight: "What a grand place New York is to study disease!"

In fact, Sunday was now his only free day, which he occupied in going to hear sermons at the New Brick Presbyterian and at other churches around the city, often going directly from one to another. On one Sunday he went to hear the great naturalist Louis Agassiz address a large crowd at the Brooklyn Academy of Music. Considering Agassiz' renown in a field of enormous interest to him, Lauderdale's response to the talk reveals the continued primacy of religion in his life. "The subject was entirely scientific," he reported to Frank, "and I question very much the propriety of such a lecture on the sabbath."

In order to graduate, Lauderdale was required to write a thesis and pass oral examinations by all seven members of the faculty. In December of 1861, he wrote to his father: "I almost tremble when I think of being examined for a degree. I feel that I know so little about some things, yes, many things." He was sorry not to have studied more in the years between terms, and despite there being two months "for cramming my head with medical knowledge," his memory was still slow, and "much that we hear is swept away like the writing on the sand."

Among his examiners were several distinguished men in the world of medicine who had won his highest esteem. His professor of Descriptive Anatomy, Dr. William H. Van Buren, was shortly to become a director of the U.S. Sanitary Commission, to whose *Medical, Military, and Surgical Essays* he contributed "Rules for Preserving the Health of the Soldier." "It is as good as a romance to hear him lecture," Lauderdale told his father. His professor of Surgery, Dr. Valentine Mott, was, at seventy-six, the oldest professor on the faculty and was formerly its president. A pioneer in both orthopedic and general surgery, Mott joined his colleague Van Buren in contributing essays—on "Pain and Anesthesia" and "Haemorrhage from Wounds"—to the volume issued by the Sanitary Commission. Lauderdale pictured him as "the grand old Nestor of American surgery," his legs too weak to stand during lectures, his hands trembling, his talk full of stories from a lifetime in the profession.[39]

Lauderdale passed his examinations without incident, and his thesis was easy to write. A handwritten essay on ten legal sheets, it was a personal meditation on "The Relation of Natural History to Medical Science and the Importance of Scientific Studies to the Medical Practitioner." It was a sincere but very slight piece of writing which contained no research and could have been written in one evening. A current candidate for any higher degree would be incredulous to think that it sufficed for an M.D., but it was typical of a time when there were no state boards to control licensing in the profession. To practice medicine, no license was required.

As the war demanded increasingly more attention, more money, and more lives, some of its clamor and commotion began to break into the customary quietude of the Lauderdale chronicle, and the reader feels the city portrayed within it becoming progressively more martial. On a cold, stormy December night, Colonel James A. Mulligan, whose Irish Brigade had surrendered to Confederate forces in Lexington, Missouri back in September, draws a large, eager crowd to hear him speak from the balcony of the Fifth Avenue Hotel. Strange metallic leviathans are afloat on the Hudson River. Boardinghouse dinners are all abuzz with the Mason-Slidell affair and rumors of French and English support for the Confederacy. Stocks and commodities are in nervous fluctuation. The New York 7th Regiment can be seen in the city streets, now parading spiritedly into Lafayette Place for a grand review, now moving somberly toward the funeral of one of the regiment's first casualties. Irish militia march on St. Patrick's Day. Civilians are making regimental flags as gifts for local troops. Cannon salutes are audible from various points in the city. Newsboys belt out extras about the victory at Fort Donelson under the leadership of the Union's new hero, Unconditional Surrender Grant. Old Dr. Spring flies a victory flag from the steeple of the New Brick Church. Sunday sermons address the political situation, with God divinely appointing now one side of the conflict, now the other. The city's opinionmakers are waging wars of their own in the daily papers and weekly journals. News of the war is so essential that even no news is news and is deeply felt as a "painful silence." Lauderdale's father, having lost a campaign for sheriff because "it is hard to persuade the Republicans to Vote for an old Democrat," is concentrating again on his medical practice. Geneseo sends out its own regiment. Willis is tapping out U.S. Army transmissions on a St. Louis telegraph. Sam, now a clerk, is working first for a fellow Geneseoan, Brigadier General James S. Wadsworth, the military governor of Washington, D.C., in whose crowded office Secretary of War Stanton pushes his way past a steady stream of petitioners;[40] then Sam is assigned to a discharge officer, Captain George Conrad, whose headquarters, formerly McClellan's, are directly across the street from Lincoln's at the White House. On March 6, during Lauderdale's commencement, a clash of troops near Fayetteville, Arkansas, begins the Battle of Pea Ridge, which results in more than 2,100 casualties. A week later, Lauderdale reads of the Battle of Hampton Roads—the war's first clash of ironclads—between the CSS *Merrimack*, and the USS *Monitor*, which had been built up the Hudson River in Troy, New York.

Around March 25, Lauderdale receives the following notice from Dr. James R. Wood of Bellevue Hospital:

> Permit me to congratulate you that your examination for Junior
> Assistant has been satisfactory to the Committee.

A week later, General Johnston's troops begin their march on
Pittsburg Landing, and two weeks after that, Dr. Lauderdale boards a
train at Avon, New York, and settles in for the first stage of his journey
to St. Louis. In seeking out the beginnings of a career, the new doctor
finds a war. He makes his rounds on wards that are carried upon its
hotly contested waters, and becomes a messenger from the heart of a
wounded country.

The Letters

April [15] 1862[41]
en route to seat of War
Buffalo Depot
Tuesday Evening 11 Oclock

Dear Sister

My ride thus far has not been unusually remarkable.... I have got tickets and checks to St. Louis here—they do not sell them in Avon.[42] I am sitting in a high back car which I prefer to a sleeping car. It is not crowded, a few are lounging about in a semi-conscious state without any one to talk to. The gong strikes the signal for a start and we move off along the shore of the Lake with a beautiful moon shining down upon us from a clear sky. There is too much motion to write or read so I will doze.

Wednesday Morning [April 16]

Just arrived at Cleveland Depot & have taken breakfast at this place. Mr. Wheeler keeps the saloon. He is an old acquaintance.... I am in the C.C. & C. Cars. I guess uncle R[obert] did not get my dispatch as he does not make his appearance. I only remain 45 minutes....

10 AM

We are jogging along. The country is looking springlike, the grass is quite green in the fields and the buds of the swamp trees are bursting. The weather is quite warm. I am reading most of the time. I find no one that I am acquainted with. We are half way to Crest Line. The boy who is trying to sell me dime novels annoys me much. It is rather dusty going through Ohio. A woman just came on cars going to see a wounded friend

41

at seat of war. At Crestline we take on a company of marines and sailors on their way to Cairo to aid Gen Foote.[43] This savors of war a little.

We come to another Caledonia.

1 1/2 P.M.

Am traveling through a low level country suitable for grazing & corn. The place we are at is La Rue.

3 P.M.

Arrived at Bellefontaine. We stop 20 minutes to give the sailors time to get dinner. The weather very warm. At every place we stop the people come out of their houses to see the sailors.

5 1/2 P.M.

We have been detained by the engine breaking something & while it is being fixed the sailors get out of the cars & wash their faces in a little brook nearby. The passengers look on & ask what is the matter & complain about the delay. In the distance are 5 women who are also looking on. They appear to be boiling sap in the woods opposite. This is a rather hard looking country through this western part of Ohio. The houses are either log or brick. I saw them raising a log house a few miles back. We are going very slow. It is 100 miles to Indianapolis. They dont go much faster than only V. RR.

Union city 7 P.M.

The dividing line between Ohio and Indianna. Train an hour behind time.

11.40 PM

I feel just like complaining bitterly with the train that I should have to stop here at Indianapolis but our sailors being in great demand at Cairo have induced the train to go to St Louis to wait & so we are going on to night.

Thursday 7AM [April 17]

We have been going all night. I slept very little. Daylight reveals extended prairies the like I never saw before. Corn seems to be *the* product besides pasturage. It has thundered &̕ lightened & rained quite hard during the night.... These prairies are immense and are seldom enclosed by fences, and being so low & level they seem to be muddy & disagreeable. Their beauty is seen only in summer. They are like the sea in a calm. You see very few trees on them. I would like to see a herd of buffalos and Indians in hot pursuit, to realize my early idea of them. The Father of waters shows itself in the distance. The fruit trees are in blossom and all things are quite far advanced.

> St Louis
> Planters House
> 3 P.M. of Thursday
> [April 17]

I made my way in the bus to this place where I found Will awaiting me. Found him well. I am too late to see Dr Hoff but shall leave for Cairo this evening on board the *Crescent City*. Then I expect to see or hear from him, and will be able to tell better what I shall do with myself. A large artillery company are going along with us whose destination is Pittsburg Landing. I shall remain at Cairo a few days awaiting Dr. Hoff who left word for me to do so.

I would tell you more about St Louis, but will reserve it for another letter. I shall not have time to see the friends for whom I have parcels. Willis will deliver them. I wish you to direct any communication for me to the care of Will & he will forward them to me.

I will close these rough notes of travel which I have so carelessly written during my ride. Hoping to hear from you soon and that you are all well I remain with much love from Will and myself your

> Affectionate brother
> John

> St. Louis Thursday Eve
> On Board *Crescent City*
> bound for Cairo.

Dear Frank

I am in a strange place to night, and surrounded by strangers. I will explain to you how I am situated. I have already dispatched you my notes of travel thus far. After dinner Will and I came down on the levee and came on board the above named steamer which is going down the river to night. Being too late to see Dr. H. at this place, at his request I go to Cairo, where I expect to meet him. Our boat is now used as a transport, and the passengers are composed of a battery of 7 guns and a hundred men with horses, cattle, ammunition etc. The soldiers are the roughest set of men I ever saw. They occupy the cabin and as I write are walking up & down, sitting down, reading, or talking, eating, playing cards. They all expect to sleep on the floor and some have been sweeping up clean places to lie down on. They wrap themselves in their blankets, and lay their heads on their knapsacks. They all together form the most motley crowd that I ever fell in with. They are quite noisy at times & once or twice this afternoon they have got into a row, and then it is necessary for a superior officer to come and restore order. Some of these soldiers are from Iowa, some from Indiana. I believe their destination is Pittsburg Landing.

I have taken a state room, and should retire very soon, because I have slept but little during my long railroad ride.

What little I have seen of St Louis does not give me a very favorable impression of its beauty. The city is looking quite black and dingy. The streets are paved with a poor quality of stone, and are rather rough. It has rained very hard lately and the mud, which is of a peculiar grey color, is very deep. The river (The Mighty Mississippi) is rising and is carrying down great quantities of flood wood. What a muddy stream it is! & how muddy or discoloured is the water that St Louis people drink!

I wish you could take a walk, through this cabin, and see these soldiers in their various attitudes and employments.

Friday 10 AM [April 18]

I am now sailing down the Mississippi—we did not leave St Louis till 7 this morning. This river scenery is now attracting my attention. As I sit on the deck we are sailing along about 10 miles an hour. The banks are skirted on one side by cotton wood, elm and sycamore trees. On the Missouri side where we are now, we have a fine view of strictured rocks, which exhibit all kinds of architectural forms, such as columns, arches, chimneys with here & there deep caves. We pass a gray stone with a square tower, the most architectural structure I have seen. There are scattered houses along the way—some are painted white and look pleasant. The air is rather cool this morning, and I find my over coat very comfortable. There are two or three medical men on board on their way to Pittsburg landing. I have just been talking with a young man who described to me some of the incidents of that battle. There is a tree which grows along the river that has a pink blossom like the peach, and this with the delicate green of the young leaf looks very beautiful. The river being very high now, it is miles in width in places. One of the cattle broke away and jumped over board, she swam to the shore but finding it very steep could not get out. The boat was turned about and she was captured with much difficulty. We must now be approaching Island No 5. This is the way they build their chimneys to the houses.[44] I see an occasional wheat field which looks beautiful. Crows are the only birds to be seen. The soldiers are taking their time lounging, talking, sleeping, smoking, playing cards, dominoes, and some are writing to their friends. We are running quite near shore, we change our course constantly. Now we see little cascades spuing foam from between the layers of rock. The soldiers long to fill their canteens at these places, and would like to get on shore.

We pass a fine large stone mill, and a neat country farm house.[45] Then a low shore with a gentle rising land beyond. The Missouri shore is the most interesting. St. Genenvieve is on our right. The Illinois shore offers nothing to the view but a long line of cotton wood & willow trees. It is a fact that those soldiers who have been in battle are much more quiet and thoughtful than new recruits. It sobers a man down very much.

12 AM

Pass St. Mary's. Persons acquainted with the river are able to tell you the number of inundations by the successive growths of cottonwood which spring up on the recession of the flood.

I am sitting now in the Pilot House where I have the best view I have had. The village of Chester is now in view, situate up on a hill on the Illinois side. Also mouth of the Kaskaskia river.

Just after dinner I am sitting on deck. I see trees on shore which have bunches of open leaves situated in different places upon the branches. I am told they are the Mistletoe. They are the first I have seen. A soldier has just whittled his pilot bread into a round shape which he calls "an extra wheel for the cannon." We carry the stars and stripes and it is answered by people on the shore by a flag or handkerchief. It is often wondered by people on shore, where the soldiers come from. A waggish soldier replied once that he came from the north pole, and that there were two regiments waiting to come when he left.

You will remember the trading boats which slip along down the shore and trade with the natives.[46] The trees & vegetation is about like it would be in June at home. The next place of note which we pass is Cape Garrydo or more correctly Girardeau where we see a fort at the top of a hill in rear of the town. It is quite a neat looking place, houses are built of brick.

We reached Ka-ro (as pronounced) about 9 P.M. Here I left the boat on which I have been a guest during a very pleasant trip from St Louis. The boat will go on to her destination, Pittsburg Landing. It being dark, those who landed had to look out for mud. It is an awful place just now, as the water is high in the river, and as the rains have been frequent, and everything has conspired to make this naturally disagreeable place the biggest mudhole in the country. Every man goes about work with his pants rolled up. It was dark when I landed & it was by mere good luck that I did not go over my head in the mud in the principal street.

I am stopping at the St Charles Hotel, the only place in town. This is full of people who are engaged in the war in some capacity. They seem to be talking of nothing else. There are many soldiers here who are relating their own individual experience to their friends, and criticizing the operations of the different generals. I begin to feel as though I was almost in hearing distance of the guns. A young soldier who was at Pittsburg battle has presented me with a bayonet which he picked up from a rebel gun. He showed me a fine sword, which he also obtained at the same place.

Saturday Morning [April 19]

The rain is coming down in great quantities. (The town seems to be well nigh inundated.) If the river rises a foot & a half more, it will wash over the levee. There were 8 or 10 transports arrived here this morning bringing Gen Popes army, or several divisions of it. With this addition to the people, we have the streets completely thronged with men walking here and there hardly knowing what they want. This portion of the

army are going up the Tennesee River. In some of the streets they go from house to house in boats. I am in a drug store near the P.O. finishing this letter to you & you would laugh to see the motley crowd that come & go buying little luxuries & medicines for their dreary camp life. With much love to all my friends & wishing you to send all communications for me to Willis to be forwarded I remain

Your affectionate brother

John

St Charles Hotel Cairo

Apr 20/62 [47]

Dear Frank

    Yesterday after I put my letter in the P.O. I came back to the Hotel and who should I meet among the great crowd of people at this place but "Dug" Tyler. He wore a cap *a la militaire* & I found he was a paymaster clerk in the army & I was right glad to meet a person that I knew. Dug is here with his father in law, a Major somebody. Soon after I cast my eye on the Hotel register and saw the name of my old friend Dr Newberry, I made haste to find him and he introduced me to a lady who was his traveling companion, a Miss Brayton of Cleveland. They had just come in from Pittsburgh [48] where they had been to look after the interests of our soldiers. Miss B. has been very active in the Ladys Relief Committee & had been making inquiries as to what could be done to better the condition of the army. All the rooms at the Hotel being taken I gave up mine to Miss B. & Dr N. & I lodged in the Soldiers Home, a place which was kindly offered us by Rev Mr. Folsom (the father of our Mr F). This Mr F. is engaged in a good work here in the way of receiving & disbursing all kinds of hospital stores to the sick & wounded. He inquired of me after his son George. Dr N. is one of the sanitary commission. [49] He left this morning with his friend for St Louis on his way to Cleveland.

    This is Sunday, but you would not think it if you were here in this hotel, such crowds of soldiers coming and going.

On board *D.A. January*

Hospital Transport

7 P.M.

    While I was sitting by the table writing you Dr Hoff came in and said his boat was waiting, it having stopped to take me out of that Cairo

Mudhole which is likely at any moment to be submerged by the river. I almost trembled at the idea of staying there another night. I am now on a first class river steamer which has been fitted up for a transporting hospital. We have on board about 300 sick and wounded taken from Pittsburgh Landing, the place of the last battle. They with nurses, crew and other attendants constitute the company on board. We are bound for Keokuk, where there is a large receiving hospital in which these wounded are to be placed for treatment. Both State Room and main deck are filled with cot beds filled with the sick lieing along just as near together as possible. Some of their countenances are pictures of despair. There are three medical men on board besides myself, who do all in our power to render them comfortable. We are steaming up the river against a strong current.

6 P.M. April 21st/62

I have just come down from "Texas" and am sitting in the after cabin, and will begin again. I must say the "Texas" is the cabin on the hurricane deck, where we dine. I have been very busy to day dressing the wounds of our patients. Their bodies are more or less pierced with balls, or injured from the bursting of shells. I have dressed three to day who have been shot directly thru the upper portion of their lungs, and who seem to be doing well & likely to recover. I did not think it possible that a man could be so riddled and survive. There are several other diseases, such as Pneumonia, Erysipelous, and low grades of Typhoid fever, but the most are the "Vulni lutulici" to be technical. Our wounded are from Illinois, Wisconsin, Iowa and Indiana regiments who were so badly cut up at Pittsburgh. It is rather a bad sign if a soldier has a wound showing the ball to have passed in to his body from behind, for it tells us that he must have been hit while retreating. When you ask a soldier if he has been shot in the back, he does not like to tell you the fact. Our wounded are generally from all grades of society, generally the humbler walks. One man who had received a gun shot through the arm, and was struck by a piece of a shell in the back, was making a great ado. I asked him what had been his business heretofore, he replied that he had lately had charge of a ladys Academy in Wisconsin, and had given up his place there, to be a soldier. It brings a strong man down to the helplessness of a child, to be a victim of war, & it is only the hardy ones that can bear up under such shocks. Two or three were breathing hard as I passed their cots just now and I fear they will not go off the boat alive. As every part of this boat has been converted into a hospital, the little room where liquor or sigars are sold, is now occupied by an apothecary who deals out the medicines ordered by the doctors. "Ordered," I say, because every thing has to be specially ordered before it can be dealt out. While the river boats in general display their stars and stripes from their flag staves, our boat has a little piece of yellow bunting flying from her bow which you remember is hospitals colors the world over. There are three ladies on board who are acting the part of Florence Nightingales. One is a Wisconsin senators wife,[50] and I have not learned the names of the others yet. These three go around to the cots of the patients, and pretend to minister words of comfort & attend to little wants. I saw one reading in a Testament to a dying one. With all these kind arts, they take some liberties such as suffering the patients to complain of the attentions of the Physicians, when they are doing their best to relieve their wants. Dr Hoff is "down" on them and says if they don't keep their mouths closed that he will set them on shore. He dont appreciate their attentions *at all* and shows them very little respect. They appear to be of the strong minded variety of femininity.

We are about 30 miles below St Louis & we may stop there a moment. If so I will mail this there. If not I will send it from Keokuk some ways above.

It has rained every day nearly since I came into this valley, and is so cold that fires are indispensible. I suppose however that this cold weather is better for our gun shot wounds than warm weather would be. I shall expect you to write me as often as ever, and direct letters to St Louis care of Willis.

Enclosed I will send you a little of the advanced vegetation of these latitudes, a specimen of lilac from Cairo, also a leaf of the cotton wood or water poplar, which grows along these rivers, also a dogwood blossom from Pittsburgh Tennesee, the place of the recent battle.

I wish to know all about the Library matters and every other item of interest occuring in your pleasant quiet village. With much love to all I remain yours affectionately

                                                                Brother John

                                          Tuesday Evening Apr. 22, 62
                                          abreast of Hannibal Mo

Don't you wish you were here to go ashore and see your Hannibal friend What's her name? I am very tired. I have been waiting on over 70 patients, dressing their wounds and stumps & relieving their numerous wants—in a word, getting them into fighting order again. These men tell us all the incidents of the battle they were in, and they talk among themselves of the incidents to which they were eye witness, and participators. One soldier told another who received a wound in the side of his foot, that he made a great mistake in not raising his foot 1/8 of an inch higher, at the same time remarking that he the speaker would not have had his arm shot off, if he had not raised it quite so high. Those patients who are suffering with typhoid fever are pretty badly off. We have lost two thus far on the trip, and I fear one or two more will be coffined before tomorrow night. It is impossible to do justice to so many, crowded together as they are in every nook and corner on both decks.

Wednesday Noon [April 23]

We have just arrived at Keokuk and the patients who can, walk up to the Hospital barracks provided for them. The remainder have to be carried in carriages. We shall leave in the morning for down the river stopping at St Louis. I am just permitted to see one little corner of the state of Iowa. There is no one here that I know of upon whom I could call.

I wish you could send me the *Liv[ingston] Republican*[51] to Willis and he can forward it to me. I am very isolated. We make so few landings that we dont get the papers regularly.

Keokuk is very much in situation like St Louis.

You will please accept this imperfectly written epistle as I have been writing at different times and under unfavorable circumstances. I will close this from your affectionate

Brother John

Thursday P.M. [April 24]

Dear Frank

When we reached Keokuk last evening the good people of the place sent down their carriages, and assisted the sick and wounded to the hospital. The building set apart for this purpose is a hotel, that was formerly used as such, but business being much diminished in the town, it is too large for such a purpose, and makes a splendid place for a hospital. I found here between five & six hundred soldiers who are recreating & recovering from their wounds. (Fine writing is impossible the boat trembles so.) Keokuk is a *right smart* kind of a place, but business has received a check, from which it will not recover till after the war.

We got off early this morning, and shall reach St Louis this evening, if nothing happens. Our boat seems quite deserted, their being no one on board but the *corps du hospital* and boats crew, say 40 persons. It costs the U.S. about 200 dollars a day to keep such an establishment. After leaving St Louis we shall go down to Pittsburg for more sick. Every thing is being cleaned up for their reception. We shall have a rest till we take on more wounded. I have been on deck to look at the scenery, but it has been so monotonous and [as] the weather is rain and cold I prefer the cabin.

As we are coming into St Louis I see over on the opposite shore the *Gladiator,* the craft whose decks you walked & which carried you down to Dixie land. The Pilot tells me that she has also been brot into govern-ment service and is now carrying troops.

Planters House, St L.

I have just arrived at this house again, but Willis is not here. I under-stand that he has gone off to a concert this evening. I may see him before I go. Our destination from this point is quite uncertain, and our time of leaving is also unknown to me. It is now rumored that we will be obliged to get off at the earliest moment in the morning.

It would please me to stay here a day or two, but those who are in the U.S. Service must go at a moments notice, wherever they are ordered.

I am having a little chat with Will. He sends his love with mine to you all.

Your affectionate brother
John

Tennesee River, State of Kentucky on board the steamer *D.A. January* April 26th 1862 3PM

Dear Frank

We did not leave St Louis till 3 PM of yesterday and that gave me a longer visit with Will. He stayed with me a long time, the boat expecting every moment to cast off. Will gave me introductions to several of his friends who came on board to see our hospital. I did not have time to visit any one of my acquaintances while in town. After we got off I went up to the Pilot house where I viewed the scenery over again which I saw on my down trip just a week before. There is a great deal of sameness, the land being very low for a long distance back from the shore, and the shore itself being skirted by a dense growth of trees, your view is limited, but the pilot says as we get farther up the Tennesee "the land will begin to hill up" some. After all, there is something rather beautiful in the long line of vegetation which like hedge rows overhangs the margins of this mighty river and its tributaries. The trees we have passed today are quite green and are nearly in full suit of summer dress. Sometimes our boat goes so near these trees that you can reach out and pick a leaf. You must remember that the water is very high now and these rivers extend over many miles of country in some places. One word about our pilot, he is a large man weighing 250 pounds & knows every nook & turn in the river as well as the position of every bar. He told us when we were passing a place that had small willows growing upon it which of course was not visible to us. I asked him what he thought of secession, and his views were correct. He has no idea of letting the Mississippi River be cut in two if he can prevent it. He knows this river as well as he knows his big fat face and he certainly has a claim to it. Slavery he thinks a divinely appointed institution and like a good many in these parts says, if he thought this was to put a stop to slavery, he should not lift a finger to check the rebellion. He firmly believes that the children of Ham are to be slaves throughout all time.

This morning at an early hour we passed Cairo and during the forenoon we have been coming from that point to Paducah. Here we have the state of Kentucky on both sides of us. At this place we see a collection of white tents and soldiers standing about, & learn that it is a portion of Gen Buells division stationed here to keep this town all right. We see also the stars & stripes waving from a pole, and wherever we see this, we feel that the people on shore welcome us as we pass.

This afternoon we are running up the Tennesee river, and nothing of note shows itself to our view save here and there a little low house may be seen among the trees which skirt the river on either side, but I doubt about this being inhabited as the water is so high that it must be impossible. We passed one house where the people had carried their goods into the 2nd story for protection. The whistle sounds! A boat must be in sight, soon the steamer *Platte Valley* approaches and passes. She is just from Pittsburg, the place of our destination.

I saw some orioles flying among the trees along the shore. There is a great scarcity of life in these woods. I wish I could look out and see an alligator raising his head out of the water or some bird or some creature moving about. In the words of the poet, "the mink he keeps below." I am sitting in the Captains office in the fore part of the boat where I can see every thing we pass. Our Captain is a very pleasant and sociable man. The nurses (men) have been very busy at work making the beds, and arranging for the next load of wounded. The saloon cabin looks very neat. Just after supper we all went out on deck to look at Fort Henry which is now garrisoned by our troops and was captured by our gun boats under command of Gen Grant.[52] It is situated at a bend in the river commanding a view of several miles down the stream. Fort Donnelson is about 12 miles distant from this place. Fort H. is placed on an elevated ground & occupies a clearing of 20 acres. When the ground was cleared the trees were used for making houses. I counted about 20 rows of these huts & there must have been about a dozen buildings in each row. They afforded shelter for the rebels during the winter. Our men who are there do not use these huts, but live in tents. As we passed we saw them cooking their evening meal. On a high bluff opposite, we saw another line of fortifications. Lying close to the shore was the remains of a steamboat which the enemy had burned when they left the fort. Some portions of the fortifications were built of bags of sand piled up one over the other, looking in the distance like sacks of coffee. But Gen Grants gun boats demolished these carefully constructed works, and it must be rather humiliating to the Rebels to think they were only able to hold this fort for an hour and 20 minutes after the fighting had begun. As this is about the first point I have seen which looks like war, it reminds me more forcibly than ever that we are getting into the enemies borders. We expect to reach Pittsburgh to-morrow (Sunday P.M.).

Sunday Afternoon [April 27]

I was awakened this morning by several blasts of the whistle sounded at intervals to prevent "a collision" as the Pilot said, it being very foggy. The carpenters had not quite finished their work of preparation, and were making some noise. There is a cool wind blowing, and I try to keep out of it as much as I can. I have been suffering a good deal of pain for several days with sore throat, but am about over it now. As we steam along, our ears are filled with the singing of birds in a distant tree top. I have been reading the *Observer* this morning & am thankful to the news dealer in St Louis who has them to sell.[53] We see now and then among the floating wood pieces of charcoal timber & this is thought to be portions of the bridge which Gen Buell burned to cut off rebel communications across this river. What a bold piece of engineering that was which enabled our army to surround the rebels at Island No 10, made by Colonel Bissell.[54] I see some boxes on board marked to his address.

We are not a great ways from Savannah & expect to make a landing there. We have been in Tennesee nearly all day. The shores on both sides have "hilled up" and I enjoy the scenery much more. I never can see any beauty in a low shore. I say, give me a hilly or a rolling country instead of Prairie. I wish you could see the beautiful hills that I am now looking out upon covered with a mantle of green, such a green as only June brings us at home.

3 P.M.

We have just passed Savannah where we threw on shore a packet of papers. We saw a collection of tents, and a few soldiers lieing under the shade of some trees. I learned that there were two regiments stationed there. We soon shall reach Pittsburgh Landing & there we who have had such a long rest, will have to go to work caring for the sick which we shall take on board. The weather is rather warm, the thermometer stands at 83°. We occasionally pass some dense jungles where vines and trees form a very dense shade. The mistletoes being of denser green than the other leaves render the gloom that over hangs them more impenetrable. We are now in sight of Pittsburgh the neighborhood of the greatest battle ever fought in our country. I see a good many steamboats in sight.

Sunday 10 P.M.
Pittsburgh Landing, Tenn.

I write it sunday, but it has been very little like the day since our arrival at Pittsburgh Landing. This place is situated on a high bluff commanding the river in a very thickly wooded country, with numerous ravines in the vicinity. A place very favorable for the enemy but rather disadvantageous to our forces. I have not as yet visited the battle ground. But who should I meet coming on board just as we landed but Dr Gordon from Cleveland, the irritable doctor dressed in the garb of a regimented surgeon. I was glad to see him and he was rather surprised to see me. He was very anxious to get some newspapers of a late date. We gave him some and he mounted his horse and rode back to his regiment 7 miles away. Gen Halleck is about 3 miles from here and they are expecting a battle soon.

Do you remember a tall sandy haired fellow by the name of Tubbs at the Normal School 2 years ago? He accosted me to day on the boat, he is a musician in a band at this place. He wanted to know if the Normal was going on this summer.

Monday Evening 10 oclock [April 28]

I have seen so many things and done so much that I hardly know where to begin my narration of events and scenes that I have witnessed to day. One of our men who came on board last night sick with typhoid fever died during the night. As soon as it was known that our hospital boat was at the landing we were beseiged with regimental doctors, anxious to get rid of their sick, and put them on our boat. They all begged the privilege, but we only allowed them to do so after they had leave from the Post Surgeon, and we would receive only the sickest of their sick. The others must do as well as they can but we can not accomodate more than 150. Oh you would sympathize with these poor fellows if you could see them walking along with feeble gait, or being carried in the arms of their comrades or on "stretchers," on their way to the boats. Poor broken down frames of men, some of them were. Some of them must die sooner or later. The exposure of camp life, arduous labor, broken rest, picket duty, excitement of war and the overcoming of that inborn horror of sheding a brotherhood (that is too tame an expression), I should say the firing of bombshells into the bodies of men, cutting them down like grass, seeing their heads torn from their bodies, limbs scattered here and there, wounded men groaning with pain, being obliged to wait long, before their wants can be relieved, suffering pain themselves and naturally disturbed by the expression of pain in others, besides other horrid scenes that a battle field strewn with dead men and horses presents, is quite enough to bring a strong man down to the weakness of a child, and render him the victim of disease. I walked over a portion of the battlefield to day (you will remember that it did not take place in a ten acre lot, but extended over several miles, during the two days fight), & how shall I describe it to you. It is some 3 weeks since the fight, and things have changed some. The scene of action is an open wooded country covered here and there by rather large black oak trees, very little underbrush except in the little ravines which latter render the land uneven. There are a good many tents scattered here & there near the landing, but the long lines of army waggons drawn by 4 horses or 6 mules, the teamster riding upon the hind mules, men on horseback running here and there giving orders or directing this thing or that, carrying goods and stores to the different regiments, some of whom you see cooking their food over fires. Large baking waggons with bread piled up to the cord almost. Pilot bread in great quantities, boxes and barrels scattered here and there, long lines of mules and horses fastened by ropes and eating their corn or oats off the ground (a great deal wasted thereby), carpenters working or repairing some broken waggons, a good many meandering about with nothing to do. Some 24 pounders stationed behind an earthwork, long lines of tents in the distance. A regiment of cavalry on the march, an old house used as a fortification & beset by crowds of men, a tent where photographs were being taken, besides many things that I don't think of just now made up the list of what I saw on the battle field of Pittsburg. I picked up some little things such as bullets and pieces of shell with which I filled a cartridge box and came away. I might have brot away gun barrells & bayonets & such things, but I should find them too heavy to carry & as there is nothing peculiar in their construction I left them behind.

Tuesday P.M. Apr 29th

Last night we took on about 150 sick men & we cared for them a while & to day we placed the sickest of them on another transport to be taken to a hospital at Harrisburg about 4 miles above here on the river. It is very wearing to the sick to be shifted around so much. We did not retain them on our boat, because we expect a battle soon & must be in readiness for wounded men. This P.M. we took on board some wounded "Secish," who tell us they are from New Orleans. There are two Medical Men among them & they represent some of the chivalry of the South. There is also a captain with his arm off & other officers & men, two or three dark complected boys who acted as nurses in the hospital in which they were taken. It is said that there is some fighting going on a few miles from here. If so, we shall know more about it tomorrow. It rained again very hard last night & the river continues to rise.[55]

Tuesday April 29th 62

You would naturally suppose that I would inspect our prisoners with more than ordinary scrutiny. I have looked at their army clothing, which is of a light grey color. One of the soldiers pulled a button off from his coat, and gave it me as a curiosity. I will send it to you. I gave a Lieutenant a *Frank Leslie*['s *Illustrated Newspaper*],[56] which had the battle of Pittsburg. As he held it in his left hand (the other being shot away) he seemed surprised that we should have such a fine picture so soon. To another he gave a piece of my *Observer*. I have not had any time to say any thing to these men on the war question, but those that have, tell me that they lay all the blame of the war upon their leaders, who they say have led them on. The youngest of the party, a dark faced

boy from New Orleans, and who has a rogueish look... in his appearance, is only sixteen years of age and he tells me there are a great many boys in the southern army.

10 P.M. same day

All is quiet along shore. The stars shine brightly to night, the Tennesee rushing along by our boat as she lies tied to the shore. The weather has been rather warm to day but the clouds have shut off the full rays of the sun. I have been around among the sick this evening giving them a few simple medicines. There are so many of them, that it is impossible to do justice to each one. We cant stop and talk with each patient, making such a careful examination as we would do in private practice or in a hospital, but we administer such remedies as we think will do them some good and pass to the next. There are several very sick men—their disease is typhoid fever. We lost one this morning, and we fear many will go off before [tomorrow] morning. Our treatment of these cases is very unsatisfactory, because we do not see them till the disease has nearly destroyed them. I would almost as soon die in battle as to fall a victim to fever, when to the movements to which I should be subject so frequently, as is the case in armies moving, I must be so much thrown about. Several of our patients are delerious, and it requires constant watching to keep them from getting up and falling overboard. The sickness which follows all armies is one of the most melancholy part[s] of the whole scene. Our "secesh" are resting quietly in nice clean bunks. They are saying but little to any one.

Wednesday 4 P.M. [April 30]

We have been taking on our boat the most broken down lot of men I have seen yet. There are a good many Fever Patients among them, and I fear we shall not get them off alive. I saw five women going along the shore, two of them were sisters of some catholic order. I suppose they are visiting the sick on some of the boats. There are several "secesh" wounded, and they are badly off. I assure you our balls and shells have had an effect on them. Their own doctors are dressing their wounds which is a relief to us.

10 PM Wednesday

I have just finished my round of visiting sick. Have administered medicines to 100 during the last two hours. I take my basket of medicines and go from cot to cot and bunk to bunk to give each one something that will do him some good. Our hygienic treatment is no doubt of the greatest good to the sick. Better perhaps than the medicines in many cases. We have lost two to day, one of them was one of the Secesh. He died from his injuries & want of proper care. The Medical director sent an order by some men to have him buried & they took him off with others of our men & buried them up the hill near the battle ground. There is no ceremony attending the burial of dead on the battle field. They dig trenches as wide as the length of a man, and from ten to twenty feet in length, and place the bodies in, as many as they can get, and cover them up. There is scarce a stake or a flat board left nearby, to mark the name of the body. In a few places I would see a name cut on a flat piece of wood or marked with a pencil. Horses and men have to be buried out of the way to prevent contagion. In some places where the Rebels were buried, the men in their haste had not so carefully covered them but that the rains have so settled the earth, that here and there a foot may be seen sticking out. The covering up of so many thousands was no light labor, and if imperfectly performed, was somewhat excusable. We have taken on quite a number of sick and wounded to day, still we have rooms for some more, and just as soon as we get a load, we shall be off. The talk now is that we will go to Cincinnatti. I am very anxious to get away from here, as it is not a very interesting place, except for the battle which has just been fought.

I have had a long talk with one of our "Secesh" doctors about the war and the prospects of its being brot to a close soon. He tells me that they feel that it is their duty to fight to the last. They cant see themselves in any other condition than we were before we as a nation declared ourselves free from English tyranny. They did not expect that the people of the northwest would turn out in such numbers to suppress the rebellion. They thought that after they should be recognized by Europe, they could then make proposals for a reconstruction of their government. That they are not fighting for the slave, but for their rights. They speak in very high terms of Stephen A Douglas. They speak well of Lincoln, but not so of Seward.[57] It seems so strange to converse in such a friendly way as I have, with these men who have so lately been warring against us, and one can hardly believe they are our prisoners of war. They smoke their meerchaums & seem as contented as if they were in their own homes. They seem to realize the fact that we are much the most powerful in war, & I think are not a little surprised with the extensive arrangements with which we are carrying on this contest.

Thursday Evening. [May 1]

This is the first day of May and it has been a very pleasant one, somewhat warm. Orders came this morning to carry our sick onto the steamer *Louisiana*, which I think goes to St Louis, which we did, and I was pained with the thought of having the poor fellows changed again to another boat, because it aggravates their disease very much. But one sees every moment something which appeals to his sympathy for suffering humanity. Today we have lost over a dozen men. Our coffins are all used, and the carpenters have been very busy this P.M. making up a lot of rough boxes to supply the place. Those who die on the boat are sent ashore for burial. Six men have been tugging the coffins up the hill from the boat to a place set apart for burial. I have written the names of several on a piece of board with red chalk to be placed at the head of each grave, so their friends may find them if they wish. Some come on the boat so near dead that they cant speak to tell us their names. We begin again to take on sick, and by sun down we got a full load of about a hundred. Among them there were a good many wounded secesh, and our balls have made sad havoc with their legs & arms. Some have been shot in more vital parts. Nearly all those who are wounded are rebels. Our men suffer from fevers, colds & diarhea. They are all very much emaciated, and need recruiting greatly. After spending a few days at this place I must say that I never fully understood the reality of war. Men become very much hardened, and bear with hardships and suffering to both mind & body which would not be endured an instant in other situations. Many officers order their men about like slaves, and it is strange to see how calmly they submit to be them.

There were several secesh prisoners who came on board to day. One was a medical student and had an arm full of medical books with him, also some blankets. Towards evening an order came from Gen Halleck to have them come to his headquarters. This poor fellow found his books and blankets too troublesome to carry about, & he gave them to me. Some of the books were valuable. I gave the rest of the articles to the Pilot of our boat. I reserved several other articles which he had rolled up with them. A soldier wants just as little as possible to carry around with him, for he is very apt to lose all he has. A great many lose their money, especially those who are sick, and can scarcely hold their hats on their heads, much less [be] able to carry their knapsacks around with them.

The separation of friends or acquaintances is a cross which they have to bear. Some would like to keep together in the same company, but you see that these things can't be done. A person who enters the army must be prepared for the worst possible, and then he will more than realize all he imagined. Our secesh doctors have left the boat. They were also transferred. We parted with a friendly good by & shake of the hand. After we got our load of sick we had orders to go to Cincinnatti, and we have been now several hours on the way. We shall probably reach that place by Saturday.

Friday Evening [May 2]

I have just been my rounds among the sick and wounded of our boat, some three hundred broken down and dying men. I believe there are no class of men so willing to take medicine as sick soldiers. I feel sorry for our little boy about fourteen years old, who was a fifer in an Ohio company. He has been sick and become very thin. His parents are to be blamed for allowing such a child to go into the service where none but strong men can endure labor and fatigue. A good many old men are on board who are not less than sixty years old. The old fellows are going home to die if they don't give out before they reach there. I wish all those men who brot on this war could see the misery and suffering of these poor fellows. This afternoon we were obliged to amputate the lower extremity of one of our prisoners. I fear that it will do no good. I am detailed for duty as one of the night watch, and it is now 12 o clock and I must go through the wards and pour some whiskey down the parched throats of the Typhoid patients. Nothing else seems to keep them alive.[58]

We sailed to Paducah today and are now making our way up the Ohio. Our progress is necessarily slow as we are going up stream against the tide.

I just came from the couch of a wounded secesh to whom I have given a dose of morphine to make him sleep, and I asked him what business he had been in formerly, that is, before he became a soldier, and he told me that he was a calico printer by trade till the war broke out, then times being pretty hard "he got himself into a trap" as he expressed it. I went to the bunk of a soldier to give him another dose of medicine, and found him cold and lifeless. There are four or five others, who will hardly live till daylight. Their mouths are getting dry and their teeth are becoming covered with black saliva. Their eyes are fixed and they refuse their medicine. It is a sad sight indeed, but what can we do? They come on board completely worn out, and we have no chance to do them any good. Some of them have been sick for months, and I suspect badly treated during that time. It is no place to be sick in any army where they are all the time on the march.

Saturday P.M. May 3 62

We have had a good many very sick men. I have just been through the wards giving them medicine and the very air is bad. I am sitting in the Pilot house where the air is very pure and bracing. We are passing along the low shores of Indianna and Kentucky. The land is for corn and many are preparing their ground for this year's crops. We see many very pleasant houses along the way, quite an improvement on the dwellings down in Tennesee. We see some hills rising in the distance. The pilot knows everybody along the way and talks about them familiarly.

I have had a little talk with a secesh wounded man to night about the cause of his being in the army, and he told me this story. I wish I could give it to you in his own words. He said that some of those great men down thar in his state came round & told the folks that unless they all should load their guns and went out to fight the yanks, their property would be taken away from them, that their all would be lost & that no man ought to do that, if he had any pluck about him & all that kind of talk. I have asked several the same questions and their story is all after this style. I asked one what kind of man Beauregard was, and he said he was a right smart little man & says he, "consarned my soul if when he talks, you would be half scared to death." The style of the language of these fellows is a good deal after the Davy Crockett order. They are very ignorant and unsophisticated, & I can easily see how designing men could move an army of such men, just by appealing to their ignorance. Another man told me that he was formerly an artist, but times getting hard he thought he could support his family better by joining the army. Take them as a company, our wounded prisoners are much more irritable and difficult to take care of than our own men. It takes ten men all the time to take care of one sick, and with this force they are unable to attend to all their wants.[59] I am much disposed to think with Dr Newberry, that one great *cause for this war is the determination of a few at the South to rule.* They are so educated from their childhood in having their own way in little things, that when they grow old, they cant bear to submit to the will of others, & it is this determination to rule, that has led them on thus far. In a word they have become an aristocracy by their whole discipline, & are unwilling to submit to a democratic rule. It is the object or should be the sole object with the North to push down this spirit of Aristocracy which is now showing itself. (The heave of our mighty engines shake the boat so that my writing is scarcely readible)

Midnight

I am on duty this evening. On my rounds I find two men dead in their bunks and have been pouring stimulus down the parched throats of others, who will soon follow them. They are watching another who is threatening with hemorhage which if it continues will exhaust him. At 2 P.M. I shall be relieved, one of my colleagues taking my place. If many more die I shall have no coffins as every box has been used to make them. We expect to land in New Albany tomorrow forenoon.

Sunday Evening May 5.[60]

This morning we reached New Albany a town of some ten thousand inhabitants situated on a hill with a fine levee gently sloping down to the rivers edge. Here we left about 25 of our patients who belonged to the state of Indiana and sent on shore the dead for burial. About noon we reached Louisville and found no difficulty in going up the falls of the Ohio at a point a little below the town. We may find difficulty returning as the water is falling quite rapidly. We intend to go to Cincinnatti as soon as possible & get back so as to have no trouble in passing these falls.

The evening along the river has been very beautiful to day especially on the Kentucky shore. We have *lost over 30 of our 300 patients.* They died principally from Typhoid fever.

Monday Morning [May 5]

We have just arrived in Cincinnatti and I will mail these notes which I have written on board this tumbling steamboat written at all times of the day & night just as I had a chance. You will please excuse all errors, as I have no time to make any corrections. You will please send me the *Republican* & letters not a few to the care of Willis in St Louis. With much love to you all I remain

Yours affectionately
John

Enclosed I send a sprig of mistlctoc.

I have just received your letter forwarded to me from St Louis, have not time to note contents but will do so in next

Yours
John

Cincinnatti May 5th/62
On Board the *D.A. January.*

Dear Sister,

I was very much pleased to receive a letter from you to day. It has been forwarded to me from St Louis by Willis and is the first word I have had from home since my coming west. I think it is but two weeks since I came on board and it seems like a month or more. I have sent you several letters from different points. The one I send you to day from this place is No. 5 although I forgot to mark it so. My letters must not be criticized, as they are oft written under most unfavorable circumstances.

We reached the levee at this place about 10 this morning and we unloaded our poor sick men at two places on this side, and the worst cases were placed in a hospital over in Covington Ky across the river. We have lost a good many about 33 I think. This may not speak well for the skill of the doctors on board but I assure you that every thing was done for them that could be done. They were nearly dead when they came on board and it was hardly possible for us to do them any good. Did you ever visit this city? Well what do you think of it? If I should compare it with St Louis, I would say that it has a larger number of fine buildings used as stores etc. than the latter place and that the location does not compare with it. The houses here have a very dingy appearance which characterizes all those cities where coal is burned. I notice that people are obliged to use dark colored goods for dress, and furniture, because fabrics of a lighter hue much as we use would become speedily soiled and smoked. The contrast between houses where we live where everything is so white and cheerful, and houses here where everything is so dingy is very striking. I walked thru the streets to day feeling as though I should soil my clothes if I touched anything. They have a good deal of dust here which adds to the discomfort of the visitor. Dr. Hoff was much disgusted with the people here, because they thought to show partiality towards our sick and pay little regard for the wounded "secesh." On our boat we had made no distinction, & have treated all alike, & we have been paid for our attention by expressions of gratitude from them. These Ohio men are disposed to show a bad spirit, which has been the cause of all the trouble, and will be cause of its continuance if persisted in by them. For instance, the sexton was very particular to know which coffins contained confederates, so that they might not be buried in the same cemetery with union men. Gen. Halleck was particular in his orders that all should be treated alike. Dr Hoff says he feels like resenting this by not bringing any more patients here. It is a humiliating fact, that the state of Ohio sent a boat around to St. Louis for some sick and they wouldn't any of them come.

I saw some very fine horses attached to the various vehicles in the streets. I never saw finer in my life.

I walked thru the various principal streets of this city. I came to one very large house and surrounded by a stone wall. I was told that it was Longworths. He is one of the Nabobs of the town, and has been largely engaged in the wine business. We saw several extensive vineyards along the river.

I got some papers viz the *N.Y. World,* the *Illustrated Harper,* and the *Home Journal.* These will be my newspaper reading for the next trip. We leave to night at about 12, and expect to return to Pittsburgh for more wounded sick. We should have quite a resting spell till we get there again. My time for retiring lately has been about 2 in the morning and rising at 8 or 9 A.M. For a while again I shall be more regular. I prefer the first watch of the night to the last as it is rather hard to get up.

You asked if I passed nicely. I did not have to pass at all.[61] I am a contract surgeon with one hundred per month & without the stripes or other uniform, which I like better. This is all to night.

Tuesday Evening
May 6th 1862.

We left Cincinnati at 3 oclock this morning and have been sailing
down the Ohio all day. The scenery along the river is very beautiful.
There are quite a good many high hills and the shores are bold. The
houses are indicative of a pretty good class of people. On one of these
high ridges Hanover College is situated. It holds a very commanding
position.

Nothing occurred of any interest till we reached the falls of the Ohio
at Louisville. When we went up, the water was so high that we had no
difficulty in passing, but a day or two makes a great difference in the
river as it falls very rapidly. We are obliged to have a pilot take us down
the rapids. He came on board at a point above. The height which the
river falls is about 30 feet in a distance of two miles, so that the commotion in the water is by no means very considerable, and a very small
affair when compared with the rapids in the St Lawrence.[62] Still there is
danger, for the place where our boat passed was only 6 feet in depth and
that does not leave much water between the rocks and her keel. The
pilot told us that the place where we went up to two days before had but
30 inches of water to day. If we had been a day or two later, we should
not have been able to have passed. We rode safely through the rough
water down into the placid position of the current, and paid our extra
pilot a twenty dollar treasury note for his trouble.

We of the surgical corps are having a very easy time of it on our
return to the seat of war. If nothing happens we will reach Pittsburgh
by the 8th, and there we shall be busy again. We spend the time as travelers are apt to do, in reading writing or visiting. Our nurses are scrub-
bing and cleaning up the boat for another load of sick.

We had radishes on our table to day. It may be that we are a little in
advance of you up in Geneseo, on spring vegetables.

When I was in Cincinnati I could think of no one that I knew there
upon whom I could call and spend the time of our stay.

I wish you were here to enjoy this pleasant moonlight night. We
would sit up on the deck of our boat & watch the changing hills, as they
throw their shadows half across the river, and I would tell you of many
things that I think are hardly worth writing down.

May 7th PM.

I am sitting in the Pilot House this fine day. The pilot is a perfect host
in his way. He is very good at telling stories. He is a Kentuckean by
birth, and is about as large a man as Mr. Reed. He reminds one of such

men as Davy Crockett or Lorenzo Dow, both of whom distinguished men
he used to know. He is good humored and affords us often a good laugh.
The weather grows warm as we get further south again....

We are coming in sight of Paducah, Kentucky, and as I can send this
to a post office I will enclose it. This town is just at the mouth of the
Tennesee river. We leave the Ohio and turn up this stream toward the
seat of war. The boat is just rounding to shore, so good afternoon from
your affectionate brother

                                    John

                          Up the Tennesee River
                          May 8th 1862

Dear Frank
    We have been floating up the Tennesee to day as fast as our panting
engines could propel us and we shall probably reach Pittsburgh landing
some time to night. The weather has been very warm almost like mid-
summer with us. The leaves of the Catalpas and cotton woods have
grown quite large and the foliage along the shore has become very
dense. A good many of the natives have come off in their skiffs and
dugouts to get any papers that we may throw overboard to them. This is
the only way they have of getting the news and they are glad to get any
thing in the shape of a newspaper, if it is not a very late date. It is common for the ladies to come down to the shore and wave their handker-
chiefs to the boats as they pass. This is answered if observed by those on
board. As I was sitting on the guard this evening I saw a female form
standing on the distant shore & she seemed to be waiting in doubt
whether or not she was seen. I thought I would satisfy her mind that
there was one who was looking at her, and I drew *my handkerchief* and
waved it. This was no sooner done than she responded by a long continued wave of her own cambric. It is policy for us to make as many
friends along the shore as we can as, there are many who do not feel
friendly, and the kind of salutation they would give would be to fire a
musket shot at us.

                          Friday Noon May 9th

    We are now at Harrisburg, a little bit of a place ordinarily, but quite
large now (you will see the place on the Map almost on the Alabama
line). This is one of the points which mark the coils of the Anaconda.[63]

We have been waiting for Mr. Beauregard to have a fight, that we might get a load of wounded. But as there is no prospect of battle very soon, we are going to take a load of sick and carry them up to St. Louis. You can form no idea of what a vast army there is here at this place, about 250 thousand. There is said to be 3000 men sick and unable to do duty. We shall carry away about 300, as that is the limit of our ability to accomodate. I have just been along the river getting some specimens of the mistletoe.

Friday Evening

We took on a part of a load of sick men this P.M. and have carried them down as far as Pittsburgh Landing, but the Medical Director thinks they are hardly sick enough, at least some of them, & orders us to wait here till morning, and he will sift out those whom he thinks well enough to stay. (I should hate to be a sick man, and be obliged to be pitched about so many times from place to place. This is one of the hardships of soldiering) There is some prospect of a battle yet, and we are in hopes by waiting a while we may get more of a load.

There are two gunboats lieing across the other side of the river—one was captured by the Rebels.[64] One of these boats is engaged in keeping the river clear between this point and Florence. Other steamboats are lieing around. Some are used as store boats, others, like ourselves, are awaiting orders.

Sunday Evening [May 11]

This has not been much like sunday at home. I have been very busy to day assisting taking on sick, taking down their names. I am sure that the day has not been observed by any one as it should be. But these war times seem to change things very much. I only know when Sunday comes by seeing Mrs. Houghton who takes care of my state room, putting clean linen on my bed. Just as I expected, we had to change our load and put on other men who looked more sick.

So this morning having discharged our men at Hamburgh, & there being none at that place very bad, we came down to Pittsburgh and filled out the load.

Before leaving Hamburgh, Capt Bartlett and I walked up to this little place which is now almost entirely deserted of its original inhabitants, and is completely over run with soldiers, tents, horses, mules and waggons and everything belonging to an army. I believe there is only one family who remained. The houses are used by our soldiers. We found the different variety of roses blooming in the yards, and we got some splendid boquets. I wish you could see the one in my room this morning. We found syringas & Honey suckles in full bloom.

This has been a very warm day, and I am glad we are on our way up to St Louis again.

Yesterday I accepted an invitation from Capt Bartlett to take a ride on horseback out on the battle field.[65] We rode out some six miles, and I had a much better idea of the extent of this great battle than I had obtained from the little excursion I made on foot at my first visit. We rode past the recently dezerted camping grounds, and among the groves of trees, which had been so splintered and torn by cannon balls & shot. They are so badly torn that the scars will never be obliterated. We picked up as many small sized cannon balls as we could well carry with us. We met a colonel who was out looking over the field for the first time since his recovery from a wound received on the day of the battle. He had much to tell us of the positions of the several forces, and what they did. Our ride through the woods was enlivened by such birds as the cardinal, mocking birds, & boblinks, who were stuffing their crops with the grain left upon the apron at the camp grounds. We saw flocks of wild pigeons & turtle doves. The graves of the soldiers [are] marked with more or less care with the names of the dead, an object which the visitor of a battle field like this may spend time at. You see also great quantities of old clothes, boxes, barrells, and fragments of everything that is used in camp. When we had reached the limit of our ride, we listened attentively for cannon or any other noise of war, but heard nothing. Corinth is at least ten miles farther on. You might think I could tell you a great deal of what the prospect is, but I heard so many rumors about the fight, that I don't believe any thing but what I read in the papers. My position is such, & my time is occupied, that I cant go around & pick up news as the reporters do, so I will leave it for them to do.

Wednesday Noon May 14/62

We finally left Pittsburgh Sunday evening, reached Paducah monday afternoon-evening at 16 miles an hour, and arrived at Jefferson Barracks this morning about one oclock. Yesterday I was somewhat indisposed and kept in my bunk. The cause of illness is some derangement produced by drinking the water of the Tennesee, which is the great cause of sickness in that country. The weather was very hot, the thermometer standing at 93° in the shade. It is at 80° to day. We have just landed the sick at the barracks and will soon be in St Louis. We had "a heap" better trip this time than last, having lost but 5 patients. We expect to stay in St Louis two or three days to repair the boat. The *Gladiator* wast at Pittsburgh Landing. When we came off our Pilot told me he saw Dorman, & that he was well. (Our boat shakes and so does my hand. Hence such scrawling penmanship.) I shall expect a letter from you when I get on shore

Yours affectionately
John

St Louis Mo. May 17/62 [Saturday]

Dear Frank

... If it were not for the exceeding hot weather and the dust my stay in town would be very pleasant. The weather is so hot that I have no disposition to move about so much, & then it is so *lime-dusty* that it is perfectly awful to go any where. I came in from a walk last evening, and my boots looked as though I had been walking through a plaster bed. Then every chimney sends out its volume of dense black smoke, which fills the air and colours everything of a black or dingy hue. I never could like such a city to reside in. How different our New York is. It is a perfect gem of a city. They have water here which might be used for washing the streets, but they dont use it much & they fail to sweep the streets as they do East....

Mr James Yeatman came in Wills office and was making up a party for a picnic next tuesday. I am invited if I remain in town. He invited us to accompany him to take tea and spend the evening. We all took the cars at 6 P.M. and reached their beautiful residence about dusk. It is situated on a high ground on the upper end of Broad way about 3 miles from the center of town. On our way up the carriage path, a little black boy was playing with some of Mr Y's younger brothers. Mr Y said to us "This is one of the oppressed." One or two others appeared & he said "Here are others of the oppressed," signifying by the remark, that it was a strange kind of oppression which allowed such privileges as these black people were enjoying. They are slaves. On reaching the house we were introduced to a Miss Allen and a Miss Powers. We walked through the beautiful garden in the rear of the house, and found flowers as beautiful as those down in Tennesee. At supper table we met the Mother of Gen Pope, also his wifes sister. Gen Popes wife is there also, and has been quite recently blessed with a daughter. The young ladies are interesting and the evening passed away pleasantly as we sat on the piazza engaged in general conversation, and when we were ready to come away it was so late the cars did not come and we had to walk back to town. Before leaving, Miss A. handed me the beautiful boquet which had been kept fresh in water since we had left the garden.

This is Saturday, the sky is a little cloudy and a fresh breeze is rendering the air more pleasant than yesterday. The carpenters say we shall be in town till after Tuesday as the boat needs more repairs than were supposed necessary. At any rate I shall be in town on Sunday and will hear a sermon, which is a treat I have not had since I left home.

Saturday Evening

I have just received from Father this week's *Republican* for which I am much obliged. I have had a good time reading up on the news since my arrival & have tried to get posted up again. About five oclock we are blessed with a refreshing rain and the air is now quite comfortable.

I called on Willis roomate, Mason, at the Governors rooms & was introduced to his Excellence Gov Gamble.[66] The old gent reminds one more of the old gentleman farmer than of the states man or lawyer.

I have read the letters from members of the regiment gone from Geneseo with interest. I am glad to know that they are actively engaged in the work of putting down the rebellion. You are right, about my wishes in regard to these scraps of correspondence which I send you from time to time—*They are not for publication at all*—and I beg of you, dont circulate the manuscript outside of our house. I am unable to pick up any information of public interest, except what I find in the newspapers, so I have nothing to tell the people.

Sunday Evening [May 18]

This has been a delightful day for St Louis. The rains of yesterday completely laid the dust, and there has been a gentle breeze just enough to shake out the folds in the flags waving from church steeples and other public places. This being my first sunday in town, it became me to improve it. Accordingly this forenoon Willis and I went to the First Presbyterian Church, Dr Nelsons. Heard a very good sermon.... The singing here was very good. In the PM attended a Baptist Church, Mr Andersons. It was the occasion of communion. In the evening Will, Capt Bartlett and I went to an old school Presbyterian church, where we heard practical discourse by Dr or Mr Brooks. I observed Gov Gamble and his family in attendance.... It has not been much like Sunday on board to day. Dr Hoff has had eight or ten carpenters at work on the

boat, and they have kept up a continual noise. I dont see the need of
working today, and Capt Bartlett said he never saw anything gained by
working sunday, unnecessarily. Dr H. is trying to do too much.

[May 19]

On Monday noon (to day) Willis proposed that we take a ride out into
the suburbs of this place. The roads were fine, a little dirty in places,
but much improved by the late rain. Our horse was a fleet animal. (Will
wont have any other to drive.) After extricating ourselves from a maze
of streets where almost every one ended in some mans barn yard, we got
on the street leading to the fairground. This is a permanent thing, and
as a matter of course is fitted up in a very substantial & beautiful manner. All its surroundings and enclosures are beautiful. After making a
circuit of the grounds we rode along the high board fence, stretching
nearly a mile, behind which was situated the long lines of low wooden
buildings which constitute Camp Benton. Will says they are able to
accomodate forty thousand troops here. There are but few here now. It
was used as a depot for a long time for the troops, before going farther
south. From this point we returned part way & rode in a direction
south across the country, which is slightly undulating though in no place
hilly. In this part of our drive we had the finest view we had yet seen of
the country around St Louis. The farms are like gardens, and the vegetation everywhere indicates a fruitful country. Situated about one mile
from the main road you can distinctly see a tower like structure situated
near a piece of woods. This is called by the proprietor Tower Grove and
we continued our ride in this direction. The roadway is lined by
catalpias & the meadows beyond were covered with heavy grass.

We found this house on our arrival surrounded by a high wall of
dressed stone. There is a very extensive garden in front devoted to flowers, greenhouses etc laid out in a style of magnificence and beauty that I
have never seen equalled any where. We drove up to the gate and tied our
horse, and then prepared to see the beauties of this place. I was much
pleased with the arrangements of walks and trees. It would seem that all
the genius of Downing had exhausted itself in laying out these grounds.[67]
Such hand rolled walks made of fragments of hand burned brick, gave
them a singular color and the border of each walk, instead of being a box
was of bricks lieing on their sides, which made the lines of fancy figures
better defined. But the richest part of this display was to be seen in the
various greenhouses. We entered one where there was a profusion of scar-
let geraniums mingled with other flowers such as I had never before seen.
We passed into another, where everything that the Tropics yield that is

beautiful was to be seen, and possessing a freshness of perfumes that is equalled only in their native country. We saw vases of fine apples with the fruit ripening. One contained a banana tree, with a cluster of fruit which would compare with the scene that I saw in Key West. I could not begin to tell you half of the beauties of this place. We left it reluctantly and passed on to the vegatable & fruit gardens in the rear of this mansion. Here we saw the same display of taste & variety. On one part of the grounds was a building of considerable size, with this inscription at the entrance—Botanical Museum. Taking it all together the owner has attempted a "Jardin des Plante[s]" and has made a very good beginning. The proprietor is Mr Henry Shaw a batchelor of about fifty and a retired millionaire. You may remember to have seen his name associated with a piece of scandal quite recently. I refer to the Shaw & Carsting trial.[68] I did not have a chance to see the gentleman which I regretted very much. But saying nothing about him, he has the finest country seat that I ever saw. We made no other calls and drove back to the city. Everitt is lecturing to night, but I dont feel like hearing him, and I am visiting in the office (Telegraph) with Willis while he writes up his days business.

To night we have word from down below *to hasten to the seat of war*, & our boat being ready, we shall get away this evening. I congratulate my self that I have had such a long vacation, and I feel like going to work again.

Let me hear from you very often at this place. Willis sends his love with me to you all

affectionately yours
John

Steamboat *D.A. January*
Tennesee River May 21, 62

Dear Frank

We are on our way to the seat of war again. This is my third trip down the river. We left St Louis on Tuesday morning. In the evening we had a hard rain and thunder storm. The flashes of lightning lit up our cabin finely. To day the weather has been very pleasantly remarkably cool, but this evening as we get farther south it grows warm again. There has nothing happened worthy of mention, we have scraped our keel over several sand bars which indicate that the river is falling. The scenery along our way is beautiful even more than the last trip. The Catalpias are in bloom now.

There is the same repairing and refurnishing going on this trip that we had last. Our upper cabin is furnished with fifty new bedsteads, which are much better than the cots we used before, and look much better. Our boats company, which consists of about sixty persons, has changed a little. There are always some going on & off of these river boats. Our *"Nightingales"* as Dr. Hoff playfully calls our female nurses, are all with us, with an additional lady, the daughter of one of them. She has come on board as a passenger only. She is a teacher of a school in St Louis, also a music teacher. She plays the piano & Guitar. She has her guitar with her, and plays for our amusement, and sings also. We think her quite an addition to our company.

I have thrown overboard to the people in the little boats who come out to meet us, quite a number of newspapers. I am sorry that Frank Blair and men of his stamp are crying so much "Emancipation." I think it only aggravates the feelings of the South, and will make them continue the fight much longer. We dont wish to get rid of the slaves, for who will cultivate these Southern lands if we send them away? It is absurd to think about white men doing this kind of work. We must have the blacks to pick the cotton and hoe the cane. And so far as bettering their condition, that can be done just in the position they now occupy & this work must begin with the white folks their "masters." I prefer the word guardian as that expresses the relation which the master holds to the slave—or should hold. And then where will they send the slaves? The Emancipationists don't know themselves. So I think they better let them remain where they are. These poor fellows don't care about going off to Central America. They have not the talent to take care of themselves, and never will have. The Creator did not so endow them, and it is no use to let them make trials. Those black men who have attained to any notoriety are not full blooded & Such persons are no criteria to judge by.[69] I have had a headache all day but feel much better to night. We took on a quantity of Mississippi river water, so that we shall have that instead of the Tennesee, which is not as good. We will probably reach Pittsburgh Landing by morning & then we shall be busy again. Our boat goes more steady since the repairs were made. But this constant trembling is rather disagreeable, particularly when you try to read or write. It doesn't prevent me from eating however.

Pittsburgh Landing
Monday Morning May 26th/62

I have not felt like writing for several days. I think I have some of my old ague feelings hanging around me. I have been taking quinine with a little whiskey, but I fancy that whiskey makes me feel worse. Don't think it agrees with me.

We reached Pittsburgh Thursday morning. We made a little stay in Cairo which put us back some time. When we arrived, found all the reports about there having been a fight false. We lay here two days waiting orders. Friday night we were ordered to go up to Harisburgh and take 500 soldiers from the hospital there, and carry them about 15 miles down the river to Savannah, where they have more ample accomodations. We discharged our load there on Sunday morning. While we staid, we went ashore and saw a little of the town. There is not much to see, there are a few comfortable dwellings & a few small buildings used for stores, one or two churches. The lower part of one of these buildings has been converted into a hospital. The people are nearly all there, scarcely any having left on account of the trouble. They gave us great quantities of flowers, chiefly roses, which are now growing in great profusion in all their gardens. We came up here yesterday P.M. and we are waiting for something to do. It is impossible to tell when the Corinth fight is coming off. We can only hear that they are skirmishing a little. Five regiments of troops from Arkansas, have passed up this river on their way to join the army before Corinth. If we succeed in whipping them out at that place, we can then make our way down to Memphis with out much fighting & would have all of Western Tennesee. We can't tell how long we shall remain here waiting. It may be a day or it may be a week. Other hospital boats are waiting here with us. The weather has been very pleasant, cloudy much of the time, and completely cool. Since we left St Louis we have found fires comfortable but I believe the store has been taken down this morning, and we shall do without fires hereafter. The watchmen on board the Gunboat lieing across the river strikes the hours and half hours. He is our timekeeper at this place. Judging from the great number of boats I have seen passing up & down the river I would say that nearly all the boats that belong on the Mississippi are engaged in doing something on this river. How anxious are we to hear of what is going on in other parts of the army. Whether we have Taken Richmond? What Butler is doing down in New Orleans? How Mitchell is doing in Alabama? We cant get papers here until they are several days old. So that news are not very satisfactory when they do come.

Tuesday morning

Yesterday I had a regular chill & fever which lasted for several hours. I am feeling quite well again this morning. I was glad it declared itself so clearly, for now I know just how to treat it. I have been feeling unwell for several days but could not tell positively what it was going to be. I am taking quinine pills, and think I shall break up the disease. I asked the Pilot if they had much Ague in this country. He replied with some emphasis, "Yes! The fish in the river die with it."

I saw a paper of date the 23rd, and got posted up a little. I see that Farragut is making his way up the Mississippi. I wish him a speedy trip to Vicksburgh, because that is an important point which we must have, and if we get it, we shall soon be in possession of the whole river. There seems to be a disposition on the part of the O.S. Presbyterians to be intimate with the N.S. Ps. Am glad to see it....[70]

The report is that Fremont is coming down this way, with troops from Western Virginia to aid in the contest at Corinth. One of our hopes is that the enemy will be starved out and thus be obliged to surrender. Deserters say that provisions are very scarce among them.

May 28, 62

I herewith send you a rough sketch of our new flag as she appears floating from the forward flagstaff.[71] It is made of yellow bunting and looks better than its predecessor which was of yellow flannel. The round hollow body which flies up and down the flag staff is of use to the Pilot in steering the boat. The Martins have come round in great numbers and we think they would like to build their nests in the hollow ball. I think they will have plenty of time to build and rear their young as our prospects of getting away from here are not good.

The lower part of the boat is being whitewashed to render it still more pure. The weather is quite warm. The thermometer marks 86° in the shade. We are still lieing under the high bank adjacent to Pittsburgh Landing. We have nothing to do but read, write or whatever we wish. I don't go off the boat because it is too warm to run about in the sun. So I try to keep as cool as possible.

We got Chicago papers this morning of the 24th which contains news very favorable to our cause.

Thursday P.M. May 29. 62

I am having quite a severe attack of the fever and ague & am suffering a good deal from headache. I expect the head pains come from the

effect of the quinine. I am in hopes to be able to break it up. We are
still lieing idle tied to the bank. Dr. Hoff says that they are fighting at
Corinth & is quite sure he hears the roar of artillery. I listen and fancy
I hear something, but it is not very satisfactory. There is so much
thumping and hammering about the boat by the carpenters, that a
sound so far off can scarcely be heard at any time. It is about 16 miles
to Corinth. But if they are fighting this afternoon they are having a hot
day for it. I am anxious to hear the result and we shall know soon as
there is a line of telegraph leading there from here. Dr. Hoff was *anxious to ride* out there and see the fight, but his superior officer advised
him to wait till tomorrow. The Dr had his spurs and everything on
expecting to go, and was a little vexed that he couldn't. If there is a
fight we shall be able to get a load of wounded men, and then we shall
get away from this place. I am very tired of staying here. If I felt better
I should not be so anxious to get away. This is a good place for ague.

Our young lady who plays the guitar continues to amuse us by singing
& playing. She has given me some instructions so that I can "pick" my
way through the Spanish Fandango. I hope I shall be better of my ague
soon.

Friday 2 PM.
May 30, 62.

Dr Schenck has just come on board and tells us that Corinth is evacuated.[72] This produced a pleasurable sensation among all, but I hope to
hear that the enemy have been so severely repulsed that they will not
fight again. But I fear that they will pursue their former policy, and go
and set up in another place farther south. Thus far we hear that our
flag waves over the courthouse in Corinth. That is all. How great losses
have been sustained, we have yet to learn. If Gen. Halleck can only give
them a good chase, and take some prisoners, it will be more satisfactory.
I am very anxious to hear more about the matter. This morning it is
reported that Richmond is also evacuated? Good news if true.

I am waiting to see whether I shall have another chill, have felt very
comfortable thus far to day. The weather keeps very warm. Once in a
while a cloud shuts off the suns rays a little.

Saturday May 31, 62
4 P.M.

We get no more particulars from Corinth yet except the humiliating report that *we took possession*, but were unable to destroy any of

the enemy and obtained about 20 prisoners who prefered to take the oath rather than go back with the Confederates. It may give us some advantages which we have not yet possessed. Dr. Hoff fairly got off for Corinth to day, and when he comes back we shall get all the news connected with the affair as it is. For a day or two past I have been drawing plans for a hospital barrack, to be erected somewhere on the upper Mississippi. Aside from reading & taking care of myself that is about all the work I have had to do for more than a week. This day has been blessed with a fine breeze which has made me feel much better.

Monday Morning June 2, 62

Dr H. returned from Corinth yesterday morning. He and his companion *lost their way*, and were obliged to stay in an old cotton gin till morning. He was about used up. He states that the fortifications in front of Corinth were impregnable and there is no blame attached to our forces for not taking it. The enemy left because they were out of water and provisions. They let their prisoners go, because they could not feed them. They burned a good many of their public buildings, storehouses, etc. We have not received any papers giving accounts of the affair, so that all we know is what comes from rumor.

If the above facts are any where near correct, we have made a pretty good thing of it. Our neighbors the gun boats have left us, and gone down the river a few miles.

The main body of the army having made a move, we shall probably change our place. We are still awaiting orders. This is certainly a very inactive life we have led for a week or more past. But I have had the Ague some every day, & a good deal every other day, so that *I* have had enough to do. *I never had it so severe* as this time. I am taking quinine for it. But I also take mullein tea and sage. I do it to please my friends here—the female nurses—who ascribe great virtues to these remedies. They surely will do me no hurt, and warm drinks of any kind are good.

Yesterday it rained a good deal, and the air was rendered quite cool. The air this morning is fresh and bracing. I expect there are a lot of letters at St Louis for me. I should have ordered them to be sent on but could not tell whether I should remain here till they should arrive. It is now two weeks since I left St Louis, and it seems almost a month. There is such a similarity one day with another that it is only by the very hardest I can remember the days of the week. And when I have a chill & fever on me, the hours drag very heavily.

Pittsburgh Landing June 5. 62.
On board Steam. *D.A. January*

This week is nearly gone, and we still have no orders to go. We have on board about 30 sick & wounded. One of our men died to day. He came on in a very poor condition.

Yesterday the monotony of things was broken up by the dress parade of the regiment stationed here. They parade every day, but this time they came out on the brow of the hill where we could see them, and they went through the manual of arms. This is more of a display than I have seen since my coming here.

In the afternoon a young colored man came on board, and entertained us highly by singing and playing accompaniments on the guitar. He came again in the evening. He was certainly one of the best guitarists I ever heard. He made the strings speak, almost.

The number of boats tied up at this place has diminished, and we hope that there will soon be a general "skidaddling" of the boats before many weeks.

The Mississippi river will probably be the way by which we will communicate with the main army.

The names of the boats here now are the *Polar Star*—she is used as a store boat. Dr Chas McDougald Med. Director lives on board of her.[73] Then there is an ice boat lies next go along the bank of the river. Then our boat is next. Lieing close along side us is the *Tycoon*, another hospital boat. Next is the *Hannibal*, used as a transport. Close against her is the *Hiawatha*, a transport which has brot a load of soldiers from Arkansas to this place. The order was countermanded, and she is going to take them back again. The soldiers have had a good time among themselves. You ought to have heard them sing. It sounded like a camp meeting. The band belonging to the regiment played very well about twilight. We are very glad to hear anything down in this wilderness country. We have not had a newspaper in 6 days, & I am very anxious to get posted. I miss the papers so much. I have had my ague again to day.

Next boat down the stream is the *New Uncle Sam*, on board of which is Capt. Wm Chandler our pay master. Across the river and some distance down is tied the small pox hospital boat. This comprises about all of the permanent fleet at this point. I was much pleased the other day to see a familiar face on one of the transports. It was that of Ed Stanley of Cleveland. He is a quartermaster in the army, and was on his way from Corinth to Cincinnatti.

Wednesday Morning June 11. 62

By sunday night we got the best part of a load, & Dr McDougald ordered us to go down to Savannah and get the balance which we did, and left there on Monday noon with a full load numbering 370 patients. Many of them convalescent. I have 119 in my division, and they are all very comfortable this morning. I have just been around and prescribed for the sick ones, and dressed the wounds of the wounded (most of them slight flesh wounds). I am sitting in my room door, where it opens on the larboard guard aft the wheel house, and the motion of the boat is here considerable—so that my writing is rather irregular.

We reached Cairo yesterday P.M. at 3 & now we are sailing up the Mississippi. We shall, Providence permitting, arrive at Jefferson Barracks this morning where we unload our sick, and will be in St Louis tomorrow some time. We have been absent more than three weeks, and it has seemed like as many months. I have had no news while away, & shall enjoy your letters more than ever. I think it is so fortunate that we staid down in Pittsburgh till I got over my ague. I have not had any of it since Saturday. I broke it with Fowler's solution.[74] Quinine did not seem to do me any good. This is a beautiful day, rather warm in the sun, but on the deck of a steamboat we always have a breeze. The river has fallen a good deal, so that flood wood may be seen sticking out of the water in places. These are called "snags."

Thursday
St Louis June 12.62

Dear Frank
    We have just arrived from Jefferson Barracks where we unloaded our sick. I have just finished reading your batch of letters which were awaiting my arrival. They have done me a great deal of good. In commenting I must say first that I am obliged for the Papers. I was much pleased with Willis friends here in St Louis. Will was so very busy that he could not go with me to Mr Fosters....

    We shall make a very short stay in town this time, and will probably return to the old place up the Tennesee. Things have not progressed far enough yet to take our final leave from Pittsburgh Landing.

    I have had no ague since Saturday, and flatter myself that I shall not be annoyed any more with this disagreeable disease....

I hope you will write me as often as once a week, and I shall write you as often as I have time. Give my love to all my friends

from Your affec Brother
John

Telegraph Office Wills Desk
St Louis Saturday Ju. 14, 62

Dear Frank

I enclosed you a letter on my arrival here which was no. 11. I wish you would look over and see if they have all been received up to this time. This is the third day of my stay in town—a longer time than I expected but you know it takes a good while to get on provisions etc, for a new trip. We leave to day at 12 oclock. Have been taking on a large quantity of provisions for the suffering people about Corinth, who have been eaten up by Beauregards army. These things are contributed by the people of St Louis. We go back again up the Tennesee river. I have had a pleasant visit with Will. I read your batch of letters with interest. I have laid in a good stock of *Observers* for my reading on next trip. Willis got me a book also at the Library on his account, so that I shall not lack for news and reading. Last evening Will and I went to the Mercantile Library to attend a tableaux vivant. It was the best thing of the kind I ever saw. The persons taking part were members of Trinity Church, and the proceeds are to be donated to paying off some debt of the church.

Your letter with photograph enclosed has just come to hand, and I have had the pleasure of reading it, and looking at the picture, which Will & I pronounce very good, and well taken....

The other day I saw a graduate of our Medical school at the Plantus Nova. He has come on to take a position on one of the gun boats. As it is about time for me to be getting down to the boat I will stop this scribbling. I should like much to be home to see all the friends who seem to be congregating from the East & West to your quiet village. When I return I hope to find Grandmother in her house in town.

The weather here is warm, but if ones health is good, the heat can be endured very well. Will is very much obliged to you for the photograph, and he joins me in sending love to you, and all the friends. I should think so much of a letter from Father. I hope he will enclose one in your next. No more at this time from

Your affectionate brother
John

Up the Mississippi River
June 23rd 1862

Dear Frank

I had nothing to send you on our arrival in St Louis, and I will drop this at the Keokuk P.O. to which place we are destined. The log book which I did not think worthwhile to write up on our last trip (because it would give very little of interest to me or you) would run something like this. We left St Louis on Saturday the 14th and ran down to Cairo thence to Paducah where we landed one of our "Nightingales," she concluding that she would like nursing in a hospital on land better than on the boat. A little above on the Ohio we stopped to wood up. There distributed a number of papers to a company of young ladies who came down near the boat to see it. We reached Pittsburgh Landing on Monday evening during a very severe thunder storm. I never saw such flashes of chain lightning. On our arrival here the prospect of getting a load soon was good. We got a very comfortable load by Thursday, and were ordered to Savannah to take on 130 more, including in all 460 sick and convalescent men. We have beds for 330, so you see that some must lie down wherever they could get a place. This is the largest load we have taken yet, but when we reached Paducah we left over a hundred, then at Jefferson Barracks about 30 more. So that we shall have a very fair complement to give over to the Keokuk hospital. We have not lost but 2 on the way, indeed the majority were not very sick.

Coming along down the Tennesee, we found the steamboat *Hannibal* aground—almost out of water. Her pilot had mistaken the channel. We found her guarded by a gun boat, for you must know that it would not do to leave a vessel in her predicament. Why? The Rebels might come along and set fire to her. They hailed us as we approached, and we sent a boat to her, which brot off her mail bags. We had no room for any more of her freight.

Dug Tyler came on board at Cairo, & told me about the report of the *Mound City* gun boat down on the White river. That was a very severe accident.[75] But we whipped them out after all. We reached Jefferson Barracks sunday morning, & discharged a few Missouri sick men. We stopped at St Louis a couple of hours, but Will was out of town, so I did not go on shore to get letters etc. Two of the doctors remained at St Louis to wait over till our return. Dr H & I are taking care of things to day. We shall reach Keokuk this evening & start back Tuesday some time.

The weather has been very warm till we got above St Louis. This day is very pleasant & temperature quite agreeable. I don't think I should ever be satisfied to live in a warm climate all my days. A persons mind sympathizes so much with his body, that if the latter is much debilitated, the former lacks its vigor. I sometimes think that Southern people cant reason as well, and are more apt to make mistakes in judgement through climatic influences than those of more temperature regions. I think a great deal of this rebellion is kept up by that mistaken judgement. I see that the farmers along the river in Kentucky & Missouri are cutting the wheat, and it seems like a very light crop, in some places hardly being for cutting. The corn which stands about 18 inches high, looks very well. The country we are passing through today is suitable for grazing, and there are a great many cattle feeding in the pastures along the shore.

[June 24]
Keokuk Iowa Tuesday Noon

Have just unloaded our sick or rather I should say broken down frames of humanity. If they can recover anywhere they will here, as the temperature is more conducive to health than down south. We had 80° & 90° of heat. This morning the thermometer is at 65° and a cold rain has been falling. We shall return to St Louis this P.M. I shall probably write you again from there. With much love to all I remain as ever yours affectionately

John

Mississippi River below
Hannibal June 24, 62

Dear Frank

I mailed No 13 at Keokuk. While there, after the sick had all got safely off the boat, I took a little walk up their main street to see the sights. Very little to be seen. Business there seems very dull. They charge high prices enough to make up for it, however. I went through the large hospital which received our sick, some 2 minutes ago, but saw no familiar faces among the patients. They have all been discharged from service, or gone to their regiments again. Some have died. I came near being left, as the boat was just starting as I came on board. It was owing to a misunderstanding about the time of starting. Not that I was so much delighted with the place that I could not tear myself away. I have been much pleased with this trip, for the weather has been so cool & refreshing. I wish I could enjoy such good air all along my travels. It must be very invigorating to the soldiers to come up here to recruit. Am glad I did not stay in St Louis as the Dr proposed. It is proposed to erect hospitals up in this country on a large scale, for the benefit of the sick of our army. I bought some illustrated papers which contain some good views (Dr Hoff says so) of Corinth and vicinity. I will send them on to you. I forgot to say that we did not lose a man on our last trip, although we had some very sick. But the majority of them were not so unwell but that they could eat all that the cooks could possibly get ready for them. This morning they had to delay serving breakfast, because they did not have bread enough baked till about 9 oclock. The kind of food must of course be plain and nutritious, and consists of bread & butter, gruel, beef tea, tea and coffee, with soup for dinner. Some days oranges in halves are passed around, and lemonade can be given to those who ask for it—or some kinds of jellies which are grateful to the palates of sick people. This afternoon I have had my room thoroughly washed & my bed cleaned of "all sich" critters, of which there was quite a number. I don't know as I should have destroyed them so unmercifully as they have never been known to attack me. They seem to be simply wishing "to be let alone." But then I don't enjoy having them around, as I prefer a state room to my self. If they contest the ground, it will be their death, as the Apothecary fixed me a bottle of poison which I generously cast in their line of attack. I told you that our beds & towels are the contributions of the Sanitary people in different parts of the country. For instance one blanket is marked as coming from "Muscatine Iowa," sheets from Ohio, pillow cases marked with the name of the owner in a neat ladies hand writing. One towel marked "New Bedford," another "U.S. Hospital," other articles such as corn husk mattresses marked again "Ladies Union Aid Society, St Louis." I have not seen anything marked M.A.L. I suppose any such articles have gone a different route to some army mans wardrobe.[76]

Our boat is sailing down the river to night in fine style, although she is breasting a pretty stiff breeze. During the whole evening we have had the most constant flash lightning that I ever saw. The time of light to dark is in the proportion of 5 to 1, so that you can see almost as well as if the moon was shining all the while. It thunders some now, and there is a squall coming on. Some of the watch talk of tieing the boat to the shore. The Captain thinks we might as well keep on our way. Now it rains down in torrents, and its leaking through the roof where I am writing, and it has wet my paper as you see. A word painter would find this a good subject to work up a picture of a thunderstorm, but I claim nothing in that direction, as I can only give you the facts as they are transpiring this minute. We conclude to tie to shore, and our boat is turned in that direction. The large torch is lit, the "roust abouts" as they call the men on deck are called to take up the large hawser, & seizing it near the end, they drag it towards a large stirrup in a field a few rods from shore. There it is made fast, and while I have been writing the above, the boat has come very quietly up to the bank, where she will lie in perfect safety, till the storm is over and the sky is clear again. The rain *pours* down now. The wind has become less violent, but the lightning flashes vividly & frequent with an occasional burst of thunder. It is some time after eleven, and I will yield myself and the boat to the care of that Providence whose voice I now hear in the thunder.

Wednesday Morning
[June 25]

I am waiting for Willis to come in his office. He is a little late this morning. Our boat got under motion again soon after she tied up again last night and has made a very quick trip of it, arriving at the levee in 18 hours—distance 200 miles.

Will has just come, and I have been reading Fathers letter. In commenting upon the remarks which he makes in regard to me, I think that a hospital would be a better place than the boat, but think they divide the labor, so that in a city like this, the pay would not be as good as where I am. It is three months till Oct 1st, when any thing is to be said about Bellevue. Perhaps time will work out something by that time. I shall try and pick up what I can in my present condition.

I have just looked over the Report. It does not contain much this week.... I will drop this in the office now. I may write again before leaving. We do not know when we shall start, or where we shall go.

I did not get any letter from you this time. I suppose you left Father to be your secretary during your absence. You must tell me about your visit in your next. No more at this moment from

Your affectionate brother
John

Steamer *D.A. January*
lieing at the levee in St Louis
Sunday P.M. June 29, 62.

Dear Frank

I have been reading the *N.Y. Observer* this afternoon, and now for a change I will bring out my paper, and pen a few notes. I have been in this town since Wednesday, & there being no orders for us to proceed to any point, we concluded to stop a few days, and make some improvements in the boat. So that I have another sunday in a town where I can go to church. This is the second sabbath that I have had this privilege since I have been in the country. Every sunday has been spent steaming or lieing at some point down in the wilderness, where no preaching is done. This morning I attended an O.S. church & heard a Mr Brooks. His preaching was very good, and sufficiently earnest, but perhaps not as thoroughly studied as it might have been. But I should not criticize preaching because I hear so little of it now days that I am hardly a competent person to judge.

I went out about 3 this P.M. to hear more, but did not find any places of worship open, and I infer that the sabbath school takes the place of the church exercise. I shall try again this evening. Evening service commences at 8 P.M. I believe I remarked upon the architectural appearance of the church edifices once before. So I need not say that I consider them very beautiful, and quite up to the times. The day is very warm, the thermometer standing up among the nineties, and I think that it would be asking a good deal of a preacher to preach during the afternoons, unless you allow him to wear a linnen coat or go before his audience in his shirt sleeves, as I once saw an old Quaker do.

The churches seem to be well attended, but I see a good many people in the street—more than looks well. I dont think this place can boast much for its morality. I never saw a city where there is as much drinking of liquor as here. *Everybody*—almost—drinks. Beer shops and gardens are numerous. St Louis has such a mixed population, that it is very difficult to control opinion on the side of right. The German people adhere so strongly to their merschaums & beer, and their miserable faith, and the French are not much better. (There are a good many of that nation mixed up with the rest.) Then the floating population—the travellers and hotel people—keep the city in a good deal of an uproar. There is no work done along the levee as a general thing, but a good many men are always standing around in little groups in front of the liquor shops, which pretend to be closed, but I guess that they let a man in and give him a drink occasionally. I think I can count from one point, as many as 30 of these holes along the levee, where sailors get all the liquor they want.

A steamboat has just come in, and she has cattle on board, and they are trying to drive them off on to the shore. This makes a good deal of noise & it affords the idle fellows along the street a good deal of amusement to see a frightened cattle walk the plank to the shore. Across the river in what is called Illinois town, there is a party of men who seem to be firing at a mark. They keep up a great banging all the time. The Captain told me last night that there should be no work done on the boat to day, as we are in no hurry just now, and I counted on a very quiet time of it on board. But I was disappointed in this. Dr H. allowed 3 men to come and nail up sheets of wire gauze over the high cabin windows, and they have kept up a hammering all day. The Dr may see a "military necessity" for having it done to day, but *I* dont see it.

The little children, the offspring of those who sell the liquor, are out in great numbers playing on the bags of grain which are piled up on the levee. I heard one ask the other if he was a rebel. I did not hear his reply, but I saw him make an effort to push him down the hill of bags. (One of our Dr's in the cabin shakes his dice a good while before he throws them.) Excuse the remark. Near the piles of bags is a quantity of heavy sheet iron for gun boats. A few feet off is the largest quantity of lead I ever saw, which when once more melted & molded is for the rebelious South—in *Minnie* doses....

[June 30]
Monday PM.

I have just returned on board from visiting Mr. Henry Shaw of the gun boat *Tyler.* I found him on board his boat, and had a very pleasant call. They are repairing some now, but he took me over the boat, and showed me 7 large guns which carry 68 pound shot but are used for throwing shell, as the most execution is done with such missiles. Mr. S. has been in 16 engagements with the Rebels in all of which they did great execution. They rendered great assistance to our army at the battle of Pittsburgh Landing, also at Fort Henry a short time before. Their boat has not been struck but twice, & they have not lost over three or four men. There are about 200 men employed on her in the capacity of officers and sailors. They will probably leave for down the river on Friday next. Mr. S. received me with great cordiality, and invited me to call every day. He said he should be very glad to have Will Ward come and go with him, as masters mate (I think he called it).

As Willis and I were walking down Vine St he stopped to talk with a young man who was dressed in light dress and black hair & whiskers. After the usual salutations had passed between the two I was introduced to the stranger who said he had heard of me before, and was well acquainted with my sister, Miss Frank. The gent was none other than the much talked of Dorman. I was very well pleased with what I saw of him. After a few words in which he told us that he had just arrived up from Memphis and that his *Gladiator* was now undergoing some repairs, during which time he thought he should go and visit his mother, we passed on. I thought that I should like to visit my mother every time I lie in port. I know if I should she *might* get tired of seeing me so often, as I have spent a good part of the time "tied up" to shore.

I am looking out of my stateroom upon the busy levee. What a great number of carts I see. They are carrying bags of grain and bales of hemp and casks of tobacco. In Gotham one horse is enough to draw a cart, but here two mules are required, and they drive them tandem— and the drivers give them some most unmerciful cuts with their short whip, to which are fastened long lashes.

These bags of grain are very liable to burst & require to be sowed up. This gives work for a lot of old women, who go about from one heap to another and with long needles & thread, they sow up the bags. How do you think they get their pay? They have all the grain that spills upon the ground & those tell me who have watched them, that they have little knives in their pockets, with which they cut the threads, and thus get a large toll. There goes one of these women with at least a bushell of grain on her head, and some more in another bag under her arm.

This morning I heard a prolonged cry of distress down on the lower deck, & ran to see what was the matter, and I found one of the white deck hands having a little battle with a black [in]fantry man. The white had the black by holding one of his fingers between his teeth. The blood was flowing freely, but as neither one called on us for surgical aid, I presume there was no serious lesions. Now while I am writing, there are two little brats engaged in fighting over the bags. One has his hair cut close to his head, the other has long hair and first gets hold of the others hair, and pulls him like a little tiger, and gives him a few dry knocks with his fist, which completely uses him up. Then they are at it again. Long hair carries a stone in his hand, but his vulnerable point is seized, and he, although frantic with rage, is obliged to yield. By this time they have attracted the attention of a man who eyes them rather hesitatingly, as if a war of extenuation were better than any interference on his part, but concludes to separate them. This suggests the question where are the Police? The answer is they are a harmless body of men, who wear no uniform, and are only seen occasionally & wear a pale silver star on their coats. When wanted they are not to be found.

I think I shall make out a week for our stay here— no day set for leaving.

Steamer *D.A. January*
Paducah, Ky. [July 4]

Dear Frank

We did not leave for Paducah till about 3.25 P.M. Wednesday and after a rapid sail of 19 ½ hours we reached Cairo. *We did* let her drive, being down stream we could "go it." We were anxious to get back to St Louis before the Fourth of July, but were so long in getting away that we gave up the idea. It was suggested that we have our celebration where we might happen to be. And it was also decided to have some of the works and the amount of 102 dollars was subscribed immediately by doctors, nurses, & all on board. I was appointed to make the selection and purchase and arrange the program of the display.

We arrived at Paducah about 3 as I said before, and there were no orders awaiting us to proceed any farther. We announced our arrival, by telegraph, & have been waiting orders ever since. Fearing that we might not be in a nonfavorable place for making a display we concluded to have our fireworks last night the third instead. It was a beautiful sight, and must have been appreciated by the natives of Paducah. It lasted about 2 hours. Our rockets were beautiful, and some of our exhibition pieces were as fine as any I ever saw in Eastern towns. (I never tried to write on such oily paper. I'll not try it again)

The Bengal lights illuminated the boat with fine effect. We had a grand *feau de joi* of Roman candles, and the whole closed with a beautiful revolving globe.

This morning, two pieces of artillery were brot on board, and a salute of I forget how many guns was fired.

Each gun was a rifled canon, and was attended by five men, who attended to the business of loading and firing. We went up the Tennesee a few miles to get some wood, and our artillery men amused us by firing shells whiz through the air, then strike the water, burst and produce an eruption like a small fountain. I noticed a beautiful phenomena during the firing, which elicited my admiration more than the rest. It was the beautiful rings of smoke which were evolved from the mouth of the guns just at the moment of firing. These rings rise, expand, & revolve as they rise, & continue to do so till they reach the height of a hundred feet, when they become discipated in the air—just like in a familiar experiment in chemistry we produce little rings from the explosions of a certain gas as it rises on the surface of the water.

We were also treated to a little display of field artillery practice this morning. You would be surprized to see how fast these artillery men ride their horses and drag their pieces around the field after them. The guns we had on board were six pounders, & so bright you could see your face in them.

Paducah Ky
Friday Evening 4th of July, 62

I was trying to think where I spent my last fourth of July. Can't tell unless it was at a picnic at the Conesus lake. Do you remember? After the artillery display this forenoon nothing occurred of any importance during the remainder of the day. It has been very warm this evening.

I went on shore this afternoon & walked up the principal street for a distance of half a mile. There has been quite an effort on the part of the people to have a city. Several streets are well macadamized and bordered with curb stones. There are several good buildings for dwellings and stores, but it has a good deal the air of a southern town. The land lies very flat, there being no elevation in any part of the town, and it must suffer from improper drainage.

This evening the hospital boat *Stephen Decatur* came down from Pittsburgh Landing. She came along side of our boat and gave us 70 sick men, which is a good beginning of a load for us. We shall take on the remainder to morrow from the Hospitals here, and our orders are to take them to Louisville, Ky. It will take us about four days to go and come back here again.

Saturday Evening July 5

Last night I went up in the town to see whether the people were doing any thing in the way of celebrating the Fourth. Did not see much. Found the office of the Quartermaster with the windows illuminated, and numerous flags flying. This was about all. The boys in the Main street were exploding crackers, and grasshoppers, and sending up a few small rockets.

This morning before eating breakfast, I took on a number of sick men, and have received a few more to day, so that we have in all about 150 sick. Orders have not come yet and we cannot be off for Louisville. We may not get off for several days.

This morning there were quite a number of soldiers standing on the wharf boat, and as one was walking along and a little drunk, he staggered and fell into the water, and scarcely rose up to the surface. The affair made a little stir for a few minutes. There was a great general rush to the side of the boat to see if they could rescue him, but nothing could be seen, and nothing more was thought of it. There was not half as much pains to get him as if it had been some article of value to its possessor. *Human life is apparently not of much account in the army.*

It has been *very* warm today. This evening, one of the sick soldiers while amusing himself fishing off the stern of the boat, and had the good luck to make fast to the largest catfish I ever saw. I should think it would weigh 50 lbs. We shall have it for dinner to morrow. Fish would be a very agreeable change for we have not had any till just yesterday, since we have been on the boat.

What a fearful time our army are having these days in front of Richmond?

Sunday P.M. [July 6]

This morning we took on some more men from the steamer *Pringle* which had just come down the night before from Pittsburgh Landing. This gave us a load of two hundred and thirty-two; and although not as many as we can carry, we started off about 10 AM, and have been steaming up the Ohio river all day, our destination being Louisville which we shall reach by about Tuesday morning. The class of patients are most of them convalescents, and require very little medicine. The most they need is good water, food & other hygienic treatment. Some of them will be fit for service again in a few weeks. There are others who will probably be discharged from the service.

After they had all partaken of their dinners I distributed a quantity of tracts among them. They were glad to get them as they seem to have very few testaments or any kind of reading matter. I do not think that this portion of our army were as liberally supplied with Bibles as the soldiers who went from Eastern states. There are some who lose their things, particularly if they have been lieing in a hospital for a length of time. I thought yesterday I should attend church in Paducah to day, but it is better for our sick that we are on our way—a floating hospital in motion is a much pleasanter place than one tied up to the shore. It is close enough even then. We are not going very far north, but the scenery is much pleasanter, and the air is better than down the river further.

The sun has poured down his rays upon us to day in full force. I can get along with warm weather if I am well as I am now, and not complain at all. I find that woolens worn next to the skin are indispensible, and I wear them all the time.

I am anxious to hear the full report of the battle near Richmond. I fear that some of the Geneseo boys have seen some fighting and may have suffered severely....

The evenings are very pleasant just at this time. This evening the moon is shining, and it sets off the densely wooded shores of the river to good advantage. The deep breathings of the engines is all that breaks the stillness of the night as our boat makes her way up the river.

Tuesday July 8, 62

We are now about 20 miles from New Albany the place where we shall leave our passengers. I thought we should go to Louisville but I forgot that this city is just above the falls, and we can't get up there. We shall land 3 or 4 miles this side.

On our way we stopped at Smith Land a few minutes. Then we landed at Evansville and discharged 28 of our sick who belonged in southern Indiana and took on about 50 more from the hospital in this place. These last belong in Kentucky and Ohio. We try to get them to the hospitals as near their homes as possible. No furloughs are granted now, so that the soldiers are obliged to remain in the hospitals or else get discharged from the service.

I lost one of my patients on this trip from epilepsy, and there was one in [the] charge of the other Drs who died from exhaustion. These are the only deaths this time.

The scenery along the Ohio is more home like than any I see elsewhere. There are comfortable houses situated on pleasant farms surrounded by thirty orchards, and shade trees. The people look more civilized than down in Dixie. I am told that the wheat crop never was better than it is this year. I can see some very tall corn on shore. A short time ago, we passed a long row of osage orange hedge rows. Where we are now the shore rises up in abrupt hills on our side, and a broad flat country on the Kentucky side.

I did not receive a letter from you when last at St Louis. I do not know where we shall go after leaving New Albany, probably back to Paducah again where we shall wait for orders. With greetings to all my friends, I remain your affectionate brother

John

Steamer *D.A. January*
July 9th 1862
Ohio River Fr. Louisville to
Paducah, Ky

Dear Frank,

I mailed my last bundle of notes at New Albany, the place we stopped at before we reached Louisville landing. We arrived at the last named placed about 1 P.M., and the Dr went up to the town to make arrangements for getting off the sick. He did not return immediately, and it was eleven oclock last night before we got them off. The majority of them were able to walk, so we had them form into a line and march double file to their quarters, distance about two miles. They arrived all safe so I conclude they were benefitted by the walk.

While I was superintending the disembarkation, there were three little girls whose ages would range from ten to fourteen came on board. They had two violins and a triangle among them, and they took their places in a row and played for us quite a while, for which they received generous contributions. They performed very well for children. They sang for us "Red, White & Blue." I was much amused with their playing.

I did not have time to go up and see the town, and the streets are very dusty so that the walking was not pleasant. I will wait till another time. We remained at our landing (Portland) all night, and got off about 7 this morning. We have had a fine breeze all day, and it has been as pleasant steaming as we could expect with the great heat that exists. The scenery along the river has been varied with mountain, bluff, low shore, & farming contry, in many places with neat little farm houses. I noticed several quarries where they were engaged in getting out a quantity of fine building stone. There are several little villages along the river of more or less interest, at one of these. Cannelton Ind, we stopped about 6 P.M. to take in coal. There is a very large cotton factory here. It has lately been constructed, and is probably the only one of the kind in this part of the country. It is certainly a very fine building and is owned by a Co. in Louisville. As I had plenty of time I determined to pay it a visit. It is only a short distance from the river and is a very imposing building. It has two high round towers surmounting the main portion, and looks a little like the Smithsonian Inst. at Washington. I got there a few minutes before work was over, and one of the employes very kindly showed me through the main portion of the building. I saw the cotton as it comes from the bales put through a series of mills, the first to clean it, another to flatten it out in sheets like wadding, another to flatten it still more, at the same time draw it out in long strips. Then by a series of this meshing, these strips are twisted loosely like candy wicking, then drawn out still smaller, till it becomes ready to be twisted into threads, which is then ready to be woven into cloth by the looms. The looms were not in operation as they have not got fairly going yet. They were obliged to discontinue work till after the cotton markets opened. They get their cotton in Tennesee. This is the only institution of the kind I ever saw, and it was a great curiosity to me.

Since our boat has been stopping here, I have been showing some of the ladies of the place through our boat. They are much pleased with the arrangements, and express much surprise at seeing a large sheet iron oven where one hundred loaves of bread can be baked at once.

The boat has not started yet, some of the Doctors and the Captains are on shore and we cant go till they return. It is a beautiful moonlight evening, and the nurses (men) have been sitting out on the deck singing and playing all kinds of songs, patriotic, comic, and sentimental. There is one who plays the fiddle and he is doing his best to add to the enjoyment of the evening. But what has amused me the most, was to see the "roust abouts" (who have just been hard at work shoveling coal) clear the deck for a quadrille. The fiddler took his position, and the men selected their partners and they danced (a little awkward to be sure) but with a good deal of spirit. The good people on shore must think we have very gay times on our hospital boat. It is now 10 P.M. and we are off again.

July 10th 9 P.M.

Our boat had a good sail down the river to day. The weather was very warm but there was every appearance of a storm brewing. The wind blew at first gentle, then it increased to a gale, and about 1 P.M. the squall came on accompanied with thunder & lightning. You could not see ahead the length of the boat, and it was no use to go on, so the order was given to turn in towards the shore and tie up. The squalls lasted about half an hour after we got under weigh again. It has rained all the afternoon, and has cooled the air several degrees.

We arrived here in this city of Paducah about 7 P.M., and expect to receive orders by tomorrow where to go. There is an opinion that we will go down the river to Columbus.

The mosquitoes are very numerous to night, and we shall be obliged to arrange our bars and bolt them out, if we expect to get any rest.

Friday Evening Jul 11, 62.

We have been lieing here in Paducah all day. The temperature is very agreeable since the rain of yester day. You had better believe the mosquitoes made an attack upon us last night. They broke through my bars, which I had supposed were proof against all "gallinippers" and sucked my blood and poisoned me. I could not sleep much till the blood thirsty creatures had got their fill. But they shared the fate of a certain fox for I found them inside my bars this morning, and I killed them before they were able to find their way out.

We expected to do something or go some where to day, but no orders have come yet, and we are as a boats company doing little or nothing. We try fishing for amusement, dont catch many. There have been over a dozen lines hanging to the side of the boat. I dont think there were more than three fish caught, one of these were a gar pike. These gars are very plenty in this river, but are difficult to catch with a hook. Catfish are the only kind which are good for the table.

Steamboats are coming and going from this place all the time, some from the Ohio and Tennessee rivers and the Mississippi. The *Silver Moon* came in just as we were at dinner, she has a caliope and played several *chunes* as she came up the river. These instruments sound well at a little distance, but our engineer says "it takes 20ths of steam to run em and they are all the time gettin out of repair." They are only found on some of the excursion boats.

There is no fighting in this part of the country, and the hospital boats are not doing much. Dr. Hoff thinks we will be ordered down to Columbus, 60 miles below Cairo on the Miss. river. News from Richmond are rather undecided. It is difficult to make out from the reports which side was victorious, and whether McClellan has or has not gained any thing by his last bloody battle.

> Steamer *January* below Cairo on
> the Mississippi July 13.62

Dear Frank

I mentioned to you that I improved the sabbath morning of my stay in Paducah in attending church. There are as many fine places of worship there, but all but one is occupied by soldiers for hospital purposes. The little church where services were held was filled to overflowing. The house was very plain, and the seats were uncushioned and had straight backs but painted. The congregation was composed mostly of females who occupy one side of the house, and the male portion the other. There was no gallery. Owing to a little difference in our timepieces I was too late to hear the first prayer (but I got a seat) and was told that this petition breathed good Union sentiments. The substance of his sermon, which was delivered extempore, was an explanation of "What is love to God." His remarks were clever, and delivered in an animated style. The weather was very warm, and the perspiration flowed freely from his brow. He said one thing which I thought sounded a little funny. He refered to the love which Hazael manifested for his Lord, when he was in a tight place, and the remark which he made, "Am I a dog that I should do this thing?" "Yes," said the speaker, "he was the very dog that did it." At the close of the prayer, he announced the hymn, found the place and led the singing at once, hardly giving the good people time to find the place. He was an old school Presbyterian minister & is doing all the good he can to keep the fire burning upon the altar during these times of war.

We got under head way about 2 o clock and reached Cairo about 9 o clock in the evening, stopping there a few moments as we generally do. We proceeded on down the Mississippi River. After you get beyond the confluence of the two rivers, the stream becomes very wide, in some places more than a mile. Our destination being Columbus only 20 miles from Cairo, we reached this point about 11 in the evening. It was fine sailing last night, and I enjoyed sitting on the guard, being fanned by the breeze, watching the play of the lightning away in the west & looking out upon the full moon, as she rose from behind the long rows of cotton woods which skirted the shore. I was in hopes the storm would overtake us and give our deck a little washing, but we ran away from it. There was rain somewhere last night, for we find the air this morning much cooler.

Columbus July 14, 62.

We opened our eyes this morning upon scenery that was new, but not unlike much that we had already met with. We have dropped down a little ways into the seats of Rebel dom, and are where we find much that looks like war.

This morning before the sun became very hot (it is now 98°) the Captain and I went out to see the town. The first thing that meets our eye is the RR Depot of the Mobile and Ohio road, which runs to Corinth or rather to Grand Junction, or as much further as the Rebels will permit it. It is expected that transportation can be had over this road without any molestation from the enemy. The principal street runs along the river bank, the rail road runs along it for a little distance. The buildings are small wooden structures and are scarcely to be called stores. There are a few comfortable looking dwelling houses but it is altogether not much of a place. It was here that the Rebels offered the first resistance to our fleet making their way down the river after leaving Cairo. The fortification which they most relied on as a defense, is situated on a high and commanding bluff just outside.... [Page missing]

Steamer D.A. January
on her way to Memphis
July 15, 1862, 8 oclock P.M.

Dear Frank,
About ten oclock this morning orders came to make ready, and go down the river to the relief of Gen Curtis' sick. Everyone was glad to hear the announcement as we were anxious to see a little more of the

Mississippi river, and it was becoming very dull at Columbus. Before leaving I mailed package No. 18. It so happened that eight of our nurses were left. They had gone early in the morning to pick blackberries some distance from the landing, but with the understanding that in case orders should come for us to leave, we could not wait long for them. The boats whistle sounded loud and long for them, but they did not make their appearance and they will have to stay there till our return.

I took the Captains glass and a book and went up to the Pilot House where I could have a good view of the country along the river. The first place of any note you meet with is Hickman opposite island No. 6. It is a cozy little place, situated on the side of a hill, which gradually slopes to the river. The houses look neater than in many of the river towns. About noon we passed the place where Col Bissell of the engineers passed the transports through or rather over a country, and through a bayou during the high water, that the army might surround Island No. 10, which lies a few miles below. The place is now very far out of water. As we came on island No. 10 all came on the upper deck to see this celebrated battle ground. Before we came abreast of it we were shown the place where the mortar fleet lay and threw shells at a distance of $^3/_4$ of a mile into the forts on the island, and the adjacent batteries on the Kentucky shore. When we reached the island there was very little to be seen that looked like earthworks thrown up. At the upper end we discovered a sand bag battery with guns pointing over the parapet. In several other places we could see guns, but everything was much concealed by high grass and weeds. There are a good many trees scattered over the island. At the lower end, on a mound-like eminence, I saw a sentinel make his appearance from behind a shelter of canvass. He was the only person visible. There were tents however to be seen, which indicated more men. On the Kentucky side of the river was considerable of a cavalry force stationed, and quite a lot of stores & provisions lay along the bank. There is no danger of the place being retaken. Two or three wrecks of steamboats were partially submerged at one side of the river, & this was all that could be seen to indicate any destruction of life or property. The island occupies the middle of the stream, and commands the river completely. The Rebels made no provision for being attacked in the rear, so that they could not maintain their ground when Gen Pope approached them in that direction.[77]

The next place was New Madrid, which has been a point of some note, and where the Rebels made a stand. It is a little town, and like all southern towns offers nothing of interest. The houses are low and no

churches to be seen with spires rising above the surrounding dwellings.
There does not seem to be much money expended in church property
here in this country, and where I see so little respect paid for religion, I
don't wonder that ignorance prevails to a great extent. Perhaps there is
an excuse for not building better houses, in the fact that they, like the
people of Santiago, are frequently visited by earthquakes. Geologists
speak of one which occurred here in 1812 that did a good deal of damage and destroyed several lives. The Pilot says shocks are experienced
almost every day (hardly) and that sand or mud volcanoes are found in
many places.

The scenery along the shore presents nothing very different from
what we see above. The fish pole cane grows along the bank in great
quantities, and the deep green of the vegetation is relieved by the bright
red flowers of the trumpet creeper, whose trailing stems festoon the
trees in many places, completely hiding them. I have seen one beautiful
tree lately, that is the cypress, which grows here in great luxuriance.

We shall probably pass Forts Randolph, and Pillow, during the
night, and Memphis possibly. Our sailing this evening is much impeded
by every little while taking soundings. The channel of the river changes
so often that this becomes necessary.

> Wednesday Morning below Memphis
> [July 16]

What a change in the air this morning! It is cloudy, the thermometer
is at 76° and quite a breeze. We arrived at Memphis at day break this
morning. I awoke early and took a walk through the principal streets
before breakfast. Knowing too that I must make my observations here
hurriedly I did not stay long in any one place. The good people of the
town were not moving about much, so that I saw little else than the
houses. The buildings used for stores are constructed with good taste
being built of brick, red as Milwaukie, & some of the light sandstone
found in St Louis. I was much pleased with the whole appearance of the
place. The streets are well laid out, and I was better pleased with it than
I was with St Louis, although it is not as large a city. There is a pretty
part in the central part of the town which is shaded by large trees.
Squirrels may be seen running about in them. The principal street is
paved with wooden blocks which, having been recently put down, look
neat. The soil is sandy, and there is plenty of dust which covers everything you touch. The shade trees are principally sycamore, which grow
here more luxuriant than I ever saw them at the north. I picked a flower
from a beautiful high bush that I passed in a yard near the street. I

enclose it. See if you can tell me the name of it. The location of the town along the river is high, but slopes as you pass back towards the country beyond. The town is under military serveilance and the sleeping sentinels, whom we found lieing on the steps of the quarter masters office, belong to the force stationed here.

The city of Memphis is protected by two iron clad gun boats, which lie at anchor in the river opposite. Just before the city is the place where the famous battle came off between our gun boat fleet, and those of the rebels. In one place you see the wheel house of one of the rebel boats out of the water, and nearer in shore lies the *Beauregard* with nothing but her smoke stack above the water. This is the work of Col Elliotts rams who persisted in their bunting [butting] so furiously that these light craft were completely demolished.[78]

The scenery along the river consists of woods, woods, woods, with here and there a plantation covered with corn. The corn is ready for roasting or boiling. I should like to get ashore and pick a few ears. Wherever you see a plantation, there is a neat little house with a veranda in front, which is occupied by the planter or overseer, and a few rods in the rear there is one or more other houses of smaller dimensions and with less of style about it, where the slaves live. A row of these houses which are usually white washed, make a very pretty appearance at a distance. In some of the cornfields you will see a high shed like this.[79] It is where the overseer sits and watches the blacks while they "hoe de corn." The command "Be ye not eye servants, etc.," was probably not intended for the blacks, hence the need for overseers. Perhaps these observations of mine are wearisome to you who have seen much more of this river than I have. I note these down as they may be pleasant to look at hereafter and there is very little else to write about.

Although the lesson taught our men that they must be ready when the boat starts or they will be left, still one of our best nurses was left behind this morning. He saw us from the shore and signaled us, but we could not turn about & he too must stay till we return.

I have been reading a very sensible morning paper which I obtained in Memphis, published there. The subject of Foreign intervention is a good deal talked of. I wish something of the kind would be carefully considered by our nation, for the two factions into which it is now divided, threaten like the Kilkenny cats to destroy each other.

We arrived in Helena about one oclock and the large army of Gen Curtis which has lately been in Arkensaw were quartered here, they having arrived at this place the day before. It seems that they were on their way towards Little Rock, and expected to meet transports at some place along the river Arkensaw, but failed to do so. I think the river fleet were impeded in some way, either by the evening or low water, so that provisions could not be sent there and for a while they subsisted on half rations. Finding it useless to try to make further advances, they turned about and proceeded towards the Mississippi river, where they found the supplies they wanted in great abundance. In coming this way they had a little fighting to do. They met a number of Texan rangers and Arkensaw troops, and killed 120 of their number, and loosing four of the yankees & wounding about 40. These 40 we shall take on our boat with a large number of sick besides. This army had a pretty hard time of it in marching, owing to the scarcity of water for drink, and to the bad roads which afterwards followed the recent rains. We have been receiving the sick on board this afternoon, and it had rained very hard all the time, and the wind has blown so that it has been rather disagreeable.

The town of Helena is a little village, on the Arkensaw side of the river, and has a good many neat dwellings. One formerly occupied by the rebel General Hin[d]man[80] and is now used as Gen Curtis' head quarters, is a very pretty house, and the ends are surmounted by a cross. I thot at first sight it was a catholic institution of some kind. An army if as large as this is a great nuisance to a place. I saw a number of fellows pulling down a tolerably good house to make fires with to do cooking. When they are off in the country and get out of provisions, they do some foraging as they have done of late. If a man is going along to mill with a grist, he is liable to have his property taken away by these hungry men. It seems to be a very cool procedure, but the soldiers must live, and it is a military necessity. The disciples plucked the ears of corn when they were likely to starve. I saw one man have a copy of Perrys *Japan Expedition,* which he had picked up in a barn (I think he had no business with it).

[Thursday July 17], 62 [81]

I arose earlier than usual this morning to finish getting the sick. After we had taken on our complement of passengers, there was a suther came on board to get us to take some cotton to St Louis. We took it as we have a place we could stove it in the hold. The roustabouts had quite a lively time exercising their muscles, as they rolled the cotton bales on board. There were 39 in all, and the average weight of each 400 pounds. The gentleman told me that each bale was worth 50 dollars, it costing him about 11 cts. He told me how he got it. The people in his neighborhood have been strongly "secesh" and their leaders have burned all the cotton they could find. One man however had 400 bales in one place which the secesh burned, but he had above 39 concealed in some secluded woods, and he thus saved a little which would yield him a few dollars. The sale had to be made under the pledge of strictest secrecy, for the poor man would be severely dealt with in case he should be found out. It has rained so much to day and I have been so much engaged on board the boat, that I have not paid this town a single visit, not so much as to put my foot on shore. The levee in front of the town is built up with a mixture of sand and cotton. We could not afford to make such a use of it at the north. I dont think there will be much used in that way even here, for a while. I noticed in a field that we passed to day, where cotton had been grown in previous years, broad strips of corn and sweet potatoes. Jeff Davis' order not to plant cotton seems to be obeyed, at least here.

As we started off up the river, we all looked out at the long line of men, horses, mules, tents, and army stores, which extend for more than a mile along the shore. They all seemed to be enjoying the rest and holi-day they are having after their toilsome expedition into the back coun-try. I have heard nothing of his plans (Gen Curtis), but think they will try again to see what they can do towards taking Little Rock.

The weather owing to the heavy rains has been remarkably cool for the season and place. Two of our men have died since coming on board, and I fear others will follow them before we reach our destination. All those nurses and others who got left along the river, who went to gather blackberries, came on board this morning and they [the blackberries?] looked cheap enough. They came down on the boat *Memphis.*

Friday July 18, 1862

We reached Memphis again this morning and stayed long enough to put on some coal and ice, which very important article had been out for a day or two. We also took on fresh meat and some vegetables, among them some tomatoes which I am so fond of. I should like to get some good ripe apples. Have seen but few and they were poor. While at Paducah the fruit women brot on a kind of plum which was tolerably good. We were detained so long at Memphis that we did not make as much of a distance as I should like to have done. The only place of interest that we have passed today was Fort Pillow this evening just at twilight. There is not much to be seen, the earth works are so over grown with grass and bushes that you can scarcely discover the outline of the works. One of Uncle Sams iron turtles (gun boats) lies out in the stream opposite, and the fort is garrisoned within.

Where we are now sailing the water is rather shallow, and they are taking soundings, thus feeling our way along, that we may not go onto a sand bar which would detain us. The deck hand throws the lead and sings out the depth to the mate who stands on the upper deck. He repeats the same to the pilot who is at the wheel. You will remember this very common experiment.

Saturday, July 19th, 1862

When morning came we found ourselves at a place along the shore where the boat landed about daybreak to bury the dead. We have lost five men on the passage thus far, and as we could not keep them on the boat another day till we could reach any place where they might receive a burial, it was our duty for the health of those on board to dispose of them as above. I went ashore to see what they were doing, & I found the deck hands at work with their shovels covering up the coffins which had been placed in a trench broad enough to receive them all. All the monument we could raise to mark the place of burial of these poor soldiers, was a simple small pine board, with their names written upon it. Their friends may come and remove them to some family burial place, but in all probability they will not. I sometimes see the friend of a deceased soldier in search of his remains. I saw those of a soldier which had been placed in a metallic coffin with a glass over the face and I could not understand what satisfaction it would be to his friends to have him brought home to them in the condition that they were. The little baggage which the soldiers leave with us when they die, sometimes contains momentos or other articles of value & always a good many letters which they have received from friends at home. These occasionally fall under my observation, and are often interesting. Letters are sent back to the friends from where they came, with a line stating the circumstances of the death of the person. The baggage is generally delivered over to the lieutenant whose business it is to send anything valuable to his friends. But the knapsack, gun, and other accoutrements are turned over to the government.

[Sunday July 20, 62]

We have had a sultry day, but have had a fine rain this evening, for which we are thankful. A good wind is very desireable to purify the air of our cabins as well as the surrounding atmosphere. We passed Island No 10. about 4 P.M. and hope to reach Cairo sometime to morrow forenoon. We shall pass Columbus in the night I hope, as I don't want them to make the necessary delay of stopping there. We have just been taking on 11 cords of wood. Wood and coal has to be consumed in great quantities to carry us on our way. I have just been witnessing one of the most beautiful sights that it was ever my pleasure to see. The woods along the shore are filled with fire flies (whose lamps are filled with better oil than those we have in the north). I never saw them in such swarms. The night is rather dark and they show off to good advantage upon the dark foliage, which seems to be densely bespangled with these little creatures. If they are as plentiful in the Dismal swamps as they are here, I can easily understand how the young lady of whom the poet speaks might, "By the flickering light of the fire flys lamp, paddle her bark canoe" and get along very well.

When we were pasing the county of Lauderdale, Tennessee, I turned my attention that way, but could see nothing of interest....[82]

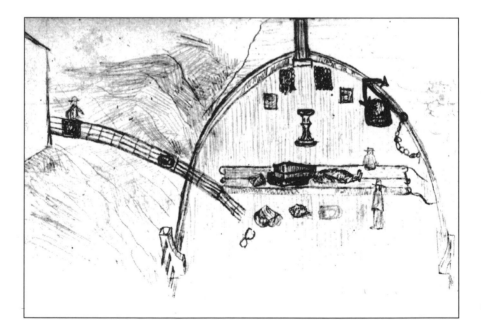

Sunday July. [20]. 62
[Under the sketch]

Taking on ice at Cairo, by sliding the cakes down the ways. Coffined and uncofined bodies lieing on the platform which are in danger of being dashed to pieces by these masses as they slide down with great momentum onto the deck.

Monday P.M. July 21, 62

We are pushing our way up to Jefferson Barracks against a pretty strong current, but we shall probably reach that point in time to unload & get to St Louis to night. We have been away just 3 weeks, and I feel quite behind on news. Shall soon be where I can get posted up. We have lost ten of our men on the trip, which has been one of unusual length—just five days. The patients are comparatively comfortable. They feel as though they had got almost to their homes. Their experience down in the Arkansaw swamps was very trying to their strength. Although they did not do much fighting they ran short of provisions, and the water was very bad.

4th, and lastly, I enclose you a letter which was taken from a dead secesh or some where else, and I think was written from Island No. 10 from the fact that the incident related of the "yankees slipping up to their guns and striking them" is referred to. This you remember was done by the sailors from one of the gunboats. I saw the guns as we passed the place. One of the soldiers with a broken leg is walking around the cabin on *crutches made from a Rebel flag staff*. They answer the purpose admirably, and are a momento besides. While Curtis' army were passing through Arkansaw, the soldiers did a good deal of foraging, and among other things, they picked up some valuable books. I have just been reading one entitled *Bible Defense of Slavery*, a book of considerable size and pretensions. The arguments used for the defense of slavery are such as you will hear from every man who is in favor of the institution, and believes it to be approved by God. I wish you could read it, it is written by Preist & Brown & was published in Kentucky. Among the commendatory notices from the Press there is one from the *Monroe Democrat*, which advises its readers to posess themselves of the volume, as it contains much that is too true, and should be considered by Northern people when they talk about this subject of slavery. The book was published just ten years ago. Perhaps the Editor of the above pages would not exhibit the same views & sentiments at this time. This book contains a prophecy of what will be the course of events if northern influence gains the ascendancy in our government, which is now being fulfilled to the very letter. It is very clear that northern abolitionists, and the southern leaders, have split our glorious union, and until they are put down, we never can hope to have a reunion of state. There is no use of talking. A sick Captain who sits near me while I write,

says that we are going *to have a pretty rough time of it*, if we subdue
them. The opinion of those who have seen the critter, and felt of him,
are worthy of our consideration.[83]

The whistle announces our arrival at Jefferson Barracks, and I must
assist in getting our sick off. How glad the poor fellows are to get here.
How they crowd the way to the guards, and look out towards the beautiful grounds with shade trees with here and there long ranges of buildings which are the hospital barracks. Within these temporary asylums I
am told every comfort is provided for the sick soldiers and we can hope
that if our sick have any vitality left in them, it will be increased by a
sojurn here. The convalescents who have just come down to the shore to
meet us are all looking like well new. We shall soon dispose of our load,
and then in another hour of steaming, the high dome of the courthouse
which is but just seen now, will rise up before our view, and the boat
will be coming up to the levee & crowd in between the other boats,
demanding a place among them, so that we can get our packages of letters and papers that are no doubt awaiting us.

                              Hospital Steamer *D.A. January*
                              From St Louis to Paducah
                              July 24th 1862

Dear Frank,
    We reached St Louis on Monday evening but too late to find Will to
get my batch of letters & Papers. In the morning, however, I was grati-
fied to get two from you, and also to read those which came to Will....

I should like very much to stop down to the "Hall" and hear the
Normal singers. I have heard no *good* music here since I have been
west. One of the nurses is sawing away at his fiddle just now, but I
should prefer to hear Cook....

Tell Mother I don't know what to say about the war. It is a game that
I can't see the issue of just now. One day I feel encouraged, the next am
doubting of our final triumph. Want to see things tried a while longer.
Dont quite like the management of things at Washington. Business
changes hands too often. Think McClellan should hold the reins in *his
own* hands. Gov. Gamble has just issued an order throughout the state
of Mo. that all men capable of doing military service, will report themselves at the various recruiting stations and stand ready for subduing
the guerrillas in the state. The oath has produced a good deal of sensation in St Louis & several are trying to leave the city, but are prevented,
the city being under martial law. Will says that he shall try and get

Mason to intercede for him, as he does not care about going into service. There are a great number of "secesh" in St. Louis whose influence is bad for the Union cause.

I have had a very pleasant short stay in St Louis this time. On the first of the month Will changed his business from the Telegraph Office to the Banking house of L.A. Benoist & Co (this name is French and is pronounced as if spelt *Benwauh*). He likes the place well and his hours for business are shorter. I think he is very fortunate in getting the situation. He has a very pleasant place for boarding. It is in one of the finest houses in the city—a select class of boarders and a pleasant lady, Mrs Haslam, is the hostess. I took up my lodgings with Will while in town. Everything about the house is elegant. The place is known as the Phinney mansion, and it is situated near sixteenth street on Washington Avenue.... My health is very good these days, better than ever, but rather thin in the flesh some think. Just as we were about starting this noon who should come on board to see me but Wm Bissell. He has been down in Arkansaw with Curtiss' Army, is spending a few days in town, and expects to go to St Paul soon. He looks the same as ever & talks as he used to do. He barely alluded to matrimonial difficulties which I did not care to know about. We are sailing down the river making very good time, and shall reach Cairo by day light Providence permitting.

Saturday P.M. July 26, 62

We reached Paducah yesterday about noon, and there received orders to steam up the Tennesee river until we should meet the steamer *J.S. Pringle*, then take off her sick on our boat, return with them to Jefferson Barracks. We met the *Pringle* about 4 P.M., very soon took off her load as they were all well enough to walk but one, and by this time we are all well on our way to St. Louis, having passed Cape Girardeau about noon. Our patients are all convalescents, but one in my division that is very sick, hence our labors are very light comparatively. Our sick have good appetites. You ought to have seen them eat their dinners a while ago, off from their (our) new service of tin, which was used to day for the first. It consists of three pieces to each man viz. a cup, plate and spoon which are all chained together to prevent their getting lost.[84] They answer the purpose very well, but the cook says they are bad to wash. When they are not in use, they are hung up on iron hooks. With this new apparatus we can have a tin wedding as well as Mrs. Wood. I had some peaches when I was in St Louis last. I also found some apples that were very good. The apples are high priced and do not equal those of our "Kedentry." Wild plums are sold in large quantities.

I never knew the fruit till I came west. A stern wheel steamboat has just caught up with us and it affords amusement for the soldiers to see how her speed compares with ours, and whether we will out run her. We have no idea of racing, that is opposed to our by laws. Our boat is slow enough, but I think for all that we shall reach St Louis first. She has drooped behind several feet already. This afternoon is delightful, the clouds intercept the hot rays of the sun, and there is just breeze enough to unfurl the flags. I have just been distributing among the men copies of the enclosed poem which all seem pleased with.[85] Did you ever see it? I found half a dozen or more that could not read. I am always startled when I find a man that cant read. It must be a great privation to such a one. There must be some portion of this great west not as well supplied with educational institutions as they should be. And it is not a pleasant thought to entertain that these schools will not be as well sustained for a while as they were before the war. How beautiful those corniced rocks are that form the west bank of the river, how they tower up. At this time their perpendicular faces are clothed with cedars which cling for a roothold, and climbing vines creep up towards their summit. There is one feature which distinguishes the trees and vegetation of the river at this place from that farther south and particularly that of the Tennesee. Along the latter river, the trees are not more numerous but the spaces between them are so completely filled with vines that they entirely mantle them, and the trees lose their identity.

Instead of jagged outlines of foliage you have graceful curves & undulations. One of the waiters that we took on at St. Louis plays the guitar and sings quite well. He takes his position upon the upper deck every pleasant evening just over my stateroom and entertains us.

We have a remarkable boy on board this boat whose business is to sell newspapers, oranges, lemons, figs, etc., to all that wish to buy. He keeps he says very good Havanna segars—although I never tried them. He is a very precocious youth, is only seventeen and very dwarfish in stature. He says he used to travel with Gen. Tom Thumb and drive his carriage through the streets.[86] I have to watch him a little to see what he sells to the men. I dont allow him to sell apples or any kind of fruit that will sicken them, although they would like well to get hold of it.

Saturday Evening

I have just been looking among our men for a man of the 59th Ill Volunteers, one who was at the battle of Pea Ridge, and if possible was acquainted with Johnson Kelly. I found 3 or 4 of the Rgt on board, and one of his company. I have been quizzing the poor sick man for information concerning him. He was able to give me nearly every thing worthy of interest to his friends. It seems that Kelly was killed or so badly wounded at the battle of Pea Ridge that he died soon after. I shall pass the details that I obtained over to Willis, who received a note from Couzen Michael making inquiries about his son.

St Louis P.O.

Am looking for Willis

Yours affectionately

John

St. Louis

Sunday Evening July 27th 1862

8 P.M.

Dear Frank

Our boat arrived in town to day about 11 oclock, too late to attend the morning service at one of the churches. After dinner I went ashore, put a letter in the P.O., then walked up Washington Avenue to Willis' boarding house, found him in his room reading. After sitting a moment he produced your letter to us, which afforded me pleasure to read. Will was surprised to see me back again so soon. Have been absent from this place since Thursday. The quickest trip we have made yet.

This afternoon I went to Mr Nelsons church cor of Locust and 14th St. I understood there was to be an address to the children of the sabbath school, and I thought I would be present and compare this assemblage with others I have seen in eastern towns. I found things conducted in a similar manner....

I have been staying on board this evening to give the others a chance to go if they wish. Dr. Hoff & the Captain went to church this evening. The Dr. said that he had not been to church in over a year. There are quite a number that can say the same thing.

Tuesday July 29th 1862

We did not get away from St Louis till about 1 oclock yesterday, it takes a good while to shovel on coal especially this warm weather, and to slide on ice, and get everything ready for a start. We changed our mate. He became dissatisfied with some thing, and when the mate goes he takes with him his squad of deck hands. Steamboat men are continually changing their places, and a Captain never knows when his new men may take a notion to leave him. It is not considered unfair if the hands leave at one hours notice. There is never any difficulty in getting more help, for the old help was no sooner paid off, than a stout broad shouldered mate brot on his squad of roustabouts.

We had a pleasant and rapid sail down to Paducah where we arrived this morning about 10 A.M. We landed along side of the *I. Raymond,* which had just come down the Cumberland river from Eddyville where she had taken an artillery company to put down a little rebel outbreak which occurred there a short time since. This battery consisted of 4 parrot guns and 2 smaller ones. They succeeded in capturing from a band of guerrillas several pieces of artillery and 3 or 4 prisoners. I stepped on board to see the plunder. The guns were dismounted and had been used (it is thought) on a floating battery up the Tennesee. But they are all safe now in our hands, and will be put to a better use. When we arrived here, we expected to find orders to go some where or do something, but there is nothing of the kind here, so we shall wait till Dr McDougall up in Corinth sends us a telegram which we expect to get very soon. We may have an order to go down to Helena again or down the river in that direction. But while we are waiting, I will sit in the office and try my new pens. It must be a task to read some of these notes, for I am sure I can hardly read them myself, but they are only "notes" and not well written ideas. They will serve to call up reminiscences of travel at another time....

Paducah is the same hot and dry place that it always is when I have been here. I can count over 50 bales of cotton, and a dozen or more of tobacco casks on the levee. This is an indication of a little business going on in this part of the country.

I have just been reading of the little assay down near Vicksburgh in which the gunboat *Tyler* was engaged and received some damage. I believe she lost 20 of her crew besides some wounded. If I had taken the position on board that boat that Mr Shaw spoke to me of I should have had an opportunity to witness the effect of shot & shell on the gunboats and perhaps on myself.[87]

I read my *Observer* with a good deal of interest. Seems to me they never were so well edited, and I like the paper for its conservitism above every other sheet that I find.... Tell Sam that if he wants any letters from me, that he must remember the Golden Rule, "Do unto others (me and Will), etc. etc."

I don't know what to tell you about my coming home, as I don't know my destination from one week to another. Army people don't know what they will be ordered to do. If I am well and nothing happens I shall stay here till October, and if nothing happens and I am well I may stay longer. So for anything reliable as to my goings or doings I shall have to refer you to subsequent letters.

I should enjoy a dish of those rasberries you spoke of. (Have had none this year.) Does the stuffed cat continue to scare away the birds from Mothers bushes? The fruit which we find out here is not as good as we get in our state. It is not so perfected by cultivation. I have been eating a peach raised here in Paducah which is very good, but I learn that the people do not graft their fruit, but raise what grows from the natural stock. We had a very good dinner of vegatables today viz. corn on the ear, beets, cabbage, beans, etc.

How does your Normal flourish this season? I wish to be remembered by all the Professors. Do you have Mrs Cook there this summer? I dont see how you can have a concert without the "orange girl" to sing for you. Is there as much strife as ever existing among the people? in regard to the two schools? The music on board the boat at present consists of two guitars and a violin, in the hands of two yellow boys, and a nurse, and when they arrange themselves up on the upper deck and fiddle & thrum the guitars they make music which I can endure very well....[88]

The Hurricane Deck of Stmr D. A. January on the evening of July 30.1862.

We have had very warm weather to day but there is every appearance of a storm coming up which will diminish the heat. The greatest annoyance that I have felt lately has been the mosquitoes. If you expect to sleep at night you must completely bar these vampires out. I have been too unsuspecting, and I have passed two or three miserable nights. A mosquito bar, to be a good one, is made box fashion, like the cover to a divan. It is raised a little above your face, and must be fastened close around the sides of your bed. I have been rigging such an one to day, and I think I am safe now from their attacks.

> With much love to all I remain
> Yours affectionately
> John

    This is the First day of August and we are still tied up to the bank at Paducah. No orders have come from Dr. McDougal. We do not know what to think about the matter. We are sure that the line to Corinth has not been cut off thereby preventing any communication coming to us. I guess the Dr. has no place to send us just now, so we will wait patiently till something "turns up" calling us to the rescue. There are no battles these days, and no wounded to pick up. The men that become sick are taken care of by the Regimental doctors in camp, and it takes a long time to collect a boat load of such that require transportation. The war news that we get these days is not very consoling to the northern mind. Everything seems to favor the rebel cause. The idea that our recruits have to be bought into the service at so much a head is certainly a bad state of things. Such men I fear will not fight well. The South are a unit fighting for a single object. We are a divided people and contending for several objects, some of which we may as well give up the idea of realizing. As near as I am able to get the mind of the people in this place, I do not think the Union cause has many friends. I think the inhabitants of the town would as leave have a regiment of Confederates quartered here as the Union forces who are now garrisoned near the city. I have visited this place so many times that I should like quite well to have a few acquaintances among the people. I would like to have a place here where I could call on someone whom I have met before at the North. I should not care to go into a family whose views were extremely southern, as the most of them are, for then I should not be received with the same spirit that I should wish to carry with me. Do you know any one here? In my walk this evening through one of the principal streets, I came along to a little boy who was playing in the sand. I started to see what he was doing, and found that he had thrown up with his little hands a miniature fortification with all the appointments about it that you would see in any of the earthworks along the river, and he had one little toy cannon (which by the way he told me was not loaded) mounted upon the central portion of it. I give you the plan so that you will see the little fellows idea of a fort was not a bad one.[89] I said to him, "you have a Union fort here?" "Oh nǫ!" he instantly replied, "this is a Secesh fort, and there goes one of my soldiers," pointing to a big black beetle that was crawling about in the enclosure. This seemed so roguish and good natured, that I stoped and had a long talk with him about his secesh notions. He told me that he got his idea of a fort from what he saw at Fort Henry. He had also been at Corinth before the evacuation. He was soon joined by other little boys, two of whom were of the same mind as himself. The next whose sentiments I inquired of was for the *Union* strong. He looked at the fort and then ran on about his play. A little girl had joined the group and I had asked her Who she would rather have for President, Mr Davis or Mr Lincoln? After a little thought she said "I should like the man that the Lord may select to be the one for President." I was a little surprised at this remark coming from a little girl of 8 years. I wanted to say more to these little folks, but it was getting late, and I passed on much pleased with the interview.

The Marine hospital situated just at the outskirts of town is quite a large and commodious building. It is used at present for hospital purposes, and since the war, has been well fortified by an earthwork and ditch extending quite around it, the entrance way being cut through the mound. Large guns are pointing over the East works, and small ones occupy conspicuous places within. Outside it all there is a row of trees and large brush lieing with the limbs away from the works. This is intended for a defense against a cavalry charge. I visited this place just at sundown and the artillery men are engaged in target practice with one of their smaller guns.[90]

   This is the rascal that has been bothering me while I have been writing.[91] I send his likeness taken on the spot by "our special artist." In my walks I inquired of one whom I met if they had any High schools or other places of learning. I was told that they had. At the same time, seeing a large brick building some distance off, I asked what it was? thinking it might be a public school. I was told that it was a "stemery." I thought my informant (a lad) had mispronounced the word seminary, so I ventured to ask what was done in such a building, and was told that the leaves of tobacco are deprived of their stems, and prepared for market by drying, etc. That is "stemery," a purely southern institution—don't forget it. Our nurses who use tobacco get all they want for a small sum. One of them is a segar maker by trade, and he makes them all the cigars they want. I was permitted to see the manner of rolling the leaves of this vile weed into cigars. It was quite a new thing to me. I have seen boat loads of cotton and tobacco lieing along the levees oftentimes in equal quantities, and *what an interesting thought* it is that one of those articles serves to clothe mankind, the other ministers to depraved taste. I am disposed to think that a cask of tobacco does more hurt to the race than a cask of liquor such as whiskey. I never look at a bundle of tobacco leaves without a feeling of disgust, and say that it is only fit to be used as a poison. All of the Doctors smoke a good deal, but one of them in particular is an inveterate smoker. You can scarcely find him a moment without seeing him holding fast by his teeth to his meerchaum. His ineffective efforts to light his pipe with a match is amusing, but he persists and finally he succeeds. I am sure that nothing but his Teutonic phlegm witholds his crying out in despair. What an indifferent race the Germans are! Give them a pipe and plenty of tobacco and beer and they care for no other happiness. I wonder if Martin Luther smoked or chewed tobacco?

                                          Steamer *D.A. January*
                                          August 5th 1862

Dear Frank
   I posted a letter to you at Cairo yesterday. We landed there a few minutes to get the mail. Our departure from Paducah after a stay there for one week tied up to the wharf was rather sudden. A hospital boat the *Stephen Decatur* came down the Tennesee River with 150 sick, which we took on our boat, and are now taking them up to Jeff. Barracks. This is the smallest load we ever started north with. Our business seems to be getting poor. I fear we shall not have enough to do to pay for running the boat all summer.

The day we left Paducah there was an election taking place, and the Military authorities compelled every voter, to take the oath of allegiance. This made the secession people mad, and some swore they would make trouble. The Military made every preparation for any insurrection, by posting pickets and planting a cannon in various places about the town. I never saw a people that seemed to feel so unhappy and look so gloomy as these secesh do. They have no confidence in the Northern government, and Lincolns last proclamation in regard to the confiscation of Rebel property is particularly obnoxious to them.[92] I do think they are in a condition not to be envied. Every man who owns slaves be he ever so loyal a citizen is liable to have his property taken from him in case any evil disposed person can bring any charges of disloyalty against him (and there are many who will do so without cause). You can see how agravating this must be to the feelings of any man who depends on his slaves for carrying on his business. I can see that the last proclamation is going to estrange the feelings of the border state men so that they will not cooperate with us as they otherwise would. I feel a little anxious to hear the result of the State Election in Kentucky.

We have three men on board that belong to the 59th Ill Rgt. I inquired again of one about Johnson Kelly. He did not know him but thought he died in a Hospital at a place in the south, part of Missouri, called Capville. I think this is more likely the place as it is near Pea Ridge battleground. We have not a very sick load this trip, and I am not going to see any interesting cases.

We passed Cairo yesterday P.M. While there I saw the gunboat *Tyler.* Did not have time to go on board of her to see Mr Shaw and see the amount of damage she received in the recent engagement near Vicksburgh. The carpenters were busily engaged repairing her. The *Carondelet* (iron clad gunboat) was floating around near Cairo as we passed. The mortar fleet is lieing along the shore opposite. When we passed Mound City we saw a good many workmen engaged on a new iron clad boat the *Exeter.* She is to be of the "ram" species of naval architecture, and is going to annihilate the *Arkansas* which proved to be the champion in the engagement referred to. (Before I write any more I must ask you to send me in a letter some of those pens which Father has called the "Falcon Pen." I have used them over a year and nothing that I get here serves me as well. Don't forget it!)

Wednesday Morning
10 A.M. Aug 6, 62

We arrived at the Barracks last night but they were so full they could not accomodate the sick and we have come to St Louis with them where we have just got them ashore. I have sent for yours and fathers letters, and just finished reading them. Am glad to see so much patriotism in your country. If we can see the same spirit every where I think we shall succeed by the force of superior numbers in squashing this rebellion. I see by the morning paper that they have had a large Union meeting in Memphis. The guerrillas are making a good deal of trouble in different parts, which is rather aggravating to Union people. An extra has just come on board which announces a rebel attempt at an attack upon Keokuk and other points near the Illinois line. A force was speedily organized and pursued these wily rebels into Missouri, and taking a number of them prisoner. Taking the oath of allegiance with a good many does not amount to anything, for they think nothing of breaking the oath, so lost are they to any moral principle. Our military *must be more severe* with these border men hereafter. Thus far they have destroyed no property, but have sought to destroy rebels. Here after it will be necessary to use both fire and sword and make thorough work of exterminating them. This plan may be too severe, but something must be done to bring these infatuated men to their senses. Every man who is the least disloyal *must leave the country, join our forces, or be uncondi-tionally a Union man.* Willis tells me that they have commenced to draft men into the service in the state. I hope they will draft a few of the secessionists, although I am not sure they will fight well. Thus far there has been a good deal of child's play in this war business, now there is work to be done at once. I read in the *Mt Morris Union* that the steamer *Collona* was captured up the Tenneese near Florence, and destroyed. I shall be obliged to object to the report as being untrue. The above boat was at Paducah one day last week "alive and kicking."

We are going to lose our Captain. He has been chosen to take charge of the Quartermasters department of Gen Curtis's fleet, the forty trans-ports which have been ordered. I regret losing him. Another has been appointed in his place to take charge of our boat. Just now the Captain [is] calling attention to what he thought were two boats running a race. We went up to see and found two boats running tied to gether. Two prizes captured from the rebels. Their names, the *Sovereign* and *Victoria*, a good haul. [93]

Ft. Columbus August 8th 1862
8 A.M.

Dear Frank

We let go our houser and spring line yesterday about 2 P.M. and in the face of a strong breeze we sailed down the muddy Mississippi. My

attention was divided between my papers and the scenery along the river.
I cant turn my eyes away from these high rocks altogether though they
have ceased to be the novelty that they were at first. I wish I could get a
chance to sketch one of these mineral escarpments. I tried to get one of
Kennetts castle, but my point of observation continually changing and the
architecture being rather complex, I did not succeed. Perhaps by taking
several observations, as the artists who take photographs of the moon, I
may get a picture. We passed Cairo this morning at sunrise. The St
Charles hotel rises like a pyramid high above the low wooden houses
which form the town. It is a short ride from the point to Columbus.
Approaching the point we had a fine view of the fort and water batteries
as seen from the river which we did not get before as we passed the place
in the night. It is a good subject for a sketch, it has the enfilade of the
river for a considerable distance, and it is the most conspicuous place you
will find any where along. Arriving here I stepped ashore, and the first
man I met was a young man of the 13th Reg. Wis. Co. I., who told me that
his Captain, Julius Lauderdale, had not returned from his furlough, and
that the impression was, he was not coming back, as he had not been well
enough to do duty much of the time. I learn that the Regiment to which he
belongs has not seen an armed rebel since they have been in the fields.
They have done some work in repairing bridges and railroads. A portion
of the regiment is quartered here. I sent for Allen (an old Academy student) and he has just been on board making me a call. It is a great pleasure to see a familiar face in these parts. A. is a private in his company.
While they are quartered in this place, he is employed in the office of
Medical Purveys, Dr. Sutherlands. I expect him to come on board this
noon and dine with me.

The weather here is warm of course, just at this moment it is 98° in
the shade. The town is lively. There are several new buildings recently
erected for the use of the army. They are light wooden structures, some
used for storing goods and provisions. There is a large amount of provisions along the shore. The rail road is open to Corinth, and I think for
some distance beyond.

7 P.M. same date.

I have just been on the shore to take a look at some dozen rebel prisoners that have just been brot in. They are laboring men, and look as if
they had just been taken out of the fields where they work. I am
informed since, that they are prisoners and are employed by us working
on the rail road near here. They keep them at the guard house during
the night.

[August] 9th 62

Last evening Allen came down to the boat and we took a walk together up along the levee, and as far as the water batteries, which are directly below the fort. If you call to mind the pictures you have of the fortifications at Quebec, you will get a good idea of the defenses at this place. We visited the engine which is used for throwing water from the river. This is a point of some interest, and we stoped in our walk to look at it. The fort alone being without any supply of water something of the kind was highly important in case of prolonged siege, or of their being surrounded on all sides. The place where the engine is located is behind a projection of the bank and is entirely hid from view by those on the river, and would be found with difficulty by one going along the shore. It is above the highest water mark. The entrance way is built up of solid brick work, and looks much like a vault. It is arched and they went to the trouble of ornamenting the cornice.[94] The passage leads in one direction for ten feet farther where there is an iron ladder that descends for 20 feet to the engine room. In this subterranean apartment is placed a small engine, which forces the water to the heighth of the fort above the hill. It is strange that the rebels in their retreat did not destroy this engine, as it could have been done very easily. But no it was not harmed in the least, except being a little rusty. It is now used by our men for the same purpose that the rebels used it. It was necessary however to make another entrance, which was done by making an inclined covered way from the front side, to admit air and convey fuel. The rebels did one foolish thing in their flight, and that was to throw their cannon balls into the river, it being highwater at the time, but soon the river fell, and we have a large amount of balls which will be so much saved for us. There are a great many cannon and gun carriages & baggage wagons lieing about which they left. Last evening just at sundown the huge black monster of a gun which I can see as I write suddenly flashed, then it was seen to be enveloped in a dense cloud of smoke, and after a brief interval, which seemed a long time, a loud report shook the air, which reverberated through the Belmont woods in the direction of the setting sun. I wish I could have seen that outpouring of shot and shell, fire and smoke, which took place at the time the battle was fought. The place is so high that the sentinels as they walk their rounds are clearly defined upon the bright surface of the sky beyond. The stars and stripes scarcely float this morning in this ovenish air.

Near us the workmen are engaged in unloading from some boat cars and an engine which are to run on the railroad from here to Corinth. This is a very important thoroughfare for us just now. The amusements of the place are held in a small tent, in which negro minstrely is furnished every night.

2 P.M.

The thermometer is higher than I ever saw, it being 102°. We shall have a storm this day, sure, I can see the nimbis gathering up their watery mists in the west. While I am writing, the sentinel on the high fortification seems to be a giant in size. I can account for it no other way than an optical illusion or mirage produced by the radiating heat from the hot hills. He is a long way off but I can see every part of him, even to the tip of his bayonet.[95]

5 P.M.

Our expected storm has come with a fine breeze and thunder and lightning accompaniments. The termometer has gone down to 80° and the air delightful. Just as it was coming on I was trying to make a sketch while sitting up in the Pilot House. The lightning displayed so lively I thot I had better get to another part of the boat.

Columbus Ky, Aug. 11, 1862

Yesterday was another warm day. It was Sunday and was very well observed by the people of this place. It was comparatively quiet on board the *D.A. January* except that some fifty bedsteads had to be put up, and the beds made, by way of relieving the quiet of the day and completing a job which could have been deferred to another day just as well. I was informed by Allen that there was to be preaching in the fort by the chaplain of the 13th Wisconsin, and I thought I would attend in the evening, it being held at that time on account of the weather. At 2 *P.M.* I heard a little bell ring down near the depot, which I at first took to be a locomotion bell, but from the way they rung it I concluded it was a bell on one of the little churches, arousing the people to some kind of service. I started out to see and first went to the depot where I was told they had had a catholic service in the morning for the benefit of the rail road employes. On continuing my inquiry I found that the sound of the bell did proceed from a church that Beauregard had not visited and crossing a common I entered it, and took my seat on a rough bench near the door. The inside of the room presented a sad appearance. All the seats except three rows had been removed for lumber by the soldiers at the time the inhabitants left the town. Since then they had put in a few boards, set up on blocks to sit upon. The pulpit had not been disturbed. There was a fine large Bible lieing upon the desk which was the only article that looked any way decent. When I entered, an old man who I am informed is the minister, was talking to and questioning half a dozen persons (three little boys, the rest were colored persons). After asking them a few general questions he said he would organize them into classes and see how well they could read. So I was invited to take charge of the boys, and the man took the rest. But just as we had fairly begun, our number was increased by the addition of several children, and the chaplin of the 71st Regt. He took a share of one of them in one part of the room, and the labor being thus better divided I proceeded to find out how well my class could read. I had been handed a childs spelling book, and I first took my pupil (a little boy of 7) on the Alphabet. I found him not proficient here. I then turned over a leaf to the alphabet with pictures at the margins of the page and he read the letters "A.P.E." The picture was not a good one, so I pronounced the word for him. Then he went on with "B.E.A.R.," "Bear," & "C.A.T.," "cat," & "D.O.G.," "dog," etc., recognizing the animals and calling them by their correct names after he had spelled a word, but when he came to E.A.G.L.E., he hesitated, and I said, don't you know this bird? The little fellow shook his head and blushed. I said again Didn't you ever see this kind of bird? Overcoming his embarassment a little, he ventured to whisper to me "It's a jaybird I reckon." I had to "come doen" at this, but bit my lip and concealed my mirth as well as I could. I spent the rest of the time in asking familiar questions which I thought more profitable. At 3, the room was occupied by the colored people alone. They consist of slaves, contrabands & a few others. They were talked to by an old "culupussun" with a head all covered with snowdrifts of many winters, which contrasted strongly with his dark face. I did not stay to hear him, as I wanted to go back to the boat and return before the services which were to be held at 4 P.M. I obtained permission from Dr. H. for as many of the nurses as wished to go to church with me. I acting as corporal started with six, and we followed on in company with the members of the 71st Regt who were just passing on their way to church. The seats were all full. I should say there were 150 soldiers, and may be a dozen civilians. I noticed but two or three white women in the audience. We had two chaplains present but he of the 71st preached, the other one made prayer. I did not learn their names. The prayer was good, the preaching was rather disconnected and pointless. He took his text on the 2nd "Sam." He read the hymns as they were sung, but pitched them too high. Before speaking he requested some of the friends to bring him some water to drink, as it would be impossible for him to go on without it. The water was brot, in our eight quart pail, and set down by him by one of the black boys, but owing to a little delay on his part another started out to get some & brot in a pitcher full, which was placed on the desk at the side of the speaker who got so much engaged in his remarks that he did not take time to drink but one swallow from the two generous fountains at his side. He detained us over an hour, although he limited himself to that time. At the close the old man who was acting the superintendant of the Sunday school made a few remarks, stating the deplorable destitution of the library & if any one had anything to give for this object it would be thankfully received. After the services the bookless shelves in the corner of the room had drawn out my sympathies before the old man said anything, and after the benediction I and my squad stepped up and gave something. Services are going to be held at this place hereafter every sunday, at least as long as the regiment remain.[96]

In the evening Allen came on board. He had come once before to have me go and attend the exercises in their camp on the hill, but it was during the time I was at church. We sat up on the deck and talked Geneseo items, and kept the mosquitoes away at the same time. The full moon as bright as polished silver rose up from behind the line of earthworks on the hill, her disk seemed as broad as a cannon wheel. She lighted the Fort and the sentinels polished bayonet reflected its light, while his form was as clearly seen as at mid day. The smoke from the smouldering camp fires which settled along the sides of the hill and down among the houses of the town received a strange colouring. The muddy river running noiselessly by had a reddish tinge. While we sat and conversed, we watched these beauties of the rising moon. Presently the thumping of the paddle wheels was heard, and the blue and red lights suspended from the high chimneys of a steamer were faintly seen, while she was making her way around the bend opposite the fort. When she had got abreast of us a band of music on board struck up most delicious music. The steamer was the *Dave [?Patum]* from Cairo with Gens. Curtis and Grant on board on their way to Helena. She rounded too, and stopped at the place a short time.

After we had passed the evening in this way Allen said he must be going back to his camp or he should not be present at roll call which takes place at 9 o clock. I accompanied him to the camp and had a pleasant walk up that corduroy road to the fort which the Rebels built to convey the caravan upon. This is another excavation which cost a good deal of labor. While at the camp I went to the tents of Co. P. and inquired after their Captain but they had not heard from him lately. I learn that the Colonel of that Regiment is going to be removed. Allen says he is a very good officer but his drinking habits render him at times a regular tyrant.

Thermometer 100°.

Notes made at Columbus Ky.[97]

All along our route we found munitions of war scattered here and there. Cannon balls are as plenty as stones on a highway. Columbiads and dalhgrens and gun carriages fill the streets. In one place near the rail road was a thousand stand of arms. Just at the side of the road I stopped to look at some curious castings which I thought at first were small mortars, but on inspection I found to be submarine shells something of this shape.[98] They are filled with some combustible material, sunk in the middle of the river channel, and then fired by means of an electric discharge conveyed through wires which are inserted in the side. A little farther on there was another variety of infernal machines like this I represent.[99]  It was made of sheet iron, and made water tight. This was sunk by means of a small cast iron anchor, which kept the torpedo suspended in the water but at such a heighth that a passing steamboat would strike her, and the concussion would be sufficient to explode her beneath the vessell and sink her. Large iron weights were used for balancing these machines in the water where the bottom of the river would not allow the use of anchor. Again we saw what was to be a hindrance to a passing vessell—an immense chain lay stretched across the river. It was the largest I ever saw, the links were at least 10 inches in length. One end was secured to the shore by a tree on one side and then some kind of machinery was arranged at the other for drawing it in, but still leaving it submerged. This contrivance offered no obstacle to our boats, as the river was so high that they passed [page torn]. *Remember all these defenses were left by the Rebels* when they [page torn]... when there was a [page torn]... pieces of waggon lieing scattered over the ground. [This] sketch will give you an idea of one of Jeff Davis' ambulances.[100] You will see that he is

very far behind the age in style and everything that you find is about off of the same piece. He did not have so much money to go to war and he studies economy.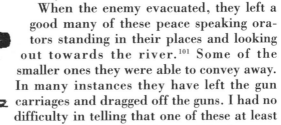

 When the enemy evacuated, they left a good many of these peace speaking orators standing in their places and looking out towards the river.[101] Some of the smaller ones they were able to convey away. In many instances they have left the gun carriages and dragged off the guns. I had no difficulty in telling that one of these at least

belonged to the Rebels as the name of one of their noted leaders was painted upon the carriage in neat white letters. Near by there were a great many large shells. I don't know the weight, but it takes two men to lift them. You see nothing but shell, the contents never having been put in. Their economy has taught them that it is not well to make up too much powder into shells at once, but to prepare their ammunition as occasion requires.

By this time we had reached the foot of the high bluffs where the fort is situated, and found the ascent quite easy, but rather long for a single exertion. Gaining the summit we were met by the guard who demanded our papers which we had neglected getting. We then had to go and see the corporal of the guard, whom we found after accosting half a dozen other guards. Guard mounting for the day was going on at the time we were there, and a full brass band were playing most delicious music at a little distance off.

The Corporal of the Guard whom we found sitting near a Sibley tent gave us full permission to visit any part of the grounds. The enclosure consists of about 6 acres of ground, with an embankment extending quite around it. The inside of this mount or embankment presents a perpendicular face. The outside is more inclined and sloped off into a moat of ditch, to illustrate by a section.[102] 1. Perpendicular face. 2. Incline. 3. Moat. 4. Hill Beyond. You will at once see the difficulty an enemy would find in scaling such a breastwork. The grounds are now occupied [page torn]... U.S.Regulars with their camp equipage, and horses, mules, waggons, etc. There are several cannon now looking out from the southerly side of the fort, in a direction down the stream. When Jeff Davis was there they showed their teeth at us, as our fleet came down the river. Now they have squared around, and are looking death at all traitors who have come up the Mississippi.

I give you the different kinds of tents in use at the fort.[103]

After we had looked at every thing of interest within the enclosure we walked to the edge of the bluff where it looks down into a frightful chasm which forms the bank of the river and up which no foe dare ascend by scaling. It would be the easiest thing in the world to prevent it by hurling missiles upon their heads. No! No! The place if taken must be taken in some other way than trying to climb such a bank. The side of this cliff which is composed of clay, has been cut away, so as to make a winding stairway to the water batteries which you can look directly down upon. Descending this passage which reminds me of what travelers tell us who climb the Alps (about rugged & narrow passes among mountain sides), we reach these important defenses near the river margin. They are constructed on this manner. The earth (which consists of sand and gravel) that forms the hill, is dug away from its place, and a level shelf is formed. Then more earth is taken and filled into gunny bags (about the same thing as coffee bags) and piled up at this shelf, which gives it greater strength, and prevents it being washed away from behind. These fortifications, of which I counted five, part the river at different angles. They are about one hundred feet in lenth, must have mounted at least four guns each, and are so deep that the guns and gunners are hid from view. At one corner you will find a door which you would think was the entrance to a cave. This is the powder magazine, and is entered by a circuitous passage, so that the bursting bombshells may not send their fire into the powder contained within. The guns used were of the largest calibre, and shells were thrown from them. There are no guns to be seen now. They have been removed, but there are great quantities of balls and shells lieing about the ground. In some places it is covered with them. They have been abandoned by the rebels. Now you would think that the position and ammunition that was held by the Rebels at this point would have rendered them secure against a foe for a great length of time, but no! they skedaddled just as soon as Commodore Foot brot his gunboats to bear upon the place. I give you a sketch of the different projectiles which I saw lieing about.[104] No. 4 were very abundant, they were the kind of shot used. No. 3 is a curious kind of hollow missile. No. 2 is a shell which explodes when it strikes the pointed end against any object. This kind  requires to be handled with some care lest by striking the end, it should explode. No 1 is peculiarly made, having a rim of lead or other soft metal at its base which when pressed upon by the expanding air completely fills up the bore of the gun, thus getting the full benefit of the charge of powder. I should like to have brot No 3 or 4 in my collection, but they weighed from 30 to 50 pounds and I could not carry them up the hill and into the boat.

After we returned to the top of the hill I was interested in looking at a large Dahlgren that had burst when fired. The split surface would measure at least one foot, that is from outer surface to the bone. This shows the great power of powder and the danger that attends the firing of such guns. I have never had the gratification of seeing a large gun fired, but those who have seen them tell me that it is terrific. There has not been such a long continued firing with such a grand display of gunnery as was exhibited at Island No. 10 just a few miles below us. I heard a lady say who was an eye witness of the seige, that it was the grandest and most terrific display of fireworks she had ever beheld.

Before leaving the grounds we took a look across the river and were shown the place where the battle of Belmont which resulted rather unfavorably to our troops was fought.[105] The broken tree tops showed that the cannon balls had rattled through their branches.

As you go along the street near the river, you will see two large anchors which you will say were never intended for river boats. They were taken from the famous Merrimac whose history you know all about. I have been writing you this afternoon with the thermometer at

100°. I never remember of seeing it fairly as high. But if we stay in this country we shall see warmer weather than this.

I have taken a sheet of foolscap to write upon as my stationary has all gone off by the mail.

The principal business going on in this town is among the soldiers and for them. There are 6 or 7 steamboats tied up to the bank, some waiting orders, others unloading commisary goods. We brot down a quantity of hospital furniture to this place. It is proposed to make a hospital station here.

Columbus, Ky. Aug 14, 1862

The other evening I had a call from the Lieutenant of "Co. J." He told me he had just received a letter from uncle Julius and that in all probabilty he would not return to his company as his health would not admit of it. I am sorry to hear it. The commandant of this place is Gen. Quinby of Rochester University formerly.[106] I have not had a glimpse of him yet. There are three Rochester boys on his staff. Mont. Rochester who is adjutant general, and two others, young Barton and Ericksen. There has been another Rochester man staying on our boat at night with whom I have become acquainted, his name is Dutton and he is a rail road man. He has been Supt. of the N.Y. Central R.R. and has come on here to take the agency of this R.R. (the Mobile & Ohio). It being confiscated property is in the hands of the U.S. and is doing a fine business just now. Mr. D. has a son with him, also a Mr. Hill a brother of your friend Mr. L.R.P. He is in his employ. I presume you know him very well as he used to attend the Academy while Mr. Nichols was Principal. I called on him last evening, and had a very pleasant talk over matters pertaining to Geneseo and its people. I tell you I am glad to see so many New York state men in this country. I have been a stranger in a strange land in my wanderings thus far. I have not seen outside of St. Louis more than four men that I ever saw or heard of before. I have no particular business with any of the people I meet, so I make no acquaintances off the boat. Almost every day I see returned men from the hospitals on their way to their regiments. The weather is hot. The quicksilver rises every day up to 100°, and after staying thus for about two hours in the afternoon it settles down to about 90°. It stops at this point till after sunset, and gets a few degrees below towards morning. This has been a long week to us. The principal thing we do is to try and get in a cool place, so we move from one side of the boat to the other selecting such a place where the breeze is the coolest. I find the pilot house a little the pleasantest place on the boat. I sat up there yesterday

Genl Quinbys Head Quarters. Columbus Ky 1862.

afternoon and took a sketch of Gen Quinbys head quarters which is near by the river.[107] Dr Chas McDougal is on board, and we are waiting to see what he will order us to do. He just arrived this morning from Memphis and is feeling rather unwell to day. He has placed himself under Dr. Hoffs care, and I guess he will recover in a few days. The mail boat has just come down from Cairo but the news she brings is about the same thing as we have had — "a movement soon expected," "guerrillas at work some where," "recruiting going on," etc. etc. It is rather hot weather to fight except they improve some of these beautiful moonlight nights. Such nights are favorable for cooning, why not for rebel-ing.

Did you ever notice *the deck hands* while they take their meals? They sit on the deck and eat off of the plates, and some use nothing but the primitive utensils. They have good food, but never eat at a table. One of them told me the other day that he used to have a pet pig on board, and that when he ate his meals he would allow the pig to step up and partake. It used to be a source of amusement to the passengers to see them eat with the pig. Some of the men took the boat and went over the river this afternoon and got a basket of peaches from a deserted "secesh" orchard, a rather poor fruit I assure you. Would be good if left to ripen a few days.

August 15, 62. 4 P.M.

We are in Columbus yet. Shall probably go somewhere tomorrow. Dr. McD. is getting better. Last evening we were visited by a storm of rain, dust, thunder & lightning, driven on by a violent wind. It began to blow about six, and increased to a gale. Clouds of dust were raised from the shore of the river over on the other side of the bend, you could see it rise high above the trees. Every sandy bar which has become dry by the suns rays was bristled into the air. The lightning was terrific. The fluid seemed to form a constant current from the clouds to the earth, and resembled a fissure through which a white heat could be seen glowing. The main portion of the storm passed to the north and east of us, but we got the benefit of it. A good wind is one of the best things we can get. We get good ventilation during such times, and the mosquitoes, dear things, are driven away before the blast. We have had a brisk wind all day. The temperature this morning was 27° below what it marked yesterday P.M. and it has not got above 80° any time to day.

I am officer of the day! Dont you want a pass to come on board? You cant get on without one? A sentinel stands at the gang plank, and stops all who would come on board. If I say he may come, he passes on. The mate we have now is great for catching catfish. When I came out on the "forred" part of the boat this morning, he had a thirty pounder by his side and his line hanging over the side for another one, which he drew up in a short time. It was one of the blue catfish of the largest I have seen. It was at least 3 feet in length. I have had several dishes of this kind of fish and am very fond of it.

I think I told you that our nurses are all men detailed from the army for that service (I think they are better than so many civilians). An order has been issued that all nurses and others employed in hospitals and belonging to the army must return to their regiments to day. Dr Hoff has just been delivering up their description rolls and passes to them. They are not very far removed from their companies. They leave rather reluctantly as they have had a very easy time of it on board this boat, particularly when we are tied up to the bank. We shall have to fill their places by convalescent soldiers or civilians. I have not much faith that convalescents will take care of the sick as they should be taken care of. But I feel the importance of having every man shoulder a musket these days that is able, and shoot as many of the infatuated rebels as possible.

Cairo, Saturday Aug. 16, 62

This forenoon telegrams came to Dr Mc. D. and resulted in our taking on a quantity of hospital property from Dr. Southerlands wharf boat. Allen who is with Dr. S. was present acting as clerk of the boat. He took dinner with me. We have come now for the purpose of getting some more hospital stores, ice, etc., and to morrow we shall proceed to Memphis with it. My health is very good. I have got so that I eat a good deal of cornbread. We have it on the table twice a day. When at any port I get fruit. I wish I had a letter to read from home, shall have to wait till I get to St Louis again.

Yours affectionately
John

U.S. Hospital Boat <i>D.A. January</i>
Monday Aug. 18, 1862
from Cairo to Memphis

Dear Frank,
I will take another sheet this morning and note down a few little incidents. Did you ever hold one of these sheets before a strong light and look at the water press mark? Look and see our poor bird, how she droops her right wing, a fit emblem of our country at the present time. I mailed a letter and papers to you on our arrival at Cairo. We stayed there long enough to get ice and the same evening (Saturday) went up to Mound City, five miles above on the Ohio. Our object in going was to allow Dr McDougal to visit the U.S. General Hospital at this place. Dr. Franklin who is surgeon in charge came on that same evening, and invited the medical department to visit the institution. The building was put up for a block of stores. At the time it was thought to make this place greater than Cairo, but they did not succeed, and the row has been easily converted into a very convenient hospital. Not equal by any means to Bellevue or our N.Y. City hospitals. It has no grounds or shade trees around it that are pleasant. A little hillock or indian mound upon which are growing a few shade trees is situated near by, and gives name to the place. We made a company of about ten and accompanied by Dr F. and his assistants we defiled and passed through several wards. Found every thing kept very neat. Every bed has a good corn husk mattress & a wire frame over which is thrown the mosquito net. The coverlids are uniform, and look very well, better than at Bellevue but they dont know how to make up the beds so well. Still I am willing to give Dr. F a good deal of praise for the effort he has made to get the institution in such

comfortable condition. It has about 80 beds. There are only 250 sick there at present. Dr. Mc.D. told them if they, the army, made the river the base line of operations they might expect to have more patients. There are several catholic women (Sisters of the Holy Cross) about the establishment, who help to take care of the sick. They have a little room fitted up for their worship. There is also a protestant chaplain who deals in the genuine article of religious truth. These "sisters" no doubt do much good here as they have charge of the cooking department, but I should not want them around my wards! They are a pale, forlorn looking set, with a down cast look which has anything but cheerfulness about it. I wish I had the chance to sketch one for you. In one of the private apartments we found the rebel Col Fry who was wounded and captured at the attack on the gunboat *Mound City.* As we entered his room he raised himself, and sat up in his bed. He has a wild look out of his large black eyes & his stiff black hair stuck up like bristles over his head. He looks some like Willis, but a man of heavier frame. He no doubt was one of the rebel tigers that they counted on. He had been shot by a minie ball through his right side, and the axillary plexus of nerves had been severed, so that his arm was paralyzed completely. As he sat there supporting his crippled limb with his left hand he looked the picture of despair. I had no chance to say anything to him as I would like to have done. We came along to another cot where lay another secesh and the Dr came up to him and inquired after his health. He said he was getting along quite well. The Dr. said we will soon be able to let you go back to your regiment among the rebels. "Oh!" he exclaimed. "Don't send me back. I dont wish to go. *I don't want to fight any more.* It was only for my grub that I was fighting, when they shot me." In another room we were shown the effects of a bomb shell upon a man in whose hands it exploded. It was as bad as bad could be. He had been engaged with two others in picking the powder out of several hundred shells which had become damaged by water, and had finished all but two or three, *when the one he was at work on exploded,* and the result was a blackened body, broken bones, and lower extremities torn into fragments. This is the first case of the kind I have ever seen, and I am not anxious to see the human form so badly torn asunder again. A shell is not apt to make a nice dissection of tissue. Strange to tell this man lived five hours after the incident.

We returned to Cairo about noon, and after taking on some meat we started down the river for Columbus. Before we reached this place we met the *Lancaster,* which boat had bedsteads that we stopped and took on our boat as being part of the hospital supplies we are now taking to Memphis. We landed a little while at Columbus, and got some more things, blankets, etc.

Last evening as we came along the Kentucky shore we saw some females, and one man standing near the river. Some one of the men on our boat waved his handkerchief which was a little rude perhaps, but oh! how one of those "phemales" resented it. She threw her handkerchief on the ground *and made believe she was trampling it under her feet.* Oh! how purty! I construed it as an insult to our flags which were floating so finely at the time. She did the same thing twice, and then turned her back upon us. This little big of secesh pantomime amused us a good deal. When will this bitter feeling be removed from the minds of these southern people? Will fighting do it? I am waiting daily to hear of something that will determine the issue of this struggle. I read a tract yesterday written by Dr Alexander which contains a prophesy that is now being fulfilled with wonderful exactness. He tells us in a word that these evils are sent upon our land because the religious state of the country has not kept pace with the increase of her population. And I believe every word of it to be true.

We passed island No. 10 about dark last evening. Have met with no detentions thus far, although the river is getting rather low. A good many snags and "saw yers" make their appearance. The weather is cloudy and cool to day and the nights are getting cool. They tell me we shall not have many warm nights this summer. As soon as the sun goes down it becomes cool, and the nights have become quite long. The vegetation along the river has faded a little in places. The sycamores are showing the effects of age first of any. The Elms are not as fresh looking as they were during higher water when their roots were better supplied. The corn fields are looking fresh and green. I have been straining my left eye to see some cotton growing, but there is none to be seen. We shall get to Memphis in about an hour and then I will continue.

Helena Ark. Aug 19 1862

We arrived at Memphis yesterday about noon and having some freight on bound for the Hospital commenced sending it off as fast as 3 four-mule teams could carry it. There were 600 cots and bedsteads (the latter a very nice article of furniture) for hospital purposes—together with mattresses, sheets, pillow cases, etc. We could not land it all before night, and we were obliged to lay over till morning. We got away about 8½ A.M. I was officer of the day and had no time to go ashore. So that all I saw of the town this time was what could be seen from the boat. I believe that the union feeling is as strong as ever there. The gun boat *St. Louis* lies out in the stream ready to protect the city in case of an attack,

and there is a large number of soldiers quartered there. A good many
cavalry horses, and it is quite a fine sight to see them, led down to the
river for watering, reminding one of a vast caravan. One of the riders
this morning had on a bright red cap, which looked quite Arabic. I
think Rob and Wat would be pleased with this part of the show.[108] We
had a pleasant and rapid passage down the river at this place, and
arrived about 3 P.M. When we had got within ten miles of the town, two
men came off from the shore and asked to be taken on board. We
stopped and picked them up. They were in a little skiff. After they got
on board they let the boat go, and our paddle wheels soon demolished it
or it floated back. After they got on board and had set down we all came
forward and gave them a good eying. They seemed to us to be men who
were escaping from rebel authorities. We concluded to give them over to
the provost marshal at this place on our arrival. The weather here is
rather warm but it partakes of the general comfort which we have experienced since the last storm.

As soon as the boat landed I went ashore and waded through the
dust up into the town. I did not go ashore when I was here before so I
determined to see something of the place. There are so many soldiers
that I could scarcely see any thing, they kicking up such dust kept the
air full. I went first up the Gen. Hindman house, which is now Gen.
Curtis head quarters, and got the material for a sketch of it.[109] I next

passed to the convent on the other side of the street. It is so surrounded by shrubbery, such as magnolias, figs, and a profusion of
other trees that you cannot see the house from the street. It must be a
beauty when everything is fresh and open, but the foliage was so
loaded with [word obscured] that its beauty was gone. The lawn in
front of this house is occupied by offices and their tents, but the trees
and shrubberies are carefully groomed by the soldiers. I passed on by
tents where soldiers encamped in booths where cavalry horses were
tied protected from the hot sun by the boughs of trees, between waggons loaded with pontoons and other bridgemaking material, by little
squads of soldiers, civilians, and contrabands, all doing something or
nothing, a good deal such a group as you would see at a country fair
or a great caravan. I came up to two young contrabands who were sitting, one on a stump the other quietly reclining upon the dirty ground
with his head in the first ones lap. As I approached I discovered that
he was doing the kindly art of looking over his head and cracking
between his nails the lice which seemed to be very numerous. He
appeared to enjoy fumbling over his friends wool as well as the one
who was being relieved. My curiosity was excited for the moment to
know what color these animals might be. If they were white it would be
comparatively an easy task finding them on such a dark ground, but
the first one he caught for my benefit *was black*. Having learned this
item of Natural History I passed on. The streets were so dusty I made
a short circuit down to the boat landing. The little stores and shops
are filled with soldiers who are spending their money all the time for
some article of clothing or something to eat. I find things are rather
high priced.

There are several steam boats here just now, and four iron clad gun
boats, besides two or three wooden ones. I went on board the *Pittsburgh*
this evening. She is one of those that you remember was in the battle at
Vicksburgh. The officer who took me thru the boat was a Mr
Harrison—masters mate—and he had a great deal to tell about the
Vicksburgh affair, about the men who were killed and cut to pieces by
the balls of the *Arkansas*. He says the *A.* is destroyed. I have seen nothing elsewhere about it. He showed us cutlasses and boarding pikes, and
how he used them, also what the steam drum was (they have just been
adding another coating of iron to their vessel), also the hose for throwing hot water upon those who would try to board her. I looked into the
muzzle of a 68 pounder, and there lay the ball ready to be driven out on
its round of destruction. I took notice of the sick men who were swinging
in their hammocks. There are several on board who were taken sick
while down on the Yazoo in a gunboat on a hot day.

Thursday Aug. 21. 62

We left Helena last night about 6 P.M. and arrived at Memphis about ten this forenoon. We took from Helena 110 patients, and since our arrival here forty more. Some of the men have been telling me of the worse than severe treatment which Union prisoners have received at the hands of Texas rangers and other guerrilla bands. The contrabands have become a floating population. Every steamboat has some of them on board, and they are all over the camp, some are good to work and others are poor help for any kind of duties. We have one on board this boat and we have him saw wood for the coal. I have not had time to go on shore here at Memphis, and I am glad that the Dr has come forward and ordered the boat to start off up the river. It is very warm being tied up to the bank. The thermometer has come within one of a hundred degrees, but since we have got under weigh it is dropping down among the lower nineties. The river is getting low and steaming is somewhat impeded by our taking the course of the channel so exactly.

On board the Hospital Boat
Aug 22, 62

Dear Father,
    I received your welcome note when last in St. Louis. We are now on our way from Helena, Ark. to Mound City hospital with 140 sick men, 30 of them from the hospital at Memphis whom it was thought best to send further north. Our business is rather on the decline just now. There were several boats engaged in transporting sick, but they have all with perhaps one exception been mustered out of the service. Our boat being the property of the Government will remain in the hospital service whether there is anything for her to do or not. As long certainly as the war continues. By the end of this month it is proposed that she shall go to St. Louis and there undergo some alterations which will enable her to accomodate a larger number of patients. It will be the middle of September before she shall be ready for service again. During the interval of repair we will remain in St Louis.
    You will remember that before I left New York I signed an agreement to report myself to Bellevue Hospital by the First of October. I did this feeling that a period spent at that institution would be of no little advantage to me in learning my trade. There are a good many ideas to be picked up at a hospital which I would take a long time to work out in private practice, and though I have not heard from Bellevue since leaving the city I am expecting to see a note come along in a few days or

weeks reminding me of an agreement, which it is my duty to fulfill, although it will not be of the pecuniary advantage that this place is to me. The great advantage that my present place affords is in the shape of the hundred dollars that is handed over to me at the end of every month. I never realized so much money for the time, and never performed as an equivalent so little labor. We have been in the service about five months, but if we put all the time together that we have had sick on our boat to take care of, 40 days would include it all. The rest of the time we have been either moving back and forth, or tied up on the levee, awaiting orders. The boat has traveled over 8000 miles and has transported to various points more than 3000 patients. The longest time that we have patients on board at any one trip is four days, and in the majority of cases 2 or 3 days. So that we hardly see our patients and make a poor diagnosis before they are off our hands. We cant see the effect of remedies, and the most we try to do is to render our patients as comfortable as possible, and promise them more thorough treatment at the hospitals. The noise of the boat forbids auscultation, and many other things are denied us which we could furnish in a hospital on shore. You must see that such kind of practice is very unsatisfactory. The first trip the boat made was after the battle of Pittsburgh Landing and then she had over 400 wounded. There were 11 amputations performed on that trip, but I was not there. I was on the 2nd trip and she carried a large number of gun shot wounds and only one amputation at that time. Since then we have seen but two amputations which were of the thigh at the lower third. So I have seen very little surgery. Have seen some interesting cases of gun shot wounds and Dr. H has put up ½ a dozen fractured femurs, that is, changed the splints. The rest of our practice has been checking diarhea, relieving pulmonary troubles, & sustaining typhoid cases. We use only a few simple remedies, never give mercury, they have generally been mercurialized enough when they come on board. A good deal of field practice is very bad owing to the disadvantages they labor under. We expect to go up to Paducah and break up the hospital there and move them down to Mound City, and thus reduce the expense of keeping up both. I have thought some of a situation in a hospital as being a good place, but here we see a limited variety of diseases and no surgery except dressing old stumps or gun shot wounds. You are aware that contract surgeons who engaged since June have been receiving 130 dollars a month since the 11th of June last, and when Dr Mc.Dougal was on board the other day Dr Hoff proposed to him to have our contracts changed to that sum but Dr Mc.D thought that as we were not doing any field service, and [were] at no expense for rations, etc., it better remain the same. I did not care about the change, though I should not refuse it if offered. I am getting all I earn or would earn at private practice. The Hospitals in and about St. Louis are attended by surgeons who have also a private practice in the city. I believe they receive 80 dollars per month. It is the same way at other points on the river where there is a Military hospital. The Dr Franklin who has charge of the Mound City Hospital has very little repute among the profession. Before he took the place, he practiced homeopathy and anything else in St Louis to get a living. I believe he has changed his practice where he is now. I dont think I should care about making any change to go into the field service as I dont feel that I am rugged enough for it at this time of the year. Military hospital practice is uncertain as to the time employed depending on the duration of the war. They are not permanent, liable to be closed if the sick are scarce. I am quite contented on the boat and willing to remain as long as the Director sees fit, although the advantages which I have mentioned are not as good as I could wish. I think if Dr Wood of Bellevue writes to me to come there I will ask for an extension of my furlough, unless I get my discharge from my present service before the first of October. I dont think it would be honorable to refuse to go to Bellevue although on the other hand I think I would be missing a good deal. I wish I knew how long this miserable war is going to last. It would seem as though things had reached a pretty bad state now. These guerrilla raids out here are more savage than any thing recorded in indian warfare, and we dont seem to be making any decided victories in any part of the country. I hope that as soon as cool weather comes something may be done towards a pacification of these difficulties.

Let me hear from you at your earliest convenience in an advisory epistle, and what you think of the state of the country, wishing to be remembered to all of my friends I remain

Your affectionate Son
John

Saturday 2 P.M. Aug. 23

We passed Columbus about the time the gunboat *Tyler* which was lieing there struck her eight bells. Do you know what time that is? It answers to our four in the morning. On a man of war the day is divided into three periods of 8 hours instead of two periods of 12 hours and the bell is struck the number of the hour. The day begins with one bell struck at five in the morning, at noon eight bells & 1 P.M. one bell again

& so on, then at 9 P.M. one bell is struck. When this was first told me I could not see through it, but is easily understood when stated clearly. The gunboats are our town clock wherever we find them.

We arrived at Mound City and sent off our sick. One only died along the way. We are now steaming up the Ohio to Paducah. The day is very pleasant, there is a light breeze which causes the awning in front of the boat to be tossed wildly about. The surface of the river is sparkling with light, reflected from the little waves upon whose crests bubbles are dancing. The trees skirting the river retain their rich foliage. Not a leaf has changed its fresh green tint. A long line of white sand separates the trees from the river and in many places there may be seen a dark band extending from some part of land across the water. These are sand bars and let us know that the river is falling and navigation is becoming more troublesome. A boat passes us occasionally. One or two whistles is the usual salutation between passing steamers, one if she passes to our left, and two if she goes to our right. This is to prevent a collision from any misunderstanding of the direction in which way to turn out. Yonder high up on the shore, and left there by some careless persons at the time the water rose above where it is now, lies a barge. It was used to transport hay to the army, but it is now going to pieces. If this was the only one of the kind I had seen in my travels I would take no notice of it, but they are numerous, and it shows how Uncle Sam's property is wasted by the quartermasters who provide forage. They seem to care as little what becomes of these heavy barges (which cost at least 500 dollars a piece) as the man did who, when he got on to the boat, let his skiff be dashed to pieces under the wheel. The destruction of property through neglect everywhere to be seen along the track of our army is immense. There would be millions saved if there should be a property police force organized to look after all kinds of army property and gather up what is going to waste. If there is not more economy used in this war, we shall be obliged to suspend operation after a while for the want of means. Uncle Sam may be rich enough to carry on the war for a while, but he will reach the end of his tether before long. I hear something that sounds like a hand organ, and looking out I find it to be the steamer *Rose Hambleton*. She has a caliope on board, and a man sits beside an instrument of this kind turning a little crank which responds by gasping in a stacatto movement the tune of the "Star Spangled Banner."[110] I have heard a similar instrument on the steamer *Lady Franklin* played upon like a piano which I think superior, though I am willing to wave my handkerchief in thanks for the patriotic music. We are at Paducah now, and shall take on some sick, and try and get them down to Mound City to day if we can.

5 P.M.

We have taken on 33 sick and convalescent men, and are now on our way back to Mound City. As soon as we landed at the wharf boat, we hailed with delight the peaches and melons that we found there for sale. I have not had a melon this year until now. The peaches are very fine fruit, and not so exorbitantly high priced as at Memphis. They sell ripe tomatoes in the same way that they do apples and peaches. A real ripe tomatoe, one that has been ripened in a southern sun, is very sweet, and rich as a peach. One man had his stack of melons in a skiff, and was paddling around among the boats at the landing. We heard of more guerrilla depredations. The steam boat *Skylark* ran aground up the Tennesee river and it was lieing there several days trying to get off. The rebels heard of it and a party of them came down and took off her cargo which consisted of provisions worth a good deal & then burned the boat. There was another boat which they destroyed in the same manner. They tried to get the *Lancaster* but failed, and about 25 were taken prisoners. They will in all probability be hung as they have been delivered over to Gen. Grant. We also hear that the Rebels have taken Clarksville and that the 71st Reg of Ohio were taken prisoner, but soon after paroled. We get these as rumors from men who have come on the boat while stopping at Paducah. Several of the deck hands from the *Skylark* will make a fine thing out of the cargo by selling it to their neighbors. They took 150 barrels of salt and burned the remainder. The ignorance of the people along the river is deplorable, and if they are a fair sample of the inhabitants farther inland I can easily see how they can embrace secession doctrines. We have occasion to buy wood from the people, and it is very common for them not to be able to write their name on the receipt. We took on wood twice yesterday, and neither of the men could read or write. I asked one, a young man, what County he lived in, and he could not tell me. I asked what town and he replied "Oh! You are too hard on me." He had a name for the bend in the river, and that was all the way he could define his location. Said he had never been to school a day in his life, because he never had a chance. I doubt if he could count the twenty five dollars we paid him for his wood. He took his "greenbacks" and rolled them up and put them in his pocket, trusting to us that the amount was right.

9 P.M.

We have just landed our thirty three sick and convalescent men at Mound City, and shall be in Cairo in half an hour. This makes the second load we have left at the former place. We have run about a good deal today. The weather is pleasantly cool to night and we shall not be troubled with mosquitoes. We will stop in Cairo a while to take on a thousand bushells of coal. The next move is not known till we reach Cairo. It may be St. Louis again for I have not had a letter in more than three weeks. How is the Atheneum flourishing this summer? With much love to all I remain

Your affectionate brother
John

Willis' Room on Washington Avenue
St. Louis Aug 27, 1862

Dear Frank,

To resume the thread of my journal, I mailed a letter to you at Cairo, also one to Father on our way up. We arrived on Monday morning and have found the weather exceedingly warm as it always is in this town if so any where. The boat has come here for repairs, and will be detained about two weeks for that purpose. The Dr thinks she can be enlarged so as to carry more sick, but I question whether it will pay to enlarge, when we are not able to fill our present number of beds. The secret of it is the Dr wants to spend some more of Uncle Samuels money in fitting out a model hospital boat, and takes a little of the credit of it to himself, and get a feather in his cap or a puff or a promotion. The boat is now vacated, and I am living with Will. When at Memphis the other day the unfortunate *Acacia* was lieing close along side of us. I heard some fiddling and slipped aboard and found a number of black boys on board dancing jigs, etc. They were having a fine time and it amused me as much as it does to see their imitators the Christies. I learn that the loss of life although great was not equal to the first report given. The river is getting low and the dangers of navigation are greater than they have been at any time during the season. I was down at Carondelet yesterday to pack my things in my trunk, and while I was eating my dinner the engine was drawing the boat out of the water. So gently was this conducted that I should not have known of its being done if I did not look out of the door and see that graded rise of the boat. She remains out of water till she is caulked, and then will come back to the city for repairs. We met on our way up the *Gladiator*. She has been painted up so white you would hardly know her. About the same time we passed the ram *Queen of the West* with a large letter *Q*

suspended between her chimneys. I hope she is in better fighting trim
than she was at Vicksburgh a while since. They are doing a fine business down at Carondelet building gunboats and rams.[111] On my way
from the Hospital boat yesterday I stayed a few moments to look at
these war vessels which are in various stages of completion. The first I
noticed was one which was being heavily coated with oak timber and
then plated with iron. I inquired of one of the workmen what kind of
boat it was going to be. He said "she is going to be a ram." One of his
fellow workmen rogueishly criticized his ungrammatical reply. The
bows of these boats are heavy and are designed for more rapid movements than the iron clad turtle backs. They run up to a boat and strike
her a blow, and then get out of the way, thus annoying their foes by
repeated attacks. The regular gun boats are expected to keep up a
steady fire all the time, and not giving up till the fight is decided by
sinking the enemy or being destroyed themselves. These boats are alive
with men who are working away in the hot sun. The boats which are
made entirely of iron are quite a curiosity. I went into the enclosure
where they were being put together. In the first place iron frames on
the ribs as we call them are placed in their proper position, then the
plates or iron are riveted fast to them, each plate being cut to fit its
place before hand. These plates are of varying thickness from $\frac{1}{2}$ inch
to 1 inch, and the thickest iron is placed in the most vulnerable part of
the boat. This business of riveting employs a great many men and some
boys. The boys carry the red hot rivets and put them in places where
they are to be pounded home. Boys are used because they can run
faster than men and do the work just as well. I was amused to see the
blacksmith with his tongs in hand pull out these more than red hot rivets from the fire and pitch them over among the boys, and then see
them scramble and pick them up, and put them in their places before
they got cold or lost their bright glow. I wondered that they did not get
hit with them. I passed one place where they were punching holes in $\frac{1}{2}$
inch iron plates. It required nine men to manage this huge sheet of
iron. In all parts of this extensive establishment you will see work done
on as grand a scale as this. Every thing being of iron, heavy machinery
is used and great numbers of men are required to manage it. The
names of all these gunboats which are in various stages of completion
are of indian origin. There is the *Osage* & the *Neosho*, which are pretty
near ship shape, and the *Milwaukie*, the *Chocta* & the *Chippewag*
whose hulls are not much more than laid.[112] One visiting the place cant
say that there is nothing being done here towards carrying on the war with
determination. I am sorry to read of the indian troubles in the northwest.
Mrs Partington says, she thinks it must be a hard place to be obliged to

live on a gun boat, since Ike has read to her that "borders" get scalding water and cold lead. Last night oh! how hot it was! The hottest weather I have seen. The Thermo-meter marked 100° all day, and it was warm all night. About day break it began to rain and we had a fine shower.

Aug. 27, 62

This has been a warm day, but this evening a fine breeze is blowing and the sky is clear. There was a fire in a large drugstore down on Main street all day and I had a fine chance to see the fire engines play upon it. They confined it entirely to the store where it broke out. There were 3 or 4 of these engines at work. They are drawn by horses, are manned by seven men each who do nothing else but "run with the machines." I think a paid fire force much better than volunteers. The work of putting out a fire goes on more systematic with such help. There is not such a hue and cry at a fire as we have in N.Y. City....

Thursday, Aug 28, 62

After Dr. McDougal had left our boat, it became evident to my mind that he thought we were having a very easy time of it (that is we doctors) and he would make some changes soon. Accordingly when we arrived at St. L. Dr Hoff said that he would have to get along with a less number of assistants, and he should dispense with the two who came on board last. My term of service having about terminated, I am thinking of returning to the East on the first of September. I thought of leaving this afternoon but could not get all my business arranged, and as I do not wish to be obliged to stop anywhere on the way for sabbath I have concluded to stay over. I did not expect when I last wrote you to change the "base of my operations" so soon, but it has become a "military necessity." We are not having any battles out here requiring the removal of a large number from the field and the Post Hospitals are sending out instead of receiving soldiers, so that there is no demand for my services in these places. There seems to be more to do among the armies of the Potomac just now than elsewhere. I shall return home by the other route viz. Chicago, that I may see some more of the country. When I came on here in April Nature had not robed herself in her mantle of green, now the scene is changed. I wish I was going to have company home with me. Will having settled himself in a good position, it would not be for his interests that I should hold out my strong inducements to him to go with me just now. You will have to forego the pleasure of seeing him for a while. How quick this summer has passed! It doesn't seem more than a month since I came on here.

... Am glad to see that patriotism burns with much vigor in your town. I wish there was as much of it in proportion to numbers in this place. Mrs Haslem was accusing Will this morning at the table of being a little that way. They are going to assess all the sympathisers of the South and the proceeds go to the support of Union soldiers' families. Have you read *Les Miserables?*[113] Will is reading the series and I have just opened the cover in a few places. It must be interesting to one familiar with Paris and French history but I have not got that far.

I have no disposition to worry you any longer with notes and will reserve any further communications till I shall have the pleasure of seeing you face to face, and I will answer all your questions that I have failed in answering

Your affectionate frere
John

Part II
Bellevue

Introduction

Upon his return to New York City, Lauderdale discovered that Bellevue Hospital had assumed he was disinterested in the positions which were available during his absence, and that he may have missed a desirable place by a matter of several days. He accepted the only immediate opening, in Bellevue's Department of Public Charities and Corrections on Blackwell's Island, a small island (now Roosevelt Island) about a mile and a half long in the East River between Manhattan and Long Island. He and another physician were assigned to about 2,500 indigents who occupied the Work House and the Alms House, which were part of a larger facility that included a main hospital, a smallpox hospital, a penitentiary, a lunatic asylum, and a place for violent patients known as the Lodge.

The Work House consisted mainly of women who had been "sent up" for minor offenses, such as drunkenness and prostitution. Arriving from the city at a rate of a hundred per day, they worked off their short confinements by making hoop skirts, a sample of which they gave to the doctor to keep for his first daughter, which he sent along to Frank with the wry comment that by the time he would have a daughter, the style would long have been out of fashion.[1] The women were commonly alcoholics who suffered delirium tremens, and many of them had syphilis. Lauderdale and his partner examined them all, referring those who required treatment to the Blackwell's Island Hospital.

The Alms House consisted chiefly of orphans, single women with infants, and the elderly of both genders, along with sick and wounded soldiers. Although acute cases were transferred to the hospital, Lauderdale treated a fair sampling of diseases, interspersed with lighter duties such as extracting teeth, attending childbirth, and lancing infections. He roomed in the male wards and boarded at the warden's house, where the surroundings were quite beautiful, and the island itself was a fine-weather attraction for parties ferrying out from the city. The

143

Blackwell's Island. Although the large building shown here was built in the 1890s, the smaller building on the right dates from Lauderdale's term on the island.

waters were vastly different from those he had lived upon in the West, but once again Lauderdale enjoyed his perspective on all of the river traffic passing around him. Travel to and from the city's churches was inconvenient, however, and he soon became restless at being "off on that lone aisle, barren of certain attractions, which the city offers in great abundance." In January he was promoted to a place in the Blackwell's Island Hospital, and shortly thereafter he was happy to be returned to Bellevue Hospital in Manhattan, where he worked for a year in exchange for room and board.

Bellevue was a teaching hospital whose college had opened coincident with the outbreak of the war. Its buildings began at 23rd Street along the East River, and Lauderdale, whose windows at first faced onto the street, was later given a room with a view of the river and of Brooklyn, to which numerous two-cent ferries left from terminals just below him. Although notorious for its squalor, its frightfully high death rate, and its population of rats who made their own visiting hours throughout the wards, Bellevue was nevertheless a prestigious institution.[2] Its college took the lead in teaching military surgery, and the hospital opened its doors to countless soldiers who were pouring into New York and who were severely overcrowding the city's facilities.

Still, as with most hospitals of the day, both junior and senior staff were constantly leaving Bellevue for the war. Hired to fill a vacancy as one of three senior assistant surgeons, Lauderdale shortly completed a trio of house surgeons under the supervision of Dr. Stephen Smith, the eminent founder of Bellevue Medical College and the author of *A Handbook of Operative Surgery*, which became a bible for army surgeons during the war.[3] There were also four house physicians and four senior assistant physicians. Although Lauderdale's was not a paid position, he was able to earn five dollars per corpse performing autopsies for the coroner, the few dollars being a small but welcome light in the gloom of record high inflation.

Most of his surgical cases were accident injuries. For emergencies, a bell would sound to summon the surgeons from their quarters. It rang most frequently for Lauderdale during the infamous Draft Riots that rocked the city for five stormy days in mid-July of 1863. At one point, in an effort to stretch their limbs, he and a colleague ventured a rowing excursion up the East River, but the outing was aborted after bullets began whistling above their heads. Perhaps only a seasoned New Yorker would not find it ironic that after an unmolested tour of the Western theatre of the war, Lauderdale should have been shot at after returning to New York City.

Letters dealing exclusively with the riots are presented here in full, along with selected brief war-related excerpts, including descriptions of two unexpected encounters with General McClellan, who had joined his wife Maria in New York City after Lincoln had relieved him of his command. A few additional glimpses of life in the city during the war have been included, but a representative sampling of the letters from this period is beyond the scope of this volume, and the reader should not imagine that the correspondence focuses exclusively on the war. Lauderdale's life, as it unfolds within its pages, centers chiefly around optimizing his aptitude as a surgeon by performing his duties diligently, by reading, and by attending clinics, lectures, and medical soirees. Now and then he discusses medical issues, such as ovarian pregnancies, with his father, and occasionally—such as after one of his first "capital operations"—his excitement overmasters his customary resolve to spare Frank the surgical particulars. More than ever, church sermons are his principal source of spiritual and intellectual guidance, and he discusses with Frank the best of them, often in great detail. Frank remains his favorite correspondent, and if he writes her less frequently, it is no less regularly, his reports issuing faithfully, like Cyrano's gazettes in Roxane's garden, every Saturday afternoon. There is much about the movements of acquaintances and family, a major development being Willis and Sam's venture raising cotton on a plantation which they leased, under the ruse of being sons of St. Louis, from a Confederate widow along the Black River near Vicksburg, Mississippi. His son's term at Bellevue nearing conclusion, the senior Dr. Lauderdale exhorts him to return home and take over his practice, but he has sung too convincingly the blues of country doctoring to persuade the younger doctor to embrace it with any warmth. There is scant incentive for setting up in Manhattan, and the prospects of joining the Army or Navy are fraught with uncertainties.

Lauderdale had barely begun to examine the knotty problem of his future when Dr. Smith recommended him for an opening in the U.S. Army's Department of the Pacific. Once again, he would be signing on as a contract surgeon under the auspices of Dr. Charles McDougall, former medical director of the Department of the Tennessee, lately fulfilling the same function for New York City. Dr. Smith, Dr. McDougall, McDougall's assistant, Dr. Sloan, and Lauderdale's former superior, Dr. Hoff, were unanimous in encouraging him to pursue the opportunity. He signed the contract at once and was slightly dazed to be suddenly bound for California, but he told his mother he felt it was God's will that he should go. "The distance I have to travel is considerable," he wrote her, "but it is only going to the other side of Uncle Sam's farm." Nevertheless, the prospect of sailing for "a more distant part of our great and glorious country" appealed to his sense of adventure, and he hoped to see "something rather more primeval" than anything in his experience.

Before Lauderdale's departure, Bellevue presented him with an inscribed case of pocket instruments; he sat for a group portrait with his colleagues; and his old spiritual mentor, Dr. Spring, gave him a warm benediction. He renewed subscriptions to his favorite newspapers, he sent the schedule for the mail steamers to Frank, and he packed all of his needs into a single trunk. He sailed for San Francisco aboard the *Ariel* on March 23, 1864.

The Letters

New York Oct 2nd 1862

Dear Father

I reached the city of Rochester too late for the first train for Albany and I had 3 or 4 hours to wait. I called on Dr Arner and he had just returned from the battle fields of Sharpsburgh and the "cornfields" where he has had a very hard time of it.[4] I never saw him looking so bad as he does this time. I do not see why he went into the service. For one so near gone with consumption it seems but inviting death already on the way....

Almshouse Blackwell Island
Oct 3rd 1862.

Dear Sister

... This circumstance gave me a chance to visit Dr Arner whom I found at home but had just returned from the battle of the "cornfields." I met his wife at the door who told me I could see him if he was well enough to see company (She did not recognize me at first). As the Dr came towards me from an adjoining room he looked the picture of an exhausted, poor, and worn out soldier, he was dressed in full uniform, and his clothes hung loosely about his shrunken frame. I thought to myself, he has done a thing which will hurry him along faster than ever to his grave. I asked him why he went into the service and he said that if he should not see much fighting, it might do him good to rough it a little. He has roughed it. He was quite animated in telling me about the scenes he had passed thro, and while he interested me, he also gave me pain, as he told me every thing in a whisper, it being difficult for

147

him to speak aloud. I should have stayed with him a long time, but I saw it gave him pain to talk, and I bade him good night at an early hour.

Almshouse Blackwells Island
Sunday Evening Oct 5th/62.

Dear Sister
... I visited the Island Hospital to day to hear one of the clinical lectures. After this was over the convalescent soldiers came into the ampitheatre and took seats. It had been arranged that Mr. Van Meter should meet them, and bring with him his singing children. They came, and each little girl had a boquet of flowers in her hand, and baskets of fruit such as peaches and grapes. They placed their baskets on the table, and holding their flowers in their hands they formed two long rows, twenty five bright faces drawn up before the soldiers. They presented an interesting appearance. They sang several of their songs, principally patriotic & they seemed to delight the soldiers greatly who looked on with astonishment and many were moved to tears, as these pleasant faces reminded them of similar faces left behind them at their homes. Some of the soldiers had their arms in splints or their faces covered with adhesive straps concealing wounds not yet healed. During the singing, remarks were made by Mr. Van Meter and others. Mr V.M. said he had two boys in the army & one, his Willie, he feared might have fallen in the late battle at Corinth. Still he rejoiced that, although he was but seventeen years of age, he was able to go out and fight to put down this wicked rebellion. After the singing was over, the children distributed their fruit and flowers among the soldiers. The whole thing passed off pleasantly. The soldiers sang "Marching Along," but the children would have the last sing, and wound up with the "Star Spangled Banner." They hastened down to the boat which was already waiting for them, and as they ran, the shout of "good bye, soldiers" filled the air.

Almshouse Blackwells Island
Sunday Evening Oct 19, 62.

Dear Frank
... I did not hear Dr Spring but Mr Binney made an appeal in behalf of the Colonization society in Africa. I dont know what you think about

colonization, but I think the plan is pretty much played out. For my part I am willing the negro race should remain in this land if he wants to do so. The majority dont want to go. Let those who do find means for so doing. Mr B. was not allowed to take up a collection but told all who wished to give something to write the amount on cards left in the seats. I fear he will not realize much.

Almshouse Blackwells Island
New York City Oct 27. 62

Dear Frank
    ... I hear a good deal of politics discussed at table by mine host Mr Anderson, who is a rampant republican. I dont say any more on such subjects than I am obliged to. I read the *Herald* so you will see what kind of instruction I receive. Mr A was so indignant to think that Prince John should call on Mrs Lincoln at the Metropolitan the other night.[5] I read all of Seymours speeches and Prince Johns too, and I cannot see that they are as traitorous as Greeley would infer for them.[6] So McClellan is waiting a forward movement to Richmond till after our State Elections? It is just as quiet as can be on the Potomac just now. The decks of the Sound[7] steamers as they go by the island every morning are crowded with soldiers who shout, and wave their hats at us. If I am on my way to breakfast and can see between the trees I return the salute. There would seem to be a great concentrating of troops some-where, and for some purpose. I hope to hear of a final blow to rebellion soon.

Almshouse Blackwells Island
Nov 7th 1862

Dear Frank
    On the table before me lies an *Illustrated News*[8] & the picture on the first page is a tolerably fair representation of the Republican candi-date for Governor, but who was defeated at our late election. Mr W. is a good friend of mine, and I regret that he should allow himself to be the representative of the Abolition party. As he was, however, I could not feel it my duty to vote for him. How did the Election go in Geneseo? I suppose Republican largely. There have been many spicy sayings in the Papers before and since the Election concerning Mr Ws history, character and liberality & which have been sadly incorrect.

Old Count Girowski figures as the second of Mr W. if John V.B. should attempt an attack upon him. It is certainly disagreeable to be up for higher office.[9]

> Almshouse B.I.
> New York City Nov 27/62.

Dear Frank

This is Thanksgiving day and I have been to church and eaten my turkey. The day has been beautiful and everything has conspired to make me very thankful. I went over & heard Dr Shedd (Dr Springs colleague). He said that the present state of the country was calculated to bind us more strongly together as one nationality than anything else that could have befallen us. For this we had great cause to be thankful. That as a people we were becoming like mortar which contains no lime to hold together the crumbling mass. He was thankful that there was so much unity of purpose in putting down the rebellion. That the States were bound together by geographical ligaments too strong to be broken. That our Southern Presbyterians should have had a little more firmness in holding on to the right, and not let go the dogs of war so soon, and after a while all would be well. He also spoke of slavery and emancipation. Said that the slave would not be bettered in his condition while out of the Union, and as the word of God teaches conclusively that slavery cant always exist—that the will of Providence is, he will be elevated while in the Union—and that fact upholds him in his view that the Almighty will not permit the Union to be broken. I think I shall like Dr S quite well after I get accustomed to his style....

> P.S.
> Sunday Evening

... War news are very interesting just now: McClellan is in town now and he & his wife go to church every sunday, so the papers say of him. No one can blame these movements of the Little General. Dr Shedd said that we ought not to triumph over any victory gained in this war, as it would be quite out of place in a civil war with our own bretheren.

> Write Soon to
> Your brother
> John

Alms House B.I.
New York Dec 10th/62.

Dear Frank

Yours of the 5th is just at hand, it has been only five days reaching me, great speed for a letter surely. I have had no papers for several days. Hope there are some on the way. My letters have not come as well as they did before Gould was arrested. Did I mention his case in a former letter? Perhaps not. Gould was a man about 40 years of age, good looking & rather a conspicuous personage from the fact of his wearing a long black beard every hair of which was nicely adjusted & of the blackest die (every one said it was colored so). The top of his head was quite bald but he always wore a nice black hat. The rest of his wardrobe would become any man of wealth. A magnificent ring glittered upon the little finger of the only hand he possessed. A costly chain swung across his vest attached to a watch which cost not less than a hundred, & his *tout ensemble* indicated one of the well to do men of New York. No one would suppose him to be simply a letter carrier for the Commissioners. He was always scrupulously neat in his appearance, but it was only lately that his friends thot he wore rather more on his person than a man who was getting but 16 dollars a month and his board, could afford to wear. He took his meals with the paupers, and his broadcloth contrasted strangely with the striped garments of the inmates. He had always maintained the confidence of the Commissioners for the several years of his stay in the Institution. He was formerly a soldier in the Mexican War, where he lost an arm, & on his return was obligated to seek a home in the Alms House. He seemed to be well enough off, but his vanity or something (the *Devil* probably) tempted him to rob the letters of the soldiers who have been spending some time at our hospitals, & when suspicions were aroused and decoy letters confirmed the suspicions, he was arrested and sent to the tombs. On the way there he got some opium (an article which he was in the habit of using a good deal) and in the morning he became a coroners case. As I passed through the dead house at Bellevue on Monday, I raised the cover from a rough coffin, and there lay the body of the unfortunate man. Having been carelessly thrown in, his long beard which was all his pride during his life, fell wildly about his features, and was matted with the ruffles of his shirt bosom. The body waited for some friend, but none came, and it was handed over to the students, who will pay twenty five cents for the privilege of dissecting it. He deserved a fate not half so good. I say this much about him because he came right under my own eyes and I always suspected there was something wrong.

As I was going up the steps of the main entrance of the Hospital the other day, I was met by more of a crowd than usual coming down. One of the foremost was a man about medium height, with light hair & mustache & perhaps a little gotee of the same colour. In form he was rather broad across his shoulders. There was nothing noticeable in his features. He wore on his head a military cap like the one I wear, covered by a glazed cloth so that you could not discover what badge of office, and a military cloak hung about his shoulders. As he passed he bowed as any well bred soldier would do, and after he reached the foot of the flight of steps, he stopped and shook hands with some convalescent soldiers who were standing near. He asked how they were, and if they were almost well again. Following close behind him was a lady supported on the arm of Dr Wood.[10] To describe her I can only say from the momentary glance I caught of her, that she was a slender figure plainly dressed, with large black eyes & an expression on her countenance of friendly sympathy for everybody and particularly for the soldiers she passed, upon whom she cast friendly smiles. A carriage stood waiting for these two persons, and after they had entered & taken their seats, the crowd gave three cheers for Geo B. McClellan, & then three more for his wife. I could hardly believe my senses that this was the individual whose name has been on everybodys tongue, and who has been the leader of our Armies during the civil war. I never should have picked him out as the Young "Napoleon of America." He had been to visit the soldiers in the Hospital. He called there twice during his recent stay in the city, and both times, he went through the different wards and spoke to each one of the soldiers, taking them by the hand, and inquiring about their wounds with as much interest as their own fathers would do. This manner of treatment at once gains the favor of the men & they love him more than ever....[11]

You ask about my situation, if it is good as Bellevue. It is one of the departments of Bellevue. It is the Nursery and Old Peoples part, and is important I change to another place in January. ?Grub dont cost nothing. ?Have no "bosom friends" but fleas and of course I have a good time with them. ?If I am considered a good doctor? The old women say if I order them an egg now & then "God bless you doctor, long life to yes! and may you get a good wife" etc etc. Then you dont like the Message? Dont you like his idea of Emancipation? I do. I would like to join Col Woods Rgt, but I can't leave Bellevue now. I learn more here than I would in the army. The army is no place for one just beginning. I am perfectly satisfied of that. And I am well enough off for the present. I wish you would say whether or not you sent the books to Newberry? Send me the papers every week! Write me as often as once a week if you have nothing at all to say. I write whenever I have any thing to tell you that is worth mentioning. But dont wait for me. We have had some very cold weather for a day or two. I hear there is skating on the ponds near Harlem. To day the temperature is mild and endurable. With these meteorological observations I close this letter. We shall have to write short letters by and by when the paper gets high. With much love to all I remain as ever

Yours affectionately

John

Alms House B.I.

New York City Dec. 22.62

Dear Sister

I have just perused the *Liv Republican* that I received to day and commenting upon it in editorial parlance *we* find not much therein. Still *we* are glad to get it. *We* are pleased to read the letters from the Editor thereof whom *we* find out on a journey through the State of Ohio visiting the pork slaughtering establishments. We wonder that he does not visit some of the slaughtering places near Fredericksburgh. The paper gives no names of any deaths among any of our friends, but if Franklins division was in the fight there must have been some. I have looked over some of the long & closely printed columns of killed & wounded at that battle, but see no familiar name as yet—& hope there is none. But it was a sad catastrophe, so disheartening to our soldiers. The Democracy of your village seems to be politically popular. Am glad to see it so....

I went down to the city to day on a little steam tug which has taken the place of the regular steamboat. We had on board quite a drove of work house women, who have been spending their time in the skirtshops. They were feeling pretty well, if I should judge from their singing and carrying on. These poor creatures go to the city and many have no homes to go to when they reach there, and although they promise to behave well, having sinned once, are very prone to do so again. They visit the drinking saloons and soon are the victims of the Police who are always on the lookout for them, and they are at once sent back to the work house. I have seen a good many that have gone and come back several times during my short acquaintance with them. Last sunday I attended the church service that is held for their benefit. They numbered about six hundred, and they were a[s] hard looking [a] set of women as you ever beheld....

Sunday Evening Dec. 28th, 62.

... This afternoon I went over to the city and heard a Scotch presbyterian on Lexington Avenue. I could not stay to the close of the sermon, if

I did I would not get back to the Island to night, so I came out in the midst of it. He talked about the number of sins that we commit and for the sake of illustrating the number he said he would allow the commission of two sins to each hour (which would, he thot, be a fair average), then allowing fifteen hours each day (the number of our waking moments), which would give 30 sins a day, 210 per week, 840 per month, 1080 per year, and so on for a life time, would give a burden of sins to carry about with us equal to the one which Bunyans pilgrim is represented as carrying on his back. This is no doubt all true and when we take this view of the subject, that huge bale of sins which the poor pilgrim is represented in the picture staggering under is not overdrawn in the least. Next Wednesday evening one of the inmates, a blind man, is going to give an oration in the Chapel on the subject of the state of the country. I doubt not it will be worth listening to. I shall attend if possible.

Bellevue Hospital New York
Jan 21st 1863.

Dear Frank and Nettie
    ... You have seen a notice in the papers of Dr McGowan who is delivering a course of lectures in this city on China & Japan. Last Sunday evening I heard him talk to the children at a sunday school aniversary and he told them a good many curious facts about the people in those countries. He said that he had seen the little boys in the street in Ning poo roll together a mass of snow, form it into an image of a man, put in pieces of charcoal for eyes, and a piece of red pepper for a mouth & then fall down & worship it. They used charcoal for eyes because they never heard of eyes being any other color than black. Dr McGowans eyes which were blue, were a great curiosity to them. He said the little Japs were much more polite than our American lads are to their superiors. He spoke about the expensive feasts which these people make to their departed friends, and after their spirits have eaten all they want, they step up and eat what is left. These people think that girls have no souls, and they destroy a good many of them when they are young. They often let the girls die by depriving them of food. He told of one who was kept on a short allowance for a good while, till she was greatly reduced in flesh, her parents hoping every day would be her last, but she managed some how to get something from day to day that kept her along. One day Dr M. heard of the case and tried to put a stop to this course. He tried to reason with the parents, but they said that it was all right. The Dr wanted to take the child from these inhuman parents but they would not consent to do this, but would sell her to

him for a small sum if he wanted to buy. The Dr did not like the idea of buying the child. So he told the parents that he would give them two dollars for the rags she wore, if they would throw in the skin and bones. This they agreed to, and the Dr has brot the "skin and bones" to this country with him, where she is being educated and gives promise of becoming considerably a woman. Dr. McGowan is a medical man, not a D.D. His remarks were very happy and interested a large audience....

Bellevue Hospital
New York City Jan. 24th/63.

Dear Frank & Nettie
... On my way up Broadway I found a great many people out, as is usually the case on a pleasant day. In one shop window I saw something quite new for children. It was a lot of little dolls that could walk. As they stepped along you would think they were alive, and they were only 8 inches in height, but dressed up in style. Near another window there was a great crowd going and coming, and I of course must go and see what was the attraction, and I found hanging up in the shop window of a tailor the wedding suit of Commodore Nutt, who is to be groomsman at Tom Thumb's marriage. It consisted of a little dress coat of black lined with white silk, a white silk vest, black pants, and patent leather boots of equally distinctive pattern. This will be a great affair. I believe it is going to come off in this city at Trinity Chappel. Bishop Potter is to be the officiating clergyman....[12]
This evening Dr Smith has his class in bandaging in an adjoining room. If you should step into the room you would see about a dozen medical students making with cotton and rags & applying bandages to a number of the patients who for the moment are supposed to have broken their collar bones. One student, after he had got his patient all bandaged up in a most uncomfortable position, was about leaving him so, when the forgetful doctor returned and apologized to the poor fellow for his neglect. You see a good many amusing things even in a hospital....

Bellevue Hospital
New York City March 6, 63

Dear Sisters
Last Friday night (I think I made mention of it) I attended a meeting of the surgical section of the Academy of Medicine held at the house of Dr

Jas R. Wood.[13] All the Medical staff of this hospital have a standing invitation to attend these monthly gatherings. The large parlor is usually filled with surgeons who meet for the purpose of discussing some surgical questions. The piano is loaded not with sheets of music but of pictures and drawings of morbid anatomy, and the photographic album is replaced by lithographic plates of all the distinguished European and American surgeons & doctors from the time of Hippocrates to the present day. On entering the room we of the "staff" are shown by Dr Wood the carotid artery which he had ligated the night before, but which operation did not save the poor fellow whose neck it supplied with blood. We looked at the pictures and chatted with each other (Dr John Hunt was present) till the house was called to order and the topic for discussion was begun. We listened to the discussion till all had stated their opinions, and after a little other business was transacted, then the folding doors were opened, and Dr Wood asked the company to partake of a generous collation, which had been prepared for our palates. This I need not say was discussed with great zeal as all could take a part. These meetings you will readily see tend greatly towards preserving that esprit du corps among the profession and are the means of communicating useful knowledge as well....

Sunday Evening 6 oclock

...This morning I listened to Dr Cook in a very good discourse and this afternoon to Dr Shedd. Dr C. directed his remarks especially to those who are continually gorging themselves with spiritual knowledge or spiritual food, but it never seems to add to their spiritual growth because they do not act upon it in their lives....

10 oclock P.M.

I dont know but I am guilty of gorging my self, for since I wrote the above, I have been out hunting up food for the mind. The first church I went to was closed, although a sunday school aniversary was advertised to take place. I came along back by way of Dr Adams church (Madison Square). Here I saw a light and a crowd of people assembling. On inquiries, was told that a Patriotic discourse was to be preached. I went in and found such a crowd that all the seats were filled and the sexton gave me a seat up quite near to the pulpit on one of the extra seats in the aisle, just where I could hear every word that dropped. Dr A's remarks were earnest, clever & full of power. He upheld the constitution, emulated Washington, frowned upon the supporters of the higher law code,[14] and recommended his hearers to cherish a christian patriotism. He said that the world demanded of us, that we should not swerve in the least from pursuing the war, and that sooner or later we will surely realize our hope. I have often wondered how it was possible for the Rebels to maintain such a bitter hatred to the government which they so recently lived under, and which they, like we, were accustomed to praise so highly. Dr A made this reconcilable by comparing the Rebels in their bitter enmity to our government, to the children of Israel with Aaron at their head dancing around the golden calf, and rebeling against the good government of Moses, which they had lived under so long and so happily. Dr A. said that he believed that the Rebels like the wayward Israelites would yet have to drink of the bitter waters of Nuribah as a punishment for their sins.

My seat in the aisle, although I know it was in rather a conspicuous place, still this first did not enable me to see why I should be looked at by so many. Young ladies especially, I observed, were looking at me whenever I happened to cast my eyes over the audience. I put my hand on my head to see if my hair was sticking up, & felt of my neck tie to see if that was awry, found my toilet all right, and I concluded the people who were looking toward me so often, thought they were recognizing in me an old acquaintance, so I was not any longer amazed. But at the close of the meeting I discovered that the man who was sitting at my elbow, and whose face I had till then only a side view of, was Gen. Geo B. McClellan, hence the attraction that way. I noticed that he slipped out of a side door near the pulpit to avoid the crowd....

Bellevue Hospital
New York City Mar 28, 63.

Dear Frank and Nettie
... The war goes on slowly, but I think favourably for the North, and we must not think of any such word as *fail* in our effort to bring back the South. As I have said before, I should like a position on Col Woods staff, but I dont feel quite ready to leave here. But if I should be drafted and obliged to go into the service, I should accept any offer of that kind. I have not thought anything of comming home, nor will thoughts of going into the country occupy my mind for a while yet....

Bellevue Hospital
New York April 4th/63.

Dear Sisters
.... The wind blew so hard just now, that it carried away one of my window blinds. I heard it strike the pavement so that I guess no one was

hurt by its descent. I have seen all the surgery I care about for one day. Saturdays is the day for opperations in this Institution, and I being one of the surgeons have had my hands in blood "some."

... Do you hear anything about the draft nowadays? I am an inmate of a public institute for paupers, and all such are exempt from military duty, hence, should I not be exempt?[15] Two of my colleagues have been in the service. One was in the army for two years, but has returned to go through a hospital practice, deeming this more profitable....

New York City
Saturday April 5th/63

Dear Sister,

... You complain of a great destitution of beaux in Geneseo. My advice to you in particular is *to get one* that you can always depend on. You should have looked out for one before the war began. The fellows are all away now on the battlefield, and they may all be dead before the war is over. In that case how many old maids there will be! Dont you feel gloomy at the prospect viewed in this light?...

Bellevue Hospital
New York City May 2, 63.

Dear Sisters

... One day this week I visited the Monitor docks where they are building the iron vessels of war. Their iron sides are rendered doubly impregnable by planks of iron, if I may use the word, securely fastened to their sides. The *Puritan*, which is now nothing more than a huge iron skeleton, is to be 200 feet long, and the largest one of the kind that has ever been built. I think she would stand the fire of Fort Sumpter or of any other fortress....

Bellevue Hospital
New York City May 9, 63

Dear Sisters

... But how we have been whipped by the Rebels again![16] Who is to blame for it? There is something wrong somewhere. I heard to day that Joe Hooker was a very profane man, as well as a hard drinker. Now if he was about half seas over, I can easily understand why he should have' been so ignorant of the position of Stonemans cavalry & thus lost the advantage gained by that powerful arm. I dont think McClellan is that

kind of a man, and hope he may be reinstated. I should not blame a soldier for deserting a commander who was conducting an attack while his
brain was stupefied with liquor....

Bellevue Hospital
New York, May 30, 1863

Dear Sister
    ... Last sunday we were in receipt of great victories acheived by
Grant. Vicksburgh was ours sure! But it has about all come to be a fic-
tion by this time. I wonder what the Papers will furnish the sunday
readers tomorrow morning....[17]

Bellevue Hospital
New York June 6th 1863.

Dear Sister
    ... I wish you had been with me the other day, when I visited the
Iron ship *Passaic*.[18] The watchman would have allowed you on board,
and Jack the sailor man who showed me around would have thrown
away his rind of tobacco, and been delighted to point out to us where
the balls from Sumter and Moultrie gouged the thick plates of iron
which formed the sides of the ship; and her massive turrets where the
two guns are placed. You look directly into their black throats as you
stand at the turrett windows. The "eleven inch" one, which throws a
solid shot weighing *only* 240 pounds, is emphatically a "big thing" and if
you fail to realize its size, climb up into the turrett, and you will just be
able to reach across the breach with your extended arms. I will not take
time to describe her to you, but will send a picture of the scene of her
action in Charleston Harbor. She is being repaired & will try Sumpter
again some day & I hope with more success....

Bellevue Hospital
New York, June 13th 1863

Dear Sister
    ... On Wednesday evening I went to the Academy of Music to attend
the anniversary of the Home for Soldiers children. The school consists
of about 150 boys and girls whose fathers are now engaged in fighting

for their country, or have died while thus engaged. It was the custom of the Ancient Spartans to take especial care of the children of their warriors, and we do well to imitate their example in sustaining such an institution. These children sang some, and they spoke some pieces, and they went through with the Zouave drill quite well. But the chief attraction of the entertainment was the songs, speeches, dialogues & calisthenic exercises of some 200 young girls from the 12th St Grammar School who very generously tendered their services to draw out a large audience, who would contribute liberally to the treasury of the school fund. I must say I was quite pleased, and that great room was crowded with young and old who seemed to enjoy it as much as I did. But as you dont care to hear anything said about talented children, I will not trouble you with any description of the stars of the evening....

Bellevue Hospital
New York June 20th, 1863.

Dear Sister
... So we have to regret now that Jeff Davis was not hung at the beginning of this rebellion. And all along during this cruel war I think we have failed in not taking prompt and vigorous action against that misguided people of the South. But as things are now, I think we must continue to fight for the Constitution till the last armed foe expires, notwithstanding we have got such discordant elements to do our bloody work for us....

Bellevue Hospital
New York, July 11th, 1863

Dear Sister
Yours of wednesday is at hand prompt as I could wish it. The *Liv Republican* is also on my table, and it tells of the rail road accident. It rejoices in the victories recently gained by our forces. Why dont *you* rejoice over the good news? It is certainly one point gained if we have taken Vicksburgh. That gives us possession of the Mississippi River nearly. We have got to keep hammering away at those Rebs or else die in the attempt. All these battles remind me that the work is going on & the successes that we have heard of this week show that it goes bravely on. The cry is now "Down with Traitors and up with the Flag." Nothing else would become a nation like our own. It would be better for us as a nation to become entirely annihilated than to look passively on and see traitors rise up and attempt to disorganize our noble Union, the inheritance of

our Fathers. Our army of the Potomac have just achieved a victory over the enemy. Although much blood has been shed, there is no doubt but that our enemy have got the worst of the battle. We are fighting for the maintainance of a great principle, that of self government, and it becomes us to give all our support to this one object. Those who are urging on the war to make money out of it solely, are as bad as pirates, but we cannot stop to complain about them now. The President calls for more troops, and we must submit to the draft in order to furnish the number of men required. Our losses have been very great, but they do not exceed the loss of life in those sanguinary engagements that we read of in Israelitish history. And although Sharps rifles and Parrot guns were not in use in those days, still when brave men fell in battle there were hearts who mourned as deeply as in these days. And it was all done to establish certain principles among nations, who would not learn wisdom in any other way....

Bellevue Hospital
New York Monday Jul 13 1863.

This morning the Draft was to go on as it had begun on Saturday, but certain riotous and law defying citizens had determined they would resist it, and it has led to a series of the most disgraceful scenes that have transpired in this city for a dozen years. The Astor place riot did not begin to be as bad. The house where the drafting took place was destroyed by fire this morning at an early hour. Mobs formed in several places, particularly in our part of the town where are located numerous factories employing a great many workmen. The ring leaders would come to a factory and drag the employees away from their work and induce them to join them. Just over the way there is situated a large machine shop.[19] About ten this morning I saw from my window a large crowd of men standing in the doorway and in front of the building. Soon all work ceased, and the engine fires went out. The doors were closed and work was done. The men had joined the mob, and they went marching down the Avenue. This afternoon we saw from our windows a column of smoke rising from the vicinity of 40th St. about 5 PM.[20] The Armory in 2nd Avenue near us was burned.[21] I visited the ruins. About the same time a fire was seen over in Broadway, said to be the Provost Marshalls house.[22] Since dark a bright fire has [been] burning far down town, which rumor says is the *Tribune* building.[23] Across town & far up, another fire lights up the sky, which we hear is the Colored Orphan Home.[24] All day the alarm bell has been sounding, calling the surgeons to cases of injuries received by participants in these scenes. Some with scalp wounds & some fractures of the skull. Some men who were badly burned have also arrived since the fires broke out. Two or three were brot here ready to land in their coffins on their arrival. Tis a pity that more of these demons were not shot down, more especially the leaders of the infuriated mob, those copperhead leaders, I don't know their names. Andrews, Editor of the *Daily News,* is said to be one, & Fernando Wood is no doubt another.[25]

Tuesday July 14, 63.

To day we have had nearly a repetition of what took place here yesterday. There were no fires but a great many people were shot down by the soldiers, and some were shot by the mob who had also armed themselves. We have had almost as great a variety of gunshot wounds brot to this Hospital as would be found after a battle.

Wednesday July 15, 63.

I had not more than written the above lines last evening, when my attention was called to the sound of fire bells. I stepped to the window & saw a light in the sky. The night was hot & no air stirring. I went up into the cupola and saw the fire just breaking out in a building a few blocks from the Hospital.[26] I took my seat in an arm chair and watched the progress of the flames. Others joined me in viewing the wanton destruction of property by the infuriated mob. The buildings destroyed were a brass foundary and a bell tower. When the latter fell the crash was fearfull. One or two pale columns of smoke were seen circling up in other places, but this grand central fire nearly eclipsed them. We looked till the walls fell and the last volumes of flames shot upwards to the sky, & then retired. Before I had composed my mind in sleep & while I was wondering at the doings of the infuriated people, a drunken man passed along the street and what he might say in such a condition would speak the sentiments of the mob. He said that "A poor man had to be drafted and go to the war, but a rich man could pay his money and stay at home. Thats whats the matter." This is the sentiment that lies at the foundation of the whole trouble as far as the rioters are concerned, and they are backed up by some of the press. But there are a good many theives and cutthroats & others made furious by liquor, who have gone on and destroyed a good deal of property in a most wanton manner. But I need not tell you of what I hear going on in the streets for I have not been out of the yard since Sunday but once. The papers are full of details but I see enough in this institution to convince me of the destruction of life. More than thirty have been brot in injured by clubs and fire arms. Men, women & children have been wounded by gun shots, so eager have they been to see the fray. One little boy of eight lies in my Ward Seven with a mosquito net over his head and breast, and if you look through the meshes you will see where the ball has gone through his lungs. Another up in Fifteen has had his thigh perforated but fortunately for him the bone was not broken. A woman in Twenty received a ball in her breast, and it passed through the tissue and can be felt with a long probe in her left arm. We shall remove it tomorrow. There are any number of broken and depressed skulls. Some will get well and others will die. They all say they were not participants but merely lookers on. For such I have some pity but I don't believe all they say about their innocence. I have very little sympathy for one man in Ward Sixteen who received several shots and bruises, upon whose person was found several bills of confederate scrip. It would seem that he had something to do with Rebeldom.

9 PM Same date.

It has been comparatively quiet during the day and people have walked the streets more securely, but business has not yet resumed. After dinner I thought I would take a row out on the river with one of the doctors for our own health. While there we heard a good deal of firing of Musketry on 23rd St a few blocks down the river, and I rowed in the direction, but kept far out from the shore. My friend thought he heard a noise like a bullet whistling in the air over head, but I laughed at the idea of any attacks upon us. But a moment after, I heard something whistling too, and I thought it was best not to stay there any longer. I asked a man on board a schooner if he heard any bullets. He said he had heard several, so we skedaddled back to the Hospital. Several regiments out of town have arrived and we feel safe. Several more cases of severe wounds have been brot in this evening. But how much longer must this shooting down of men continue? I hope they will continue it till this rebelious spirit is put down. I have not a particle of sympathy for such disloyal wretches.

Thursday July 16

A few men have been brot in to day, but were those who had been shot yesterday. About one o clock to day I went up into the 3rd story of the wing looking out on 28th St & 1st Avenue and saw a specimen of what has been going on all over the city.[27] Just across the street was a party of

men and boys in front of the liquor store. One or two of them had car-
bines, and as fast as they could get sight of the soldiers who were at the
time stationed farther up the street, they would fire upon them. Two or
three of the soldiers would now and then return the fire, but these
hounds were so protected by a pile of stones, that they were not hit. Oh!
how I wanted to see that fiend in the red shirt and slouched hat knocked
over. We were not more than 5 rods from him, and we saw all his
maneauvering. He would look out from his place of concealment and
when the soldier fired he would drop down again, then he would place
his hat on the top of the wall in hopes to draw the fire of the soldier, after
which he would fire. Oh! how I wished they had run that mountain howitzer that was standing on the corner of 2nd Avenue down here, and by a
flank movement fired into these fiends. They feared some such attack,
for a short time after they skidaddled and we have not seen them around
here since. The number that have been brot to the Hospital by this time,
including dead & wounded, is upwards of seventy.

7 P.M.

Just now a little girl was brot in with her nose shot away by a ball
which had first passed through the wall of her house. A little later a
company of the seventh Regt. have been standing on the corner opposite
the south wall with their guns pointed at any one who should offer to
show any riotous demonstrations, but more especially to fire into those
fiends who are skulking here and there along the street, firing at the soldiers. It dont seem possible that the numerous discharges of musketry
that I hear at this moment is the attempt to kill riotous men or those in
turn firing into those who would seek to put them down. The people
seem to be perfectly crazy, the women and children can scarcely be kept
out of the way of the guns. As I write I hear a succession of death dealing volleys. The rain which is now falling does not seem to restrain their
rage. The gong rings and another man wounded and bleeding was brot
in, a police man, and he was attended by an escort of police & soldiers
to keep off those who would like to finish him.[28] The negroes, the police
& the soldiers are the ones they fire upon. Other citizens are not
molested, but they have to run their chances of getting hit. I saw one fellow run across the street and hold his umbrella between himself and the
soldiers so that he should escape being hurt. One ball did come into the
Hospital. Mr. White picked it up in one of the lower wards. Twas acci-
dentally fired at us. There are a good many relatives sitting around the
bedsides of their wounded friends. Some are mothers and they watch
over their foolish, reckless sons, whose disloyalty has brot them to this

helpless condition, with all the tenderness that mothers can bestow. The gong has struck again. A large man is carried up. We visit him. A ball has gone through his body. In a moment after he is laid in his bed, he vomits blood. All we can do wont save him. We leave him to Father Larkin the priest, who will get him to answer a few questions concerning his faith in the Catholic Religion. This wont save him either for time or eternity, I fear.

Friday Noon [July 17]

Have received a few more cases this morning but they were shot several days ago, their injuries proving to be more grave than they first supposed, or they would not have come here for treatment. While we were dressing the wound of the little girl referred to yesterday, she said to her Father who was standing by, "Dont cry, Father! You wont, will you? Tell Mother not to cry!" Then to the Doctor she said, "Will I die?" "I will be tip top in the morning." Then she inquired about the children, her brothers and sisters, calling each by name.

Saturday Noon [July 18]

It is more quiet today in this the 21st Ward than on sunday. Bishop Hughes spoke yesterday, no doubt had a good effect upon the catholics. The police and soldiers are roaming about searching the houses and when they find a musket or fire arms they take charge.

Bellevue Hospital
New York July 18th 8 PM, 1863

Dear Frank

Your letter of Thursday is at hand and I will begin a reply. I can assure you positively that I was not one of the "rioters" as I have not been out of the hospital yard since Monday evening when I went a few blocks to see the ruins of a fire. I have no sympathy for these rebelious people who have allowed their passions to run away with them. It is the duty of every man to come forward at this time and help put down the rebelion. For what other course to pursue is there? Then who is to fill the ranks? It is apparent to all that wealth is unequally distributed among our citizens, but life is the gift of every man and no one can say to his neighbor that his life is of more value than his neighbors, & we may argue from this that the valuation of ones life is equal with every man, and they all stand on equal footing, and so far all would be alike subject to be drafted. But the rich man has a chance for saving his life which the poor man does not possess. Nor is the poor man responsible for his lack of that power, which if he possessed would place him on an equal footing with the rich man. Now in such a crisis such as this how is an equality of responsibility to be effected so that both rich and poor can do as they see fit about offering up their lives for the salvation of our country? Certainly there is no other way than for the rich to be taxed to an amount sufficient to enable the poor man who is drafted to do as he pleases, go or stay. If you cannot infuse sufficient patriotism into mens minds to go to war when they have been fairly drafted into the service of their country, then there is no hope left. It is absurd to think of forcing men to take up arms in their countrys defense against their will. The poor will make a fuss about it, and just so they have done. The events of the week I think will satisfy any one on this point. I read in the papers that an amount has been appropriated by the city which will enable all poor men drafted to pay their exemption if they dont choose to go to the war. That is as it should be. Why was it not thought of before? It shows what a shortsighted, blundering set of men we have got to control the affairs of government. I hope the scenes that have been enacted in this city this week will remind them that people no matter how humble are not to be trifled with. It is true, there have been base men, who dont deserve the name of men, operating to a great extent in these horrid scenes, but they were backed up by the aggrieved ones, who in their madness for the time were bereft of reason. Excuse these reflections about the *draft*, which I think is not exactly as it should be. (I sent you 3 *Heralds*.) One other thought or analogy suggests itself. The highwayman meets you with these words: "Your money or your life." Uncle Abrahams officials say to you if drafted your $300 dollars or go to the war which may cost you your life. There is this difference, the robber may be defeated, but Law is irresistable. Such opinions in regard to the draft held by many people & expressed publickly could not but influence the people to deeds of violence. Gov Seymour reminds the people that if they are aggrieved they can appeal to the courts. This method would at once satisfy men of understanding, and ability to comprehend, but the rabble would be more ready to make a physical resistance to the law than to resort to it. So it was with the rioters this week. I send you a few notes of the stirring events of the week as they came under my observation.

Bellevue Hospital
New York Saturday July 25, 1863

Dear Sister

Yours of wednesday is at hand and I read it with interest. Are the people of Geneseo, that quiet place, going to take pattern after this city and burn houses, shoot people down in the street, hang negroes to lamp posts etc. etc.? I should think they better not try it. It has been very quiet here during the past week, business has resumed, and a stranger would not know that there had been the slightest trouble in town. It looks rather strange, tis true, to see that long row of cavalry horses tied to Grammercy Park fence, the horses eating hay and switching their tails, their riders lieing on the grass or swinging on hammocks from the trees. Or in Madison Square the groups of Sibley tents with horses and men. All these are in readiness in case there might be a little trouble again. But I hope not!...

Bellevue Hospital
New York, Aug 1, 1863

Dear Sister

Yours of the 30th came to my hands yesterday. Wonderfull how prompt you are and how speedy the mail coaches. The draft seems to be all the talk in our town. I read over the list of drafted men in your town, and I see they want Fred Vance to go again? Herbert heads the list.[29] He would make a first rate captain. Tell him he had better go. There is a good representation from the Barrows family. How many I see among them who never would go or hire any body to go in their places if there was not some means like drafting started to make things go. I see also some whom I should have thought would have gone as volunteers before this....

Bellevue Hospital
New York Aug 8, 1863

Dear Sister

... It is sometimes amusing to see how people will try to smuggle liquor into the Hospital for their friends who may be patients. One of the nurses found a bottle of gin inside the body of a roast chicken. Just the other day I saw several bottles on the office table, and one of them had been filled with whiskey and put into a loaf of bread and then baked. It would not have been discovered except by the weight, it was so snugly concealed....

                                         Bellevue Hospital
                                         New York Saturday 1863
                                         [Early October][30]

Dear Frank
    ... You have heard of catching a Tartar? I dare say. Well we New Yorkers have got more than two thousand among us just now. The Emperor of Russia has sent a fleet to this port, and five vessels of war are lieing off the battery. We have been very civil to these strangers during their stay among us. On Wednesday we turned out and gave them a reception, that is, to the officers of the fleet. The sailors staid at home on shipboard to keep house. There were the Captains Skis & Skoys & the Lieutenants Novs & Noffs & Nifs & the Middies Nins & Gins & Lins & Zins & Fins. I will send you a list of them and you may study them. I never saw such a list of strange sounding names. You would think they would be a strange looking lot of men who bore them. They looked to me like Frenchmen or the higher class of Germans. The old Admiral himself looked Frenchy. They all wore black with a good deal of gold lace. The Admiral had some kind of badge dangling from his breast, but the carriage moved along so fast I could not see what it was. They all wore cocked hats like Napoleon wears in the pictures. These they doffed very gracefully to the ladies who were looking down upon them from the windows of the Fifth Avenue Houses. They rode in about a dozen open carriages. After them came the military extending more than a mile. The *Herald* tells the story and I need not say more. A ball is announced in honor of these Tartars at the Academy to come off next week. Dont you think the Emperor will love us now better than ever? I hope Napoleon will feel a little anxious when he hears how we received the Czars sailors!

                                         Bellevue Hospital
                                         Saturday 1863
                                         October

Dear Sister
    ... On Wednesday evening I sought the Halls of Science, but fell in with scenes of pleasure and conviviality before the night was far spent. I

attended the Academy of Medicine to hear Dr Leaming read a paper, A
Memoir on Dr George Cammann, his particular friend (and the inven-
tor of the Stethoscope)[31] but at the beginning of the meeting it was
announced that the Surgeons of the Russian fleet were to be present at
the meeting, and would be received in a particular manner by the
President of the society. Dr L had got fairly going with his very interesting paper when the rattle of carriages announced the arrival of somebody. With all due ceremony the committee of invitation introduced the
four Russian surgeons to the society, after which President Anderson
read them his more formal & lengthy address. How much of it they
understood we could only infer. If they did not get it all at the time, they
only have to get their dictionaries and translate it, as they find it in the
columns of the *Herald* of the following morning. We listened to the Drs
address, Dr Leaming standing before his partly read paper and, looking
as if somebody was trespassing a little, made believe he was attentive,
and the Russians kept their eyes fixed on the Dr until the close, after
which they rose and made their very profound obeisance. They could
not say anything in return unless they spoke in French or their own
tongue, which would be as familiar to most of us as the French. After
this was over, Dr Anderson invited us, Russians and all, up to his house
where he had a reception for us. The Tartars were the center of attraction to all who could converse with them. The evening passed very
pleasantly. After coffee was over I had an opportunity of taking one of
them by the hand, and exchanging a few words (badly pronounced
French words), I found Dr Johansen, surgeon of the Frigate *Peresvet*, a
very agreeable young gentleman. He wears glasses and looks like a
German. I should also say that he wears like his confreres very heavy
epauletts, and buttons of silver on his coat. We exchanged cards. I shall
see him again when the whole company visit our Institution on Tuesday
of next week. I have not had time to go down to their ships yet.

New York, Oct. 17, 63

Dear Sister,
    ... On Tuesday the French, Spanish, English and Russian naval
officers were expected to visit our institution. But when the steamer
came up there were none of the Tartars on board. What could it
mean? Did not the Bears wish to come and fraternize with the British
Lions & the French and American Eagles just for a day? We could not
exactly see the reason, accepted their apology and they agreed to
meet us on Thursday as important business demanded their attention

on board their ships. The Hospital had been scrubbed and dusted
and swept and whitewashed the day before so that the little Admiral
could commence his tour of inspection. There were about fifty of his
officers and midshipmen with him. All fine looking men as I ever saw
come off from ships. Their countenances did not present those marks
of dissipation which is so characteristic of navy men. Their mouths
looked clean & sweet as if no vile weeds were macerated there & their
eyes were not red with wine. My friend Dr Johansen was not of the
party, he having as I was told by Dr Frost got a leave of absence and
gone to the Falls of Niagara. I labor under a good deal of embarassment in not being able to speak their language and they do not speak
our language very much. It seems strange that men who look and act
so much like Americans can not understand you when you speak to
them in English. The party proceeded to the institutions on the island
after they left us, and as the *Herald* tells the story I will just send it
to you....

Bellevue Hospital
New York, Nov 8th, 1863

Dear Sister
    Tis sunday night and I must prepare my letter to you. I should
have done it before but last night I was in blood up to my elbows. It
was my first amputation. Fingers and toes have fallen to my knife
before, but last evening through the indulgence of one of our surgeons,
the scalpel was handed to me and an unfortunate man was relieved of
a horribly lacerated leg. Excuse this mention as it is my first capital
operation and my friends of the staff think me lucky. (Patient is doing
well.) It is *very* seldom that the house staff are allowed to do anything
of the sort....

Bellevue Hospital
New York, Nov 14, 1863

Dear Sister
    Tis saturday evening and the usual bloody engagements in the the-
ater have transpired this afternoon. There was a large number of students & medical men to look on and see us. The patients operated on
are doing well I thank you. There is a good deal of excitement always
attending these affairs, and I am somewhat tired when the day is

over. Some of the staff are fond of dancing & thought we had better get together in the Governors room and have a "stag dance." So for music two of the patients were invited out from the wards to play. One old man (who is my teacher on the guitar & who used to be in the Julian troop in his more palmy days), and another your German. One played on Charley Foxs fiddle and the other on my guitar, & I must confess that the music was a good deal better than the shuffling about on the floor.

Bellevue Hospital
New York Dec. 5th, 1863.

Dear Frank
... Last Wednesday evening I went over to Carries but had no difficulty in finding the place. But Carrie was not at home. She had gone down to the Island to see the boys. So Mr Ernst and I had a long, dry, inanimated discussion, about politics, war, & the certain ruin of the country if the war is continued much longer. Gold is going out of the country faster than it is coming in and when its all gone? Sure enough what will we do? Europe will not take our greenbacks. Do you know that a dollar greenback is worth in reality no more than sixty five cents in England? Mr Ernst being quite familiar with international exchanges sees the shape which things are assuming and he is more apprehensive than we who are not so well posted. But there are a few more five twenty bonds left, and we will wait till they are all used before we did ourselves bankrupt. Mr E. puffed away at his sigar, and as he returned from depositing the ashes from it in the little tray on the mantle, he suddenly inquired after you....

Dec 21st/63.
Monday Afternoon

Dear Frank
... At Goupils I found the engraving just in the place where Mr Neill saw it (same one no doubt). I asked the price & was told 17 dollars but I asked him to put the price down to the figure you gave me ($15) which he did without much hesitation. I found the Rev Mr Tompkins here looking at the works of art, and I called his attention to the picture I had just purchased and he commented in favorable terms about it. Henry Ward Beecher was here also looking at the pictures & making himself agreeable to his lady friends. I should have asked his opinion

also had he not been a stranger to me. How much Beecher reminds me of Mr Neill in his way of talking with his friends, and his voice sounds very much like Mr Neills....[32]

> Bellevue Hospital
> New York, Jan. 9th, 1864

Dear Sister

... What a good time our army must be having these days, no fighting to do, everything quiet along the lines. Have you made up your mind who you want for next President? Is it Grant? or are you satisfied with uncle Abraham? It would be a good joke for a rebel splitter to succeed a rail splitter....

> Bellevue Hospital
> New York Jan 23rd 1864

Dear Sister,

... I see [Stephen] Fosters funeral noticed in the paper. I dare say you are familiar with one of the tunes which was played at his funeral. I wonder if "Gentle Annie" will mourn his loss. He was very eccentric....[33]

> February
> Bellevue Hospital
> New York, Saturday 8 PM, 1863

Dear Sister

... While gazing at the fire and alternately writing to you, an accident case came in the Hospital. A little boy had been run over by the cars crushing his leg very badly. He was carried to one of my wards & as it was a case for amputation I sent out for Dr Smith, my counseling physician, to come and cut it off (the leg). When he came he told me to go ahead and amputate, which I did with that kind of pleasure which no one but a surgeon can feel. This amputation was made at the junction of the lower & middle of the thigh with a double flap of integument & a circular incision of the muscles. Dr Brownwell tied the vessells, and we made just the finest stump you ever saw. *I suppose you will enjoy these particulars.* I am a little ahead of the others of the staff on capital operations, but I only tell *you* of these things....

Bellevue Hospital
New York Mar 5, 64.

Dear Sister
    ... I saw a novel sight to day, and it was a negro regiment of
Infantry. They landed from the boat at the foot of 26th St, and paraded
up to the city. I never saw so many "niggers" to gether in my life, and
they made a very fine appearance. Their uniform is the same as other
privates wear and with their white gloves and white leggings they looked
well. There was every shade of colour from a light tan to that of a charcoal black. An escort of two hundred police men cleared the way as they
went "marching along"....[34]

Bellevue Hospital
New York March 12, 64.

Dear Sister
    ... Ramsey Newton calls the attention of the people to himself. He is
certainly a very enterprising young man to go away off into the center of
the Rocky Mountains, and dig for gold. Perhaps he will make as much
money as the cotton planters. In fact I am unable to prognose anything
in regard to this cotton speculation. I never had heard anything about
the thing till these letters from the boys came to hand.[35] There is no
doubt but that cotton is as good as gold when you get it, but the thing is
to get it. I shall send the *Observers* to the boys care of Washington
Hotel, etc. Be sure and send me their letters and I will return them if
you wish. Do you understand that they have thrown up all their interests in St Louis? Sam does not seem to have liked St Louis very much. I
wonder if a more Southern point will agree with him any better? I shall
be done with this Hospital by the first of the month and I wonder if I
had not best go down and raise cotton too....[36]

Part III
The Devil and Mr. Lincoln

Introduction

During his voyage to California of nearly a month's duration, the war was much on Lauderdale's mind, perhaps all the more for the lack of any news. He wrote to Frank from the Gulf of California on April 10:

> Just think of us passengers who have been without a single item of news for nearly three weeks! What may not have happened in that time? What battles may have been fought? What victories won? What victorious general has made his triumphant entry into Richmond? Who captured Jeff Davis? What day has been set for his execution? An account of his penance in his cell? What his confessions were to his ministerial attendants? All these events as portrayed by Frank Leslie's ubiquitous artists have not been furnished us. We are entirely cut off from that part of the earth called the United States, although our good minister forgot his temporary isolation yesterday, when he prayed for "these states in which we live that are rent with civil war," etc.

Posted to what he referred to as "Tent Life in the Holy Land of Mormonism" in Utah Territory, Lauderdale lived in spare quarters under extremely raw conditions, but his medical duties were generally not heavy. Writing in May from Camp Conness, he told Frank: "I wish I was in Washington to attend some of those poor fellows who have been mutilated in the recent battles. There must be a demand for Surgeons in the East just at this time." Ironically, nothing he witnessed among the sick and wounded soldiers aboard the *January* seems to have brought home to him the tragedy of the war as much as the loss of his brother Samuel, in June of 1864. Samuel's death in Vicksburg, of a combination of dysentery and typhoid fever, had nothing directly to do with the war and was thus a powerful shock to the family. In a doleful letter, beginning "Last evenings mail brought to me the saddest news that I ever received from home," Lauderdale wrote to his mother: "If dear Sammy

177

had been a soldier in the army, or was in any position where his life would be endangered, I should have been prepared for the sad news." But this civilian death, partly because it was, in fact, so swift and unexpected, plunged him into a deeper level of empathy with those who had lost loved ones in the war.

> I have often thought that we do not fully realize the amount of grief which is felt by those who mourn, untill we lose a friend ourselves. Now, we can 'weep with those that weep if we never could before.' How many times during this war, have I thought, when hearing of the many instances of families mourning the loss of a son or brother killed in battle, what a kind Providence was watching over us. The arrows of death have been falling thick and fast of late, and we could not expect to move along unharmed.

Lauderdale was markedly devoid of any sympathetic feeling toward the Mormons. He found them completely at odds with the Federal Army, who regarded the area's large Mormon community as an avowed archenemy of the United States Government, an enemy who would not shrink from aiding Jefferson Davis to bring it down. In Lauderdale's view, this was not because Mormons supported slavery—Mormons, he felt, would never associate with blacks—but because they wished to establish a government of their own. "The Mormons cherish a *saintly* feeling of ill will towards the people of northern states," he wrote to Frank on May 8, 1864, "by reason of the persecution which they suffered at their hands while seeking to propagate one of the most sinful doctrines that ever was known in the minds of any people." He was dismayed to find Brigham Young and his followers using the chaos of the war to support a doctrine of imminent doom for the federal government. "Jeff Davis stands as the representative of one kind of human bondage and Brigham Young of another. Both are said to be divine institutions, and for the good of the human race." Young, he felt, had become a millionaire at "the game of swindling the ignorant and degraded portion of mankind" and from "base traffic in human flesh." He explained to Frank that the Army planned to destroy the Mormon stronghold in Utah by protecting all non-Mormon interests in mineral mining, which it was hoped would create a majority that could control electoral power. Practically every soldier owned "feet" in the mines—which were known as "the ledges"—and the Army was doing its best to encourage every prospective miner who was a "gentile."

Lauderdale had always abhorred Mormonism, ranking Mormons, along with bogus spiritualists, as a "dangerous class of believers" who should be hunted out of the land. It is therefore not surprising that, living in camps close to the Mormon center in Salt Lake City, Lauderdale sanctioned the Army's policy, especially now that he looked upon even a trace of Confederate sympathy as delaying the long-awaited end of the war. What is surprising, however, is the sudden complete turnabout in Lauderdale's position with respect to political parties. Between mid-July and early September of 1864, he stopped ridiculing Lincoln (who for the first time he referred to as "Mr. Lincoln"); he saw the Copperheads as traitors who were doing the Devil's work; and, seemingly overnight, he became a staunch—even radical—Republican. The record of this shift, and Lauderdale's response to the end of the war, comprise the final section of letters in this volume.

Lauderdale officially joined the Regular Army in 1866. He was appointed Assistant Surgeon in 1867, and in 1880 he became a Surgeon and a Major. His long career encompassed a richly varied itinerary, including Camp Douglas, Camp Relief, and Camp Conness, Utah Territory; Fort Bridger (then in Utah Territory), Wyoming; Fort Wardwell, Colorado; Fort Yuma (then in California) and Camp Lowel, Arizona; Fort Wood, Fort Hamilton, and Fort Wadsworth in New York Harbor; Presidio Barracks in San Francisco, California; Fort Adams, Rhode Island; Fort Leavenworth, Kansas; Fort Wingate, New Mexico Territory; Mount Vernon Barracks, Alabama; Newport Barracks, Kentucky; McPherson Barracks, Georgia; New Orleans and Jackson Barracks, Louisiana; Fort Sully, Dakota; Fort Concho, Fort Clark, and Fort Davis, Texas; Fort Ontario, New York; Fort Omaha, Nebraska; and Fort Wayne, Michigan. He went with General Sherman to Zuni, New Mexico in 1878; in December of 1890 he was detailed to the Pine Ridge Agency, South Dakota, to treat wounded soldiers after the Battle of Wounded Knee; and in July of 1894 he was sent with troops dispatched to extinguish the Chicago Pullman Strike. His journals and letters comprise a fascinating portrait of the life of an Army doctor in the nineteenth century, featuring finely detailed descriptions of his encounters with various Native American peoples, in whom he took an intense interest and concerning whom he wrote one of his few published essays. In 1896 he retired to a house on 84th Street in Brooklyn. When he died in January of 1931 at the age of ninety-nine, he was the oldest officer in the United States Army.

The Letters

Camp Conness, U.T.
July 8th 1864

Dear Frank
   ... How do you & Father feel about Mr L for the next President? I have not heard that there is any other candidate in the field except Fremont and none but the radical abolitionists will support him. McClellans monumental speech at West Point was good. He can attend to the production of literary effusions nowadays as he is retired from any duties involving effusions of blood....

Camp Conness, U.T.
July 14, 1864

Dear Frank
   ... I had about made up my mind to let Lincoln keep his seat in the Presidential chair. I never gave L any credit for his proclamation because I never could see that it did any good. Everything could have been done for the slave that has been, if there had been no proclamation, so I cannot give him credit for that. So what has he (Mr L) done to recommend himself more than any man would do in his official capacity? I don't see anything! What has McClellan done to recommend himself? I do not know of anything in particular. He has always "behaved himself like a gentleman" I believe. This very fact is made light of by his enemies. His fighting qualities never will allow him to be equal to Grant because he is differently constituted. But I should think him as well qualified for the Presidency as Grant and better still. I had thought as the war began with Republican rulers in office I

My tent at Camp Conness, N.Y. May 20th 1864

would allow them to remain until peace was established. But this is not the way they have done with their military commanders. Since Genl Scott was removed they have made several changes. How would it do now to make a change in the occupant of the Executive chair? with a host of changes in positions of minor importance?.... As a Democrat I do not know of any man who is more prominent among the Democrats than McClellan or would receive more votes than he if he should be bid on for President.... But I am no politician and cannot discuss the subject well. I am a long distance from headquarters and have no papers which discuss politics with any degree of wisdom, but each clamors loudly for party & position. Send me something which you think is good!

Camp Conness
Saturday Evening, Sept 3rd, '62

Dear Frank
...The burden of the telegrams is the proceedings of the Democratic convention held at Chicago. The resolutions passed, are about as I

thought they would be. Democratic enough to suit the most ultra. But I have very little idea that McClellan will be elected. It does not seem as though the Rebels would consent to the Chicago platform, and come back into the old Union and join hands with the Yankees of the Republican persuasion. And I am quite sure the administration party will not come over to the Chicago platform. So here we stand a divided North, the same as we were five years ago, and if Fremont does not withdraw we are in just as many pieces as we were on the eve of the Election of Mr Lincoln.... The Republicans and all who join hands with them are in reality a revolutionary party. They have not lived up to the constitution, and they have made no more use of it than was necessary for them to carry out their plans. They have made some pretensions to carry out the principles of our civil government, but only such as did not touch the Slavery question. When they came into power their sentiment was written upon their banners, "no extension of Slavery," which means "Death to slavery," in a word. The will of the majority touching this question, Slavery, shall not be decided by the ballot box but by the sword. The Chicago convention shows [the Democrats] are not willing to join in the revolutionary movement against slavery. I do not know whether to blame them for adhering to their principles or to admire them.... The convention seems to be silent on the slavery question. I would like to know... whether they will if they get into power do anything for or against that institution. I think that we may as well set aside all Constitution, Democratic principles, and everything else, and let all the North join forces against the Slave Power and destroy it out of the land. Then we can begin anew. Make a new Constitution, and let it be our guide for a while until something else turns up, Popery, Idolatry, Polygamy, or some other evil gains an ascendancy, then let the people wise up again and overthrow that condition of things. But let us see the hand of God in all this for he has said He will overturn & overturn until he shall have brought all things under him. There will be rebelions and revolutions just as long as the Devil continues going up and down in this earth. Remember that the arch rebel of the universe is poisoning the minds of men to do evil. He made trouble in Heaven and was driven out and since [then] he has infused a rebelious spirit among the people of our country. Now as the Democrats have not appeared to take the right position against the slave power or the rebels, I think that I must leave them and join that party who have for their object the extermination of slavery. The object is a good one, it seems to me, and if death comes while thus engaged, I do not know of a more glorious death to die. It will be a very easy thing to draft another Constitution and we will remember and acknowledge the existence of God in it. Civil government is a human creation and is not infallible. I am sure that the principles of the

Democratic party can be improved upon & I would advise my friends
who have clung to them for so long to lay them aside for the present and
strike a blow at the demon slavery. I know it is hard for them to part with
time worn and honoured institutions but let them summon up courage as
I did the other day when I put off a pair of old scratched boots and put on
a better pair....

> Head Quarters 2nd Cavalry
> Camp Conness, Sep 7th/64

Dear Frank
   ... Last news says "Atlanta is taken." Thats good! Now let us hear of
the taking of Mobile & then Richmond. It is too late to talk now about
Peace negotiations. We must keep the ball rolling until it has crushed out
the spirit of rebelion and we can dictate the terms of peace ourselves....

> [Camp Douglas, Salt Lake City, U.T.]
> Friday Evening Oct. 7

Dear Sister,
   It was reported in Camp to day that our eastern mail has come. It
turned out to be a rumor only. It is a miserable state of things to be on the
line of a mail route and get no communications of any kind. But I do not
feel so bad about this matter as I do when I think how our country is
fairly *drenched in blood*. Was there ever a nation thus called upon to sac-
rifice its sons? It seems as if the entire generation of fighting men will be
sacrificed before the end sought will be obtained. I presume you have
read the account of the interview between Cols Gilmore & Jacques and
the Rebel cabinet in Richmond. Did you ever hear of a more determined
set of men and withall so artful in maintaining the justness of their base
designs? The question of slavery is hardly broached, all they contend for
is the right of self-government? Nothing but the entire extermination of
such men will do. The slave oligarchy must be crushed out, we cannot
allow our country to be governed any longer by a lot of aristocrats. We
had better choose a king and be done with Republican principles. This is
not so much a rebellion as it is a great revolution. I wish that the whole
North might see it in just this light, and then I think there would be no
division of sentiment in our present political platforms. I cannot believe
that you are looking forward with sincere hopes for the election of
McClellan and his den of Copperheads. If you are, I would like to know

where I could have a talk with you, and convince you that you are not quite right "on the goose." I hope my first letter from you will contain your political sentiments, and I would like to hear Fathers opinion on the war, and Willis, I would like to know how he views things relating to politics and our present struggle. I hope you are on the side of the administration, at this time any way. I regret that I am so far away from you, that I cannot advise with you, and still more do I regret that I am living in a territory where (I learn) there will be no election. I think that all those connected with the army should be allowed to vote, no matter where they happen to be stationed. I have no late papers so that I know very little of the political discussions that fill the pages of your political journals.

Saturday Morning [October 8]

I have just been reading an article in an old number of *Putnams* magazine (Dec/54) entitled "Our Partys and Politics." It is full of treason and secession prophecy which is now finding its litteral fulfillment. It seems strange to me that when there were so many prophets at the South foretelling secession... there were not an equal number of them at the North foretelling the same event and making preparations for the great conflict which must inevitably follow. The North must become a unit otherwise we can never expect to gain any ascendancy over the South, which has always been united so far as its leading and influential men are concerned. Here is a "sentiment" from a historian whose observations have been world wide and which may cheer us in this our great struggle for a permanent peace.

[Journal clipping attached to the letter] A Sentiment from Motley.—There was never peace well made without a mighty war preceding, and always the sword in hand is the best pen to write the conditions of peace.
Buckhurst to Queen Elizabeth

Fort Bridger, Utah Territory
Lat. 41°, 18'. 12" Long 110°, 32', 23"
Barometric Altitude above the Gulf
of Mexico 7010 ft.
Wednesday October 12th 1864

Dear Frank
.... Am sorry to hear that you are for Little Mack, for President! I have already given you my opinion on the subject of the next President

and it is useless for me to say more. This letter could not reach you in time to do any good as an electioneering document, but from my point of observation "away up here among the mountains," I think you are not on the right side of the fence, and I hope ere this you are hurrahing for Uncle Abraham to be our next President.... I regret exceedingly that there are two parties striving for the Presidency. The news by telegraph today from Missouri is dark. The Rebels are gaining ground in that state more than I like to hear of....

P.S. In case this reaches you before the election let me entreat of you to do all in your power for the election of Uncle Abraham and bringing an end to the war. I wish you could vote for me and I would have you poll a vote for old Abe. I cannot see that the so called copperhead party are anything but traitors, and they must not succeed. I know they will not any way. I wish they would just join hands with the Republicans until the rebelion is crushed, and then they may vote for whom they please....

Fort Bridger, U.T.
November 8th 1864

Dear Sister [1]
This day decides who is to be our next President. As soon as Lodge meeting is over I shall step over to the telegraph room and with Mr Eddys permission will read the news that may be pressing along the wires. I expect to read of nothing but defeat to the friends of McClellan. I regret that any of my friends are working about the polls today for his election. I did tell you once this summer that I thought a change in the administration would be well but of late I think different. I am sorry that there are two candidates in the field, not because I fear that the result will be a defeat to Mr Lincoln, but the fact that we of the North are a divided people still. I hope that the returns from this election will show that those opposed to the present administration are *greatly* inferior to those in favor of Mr Lincoln. The Nevada troops who are at this post have been casting their votes to day. I, belonging to the State of New York, and not having received any votes, am not allowed to do any balloting. The one great fact is this. *We must conquer the South*, we must "make them come down," however rebelious they may seem. In order to do this handsomely and effectually, we must be a unit and act as one man led by a single motive, that of putting down this giant rebelion or *rebel lion*.... This very day, the Rebels are hoping that McClellan will be elected in order that they may influence him in their behalf and

get him to make some concessions to them. There are a great many people talking about the constitution and squaring everything by that rule. But I tell you that there is no constitution any more (what applies to all people north and south). The very *first bombshell* which the Rebels sent across Charleston Harbor into Fort Sumter broke the constitution all to smash as if it had been an egg. Who ever heard of mending a broken egg shell, replacing its contents, and making it as good as it was at first? The thing cannot be done. Uncle Abraham has been trying to patch onto the sides of this broken Constitution egg, but it is no use, the thing is spoilt for all future use in its present demolished state. Shall we save the elements of this broken egg? Certainly. We will lay them by for the present and when our national bird shall have recovered from her present illness she shall have them for food, and in obedience to Natures laws she will produce another egg, perfectly fresh and pure, which will be in embryo and miniature an expression of her entire self.... It is no use for us to be fettered by the rules of an old tattered & torn and patched up Constitution. I go in for a fight, the entire North pitted against the South or as much of it is in arms against us. We are clearly justified in this course because the South began the fight. And not until the victory is fairly won need we talk about the constitution, or discuss state rights, or the slavery question.... Some of the anti-administrations papers speak of Mr Lincoln as an autocrat and a despot, but I would like to know if he is any more of a despot than Jeff Davis? I hear that you have taken your position on this great subject from the statements made in the McClellan journals. You must remember that such documents are written in false colors and are intended for electioneering purposes, and are not to be believed altogether. I have looked upon the election as a useless proceeding. Defeat to McClellan has been a foregone conclusion. He knew it would be so, otherwise he would have resigned his position in the army.... I have read all the clippings which you have kindly furnished me from the McClellan journals, but I can not find one sentiment that I can endorse, or sympathise with the writers thereof. I hope we shall get the returns in a few days that will decide who is to sit in the Executive chair for the next four years.

Fort Bridger, U.T.
Saturday Evening, Nov 12th 1864

[Dear Sister]
    ... *I admit that the administration has made many blunders*, but what people would not, if undertaking such a new and mighty business

as putting down this great rebelion? It takes a wise and good man to rule a wayward child, and it requires the same virtues in a people who would seek to bring a rebelious people to their allegiance. If we of the North were a better people I dare say we should have succeeded in our purpose before this time.... The war of our former revolution was a ten years struggle, this has lasted but less than four years. See what we then effected? And this is but a circumstance compared to what we shall bring about before the close of the present war. *We can endure the struggle* quite as long as our enemies, and dont let us give up yet....

Fort Bridger, U.T.
Saturday Evening Dec 3rd, 1864

Dear Sister,
...Well! "They that go to sea the gods forsake." I am sorry that the election is such a bitter pill for you to swallow. A "military gentleman" and a "christian statesman," will do well enough in time of peace to construct fortifications, and sit in the executive chair. But in time of war we want men of fighting ability like Grant & Sherman & Sheridan with an executive who will let these men have the men and means at their disposal to decide the great question by the force of arms. You censure the Proclamation of Andy Johnson. I agree with him that "Rebels must be dumb" or go South, & I think when he proclaims freedom to the blacks of Tennesee that he is fully satisfied that these same slaves are in the possession of rebel sympathisers....

Fort Bridger, U.T.
March 4th 1865,
Saturday Evening

Dear Sister
This is the day that was to have been a very interesting occasion to the friends of Genl McClellan? But man proposes and God disposes....

Fort Bridger, U.T.
April 7th 1865

Dear Sister,
But what glorious news have come over our wire this week? *Richmond* and *Petersburgh* evacuated! On wednesday at twelve o'clock,

our light artillery assembled on the parade ground, and our two howitzers opened their mouths thirty-six times and proclaimed our victories
over the rebelion.... To day we hear that *Lees army has surrendered*! If
that is so, our four years war is about ended, and the prayers of this
nation are soon to be answered. But I wait anxiously for the particulars
of this grand conflict. The mails come along so irregularly, and we have
to wait so long before we get the details of news, that I become very
impatient. How great the contrast between this place and New York. I
have no *Herald* or *Times* to read or Extra to buy that I may read the
latest dispatches. We have no newsboys running through our streets in
breathless haste to sell their papers. It is hard for a New Yorker to come
down to such slow coaches we have to wait upon out here....

Fort Bridger, U.T.
Saturday April 15th/65

How unexpectedly and suddenly is our rejoicing turned into mourn-
ing! The announcement this morning in garrison that Our President was
assassinated last evening while sitting in his private box at the
Washington Theater was scarcely believed by any of us. I went immediately to the Telegraph office and there it was on the strip of paper in
Chicago's writing. And a little later, word came that Sewards wound
proved fatal also. Is this the commencement of anarchy? I cannot think
so. But rather I believe it to have been brot about by some desponding
rebel clique who would make one more mad effort to sustain their hope-
less cause. The heroic gladiators of the old Roman ampitheatre would
sometimes fall a victim to the last dying stroke of the infuriated wild
beast, and the slayer and the slain would breathe out their life at the
same instant. Thus has the hydra headed monster rebelion perished and
this last act pronounces it to be more than ever the child of the Devil.
Our flag will float today at half mast all over the land, and will commemorate an event the like of which in all its parts was never equalled
since our nation became a republic.[2] What chief magistrate ever fell a
victim to an assassin? Looking over the history of kings and emperors
we find those who have perished in this way. But who would have
thought such a bloody deed could have been enacted by any but some
fiend let up from the infernal regions, much [less] by a citizen of this
would-be christian land. A deep gloom has hung over our garrison to
day. Every soldier feels sad. The minstrels have no heart to sing, and
the concert will be postponed....

Yours affectionately
John

Appendix A

Walter Lauderdale on the Draft

Geneseo Aug 13th/63
John V. Lauderdale

Dear John

Your last letter I have laid away so carefully that I cannot now find it, but I will try to answer from recollection. In reference to the Draft, if you should be so unfortunate as to be drawn I would advise you at once to make application for a Commission as Surgeon or Assistant in some Military Hospital or Regiment. If you do not succeed your next best plan would be to commute by payment of $300. The latter would be better than to serve as a common soldier. I do not believe that you can endure the fatigue & hardship. If you are drafted get a recommend from some of your head Surgeons for a situation. If I could assist you by going to Albany & seeing the Governor & Surgeon General I would do so. If you are drafted would not the Commissioners of Public Charities ask the Government to excuse you inasmuch as you are rendering service & time gratuitously in the position you now hold? I do not think the authorities would be so unfair as to compel you to leave your hospital as long as you get no pay. How is it have you had any conversations with any of the managers of your Institution on this subject? Of the drafted men in this district I do not think that over one in five will go into the Service. All would get exempted if they could & of those who are not exempted only those who cannot raise the $300. will go, which will reduce the number who will actually go into the Service to a very small per centage.

191

We could have raised double the number by Volunteer enlistment in this Town to those who will go under the Draft, especially if a small Bounty had been offered. Our Army needs reinforcing & it should be done as speedily as possible, but the compulsory plan is liable to many grave objections & I fear it will not be popular nor effectual.

... The mail is just in.... [Willis] is undecided about coming home, may come in September. Says if he is drafted he will go into the service, thinks the Democrats not as patriotic as they ought to be, thinks they should rush [to] the rescue....

Trul & Aff. yours

W. E. Lauderdale

Appendix B
The Plantation Letters of Willis and
Samuel Lauderdale

[March 1864][1]
On board the *J.C. Sevon*
bound for Vicksburg Miss

My dear Sister Frances,
    [Willis] has hired a Plantation of about 300 acres and is going to raise cotton. He engaged two Plantations but was afraid he would not have time to get so large a crop in and he released one to some Yankees from Maine. We of course were born & brought up in St. Louis—at least so the people in Vicksburg think. The Plantation is on the Big Black River on the Railway running to Jackson—you can see it on the map or at least the vicinity. The Plantation is owned by a widow lady whose husband was not killed in the Rebel army but died a natural death. There are right about there Vg widows, all twenty nice plantations and without the means to work them, so you need not be astonished if we marry some of the plantations. Willis was fortunate in finding a nice farm with all the fences and cabins, the House etc. in splendid order and not the least of the considerations is the fact that the house is a very fine one, elegantly furnished, Grand Piano and all that sort of thing. The lady is to keep house and we live with her.... Adjoining Willis' plantation a Mr. Sherman has hired 1500 acres and proposes to go into it extensively. He is of the firm of Sherman Bros, New York City. He came up to St Louis to purchase mules & all articles necessary to

such a large farm. He has on board 90 or 100 mules, 60 tons of freight, and they are in my care. He is going back to N.Y. leaving in Vicksburg his brother in law to take charge of things there, Willis following tomorrow on the *Pauline Carroll* with his things, 16 horses & 40 or 50 tons of freight.

... Mr. Sherman is a splendid man, perfect gentleman and a churchman. Am perfectly delighted with him. We dined with him two or three times at the Lindell Hotel. He has more confidence in Willis, I think, than in his brother-in-law and I will probably render them assistance, at least Mr S insinuated something to that effect....

I had to resign my position in the Bank on account of my health but am now in splendid health. St Louis is such a miserable climate, I dont know how any one lives there & enjoys good health. (This boat trembles so I cant write it so you can read it, I'm afraid). One manages to take on any quantity of dirt. What he does not from the awful dirty streets he will in the water he drinks....

> Love to the family
> Good bye
> Yours affec
> Sam

> On Board Saint Louis and New
>   Orleans
> Passenger Steamer *Pauline Carroll*
> Between St Louis & Cairo 1864
> March 4th

Dear Sister
  You would like to know the reason of my long silence. Well I have been travelling for six weeks constantly. I left St Louis the last of January for the south with no definite object in view except to see if I could better my condition in a worldly point. My first locality was Memphis. Nothing there presented itself worthy my attention so I pushed on down to Vicksburg. Here I found hundreds of Northern speculators who were engaged in all sorts of trades, Cotton carrying being the great business. I also found many going into Cotton raising. This struck me as the best thing I could go into, so getting a horse and several letters of introduction to once wealthy Planters, I started on an exploring expedition. I was well received wherever I went. For a circle of six

miles around Vicksburg the fences are all gone, also the houses. As you go further into the country the Plantations are in good order minus the Negros and Mules. If you look on the Map of Mississippi you will see running east from Vicksburg the Jackson rail-road. This is a military road and is in good order as far as Big Black River 12 miles. About 3 miles south west from the junction of the Rail road with the river and on the west side of the river there lives a Widow lady by the name of Bolls, who has a beautiful Plantation of 250 Acres under cultivation with fine gin house, good Negro Quarters, good fences, fine Residence, and house handsomely furnished. Mrs Bolls is 39 years of age with 5 interesting children. The war has left her as it has all the Planters without money, Mules or Slaves, consequently she is unable to grow Cotton. Now Mrs Bolls and I were pleased with each other and have entered into the following agreement. "Know all men by these Presents that I Susan Bolls of the county of Warren in the State of Mississippi have this day granted bargained and leased unto Willis E. Lauderdale of the county and State aforesaid the Plantation upon which I now reside, situated about 10 miles from Vicksburg, about east and adjoining the Plantation of Mrs etc. etc. Brabstons, said lease to continue until January [page torn] 1865. The terms and conditions of the above [page torn] that the said Lauderdale is to have the entire use and control of said Plantation, The Tools and farming Implements thereon, The Cotton seed for use of the Place and Wood and other things thereon which is or may be necessary for the Plantation, and the said Lauderdale is to pay to said Bolls the one fifth part of the Cotton Crop so raised or the nett proceeds thereof, and allow her to reside on said Plantation, and to furnish her Table with usual supplies and she with her family to have egress and ingress to and from her said residence, said Bolls to pay at the end of the year for the supplies furnished her by said Lauderdale. Witness our hands and seals on the 13th day of February A.D. 1864."

| Attest | Susan Bolls (Seal) |
| Lee Houghton | Willis E. Lauderdale (Seal) |

So you see I am a resident of Warren County Mississippi and a Cotton Planter, quite a sudden change you perhaps think. I left Vicksburg February 20th and reached St Louis the 26th. After purchasing my supplies I left St Louis yesterday for my new house in Mississippi. I have on [? board] of this Steamer (which by the way is a new Boat, this being her second trip, and the finest Steam Boat that ever floated on the Mississippi river, she is magnificent) some 20 Tons of freight and 16 head of fine horses. My freight consists of Plows Harrows Corn Oats Hay

Molasses Coffee Sugar Cotton Cloth Boats Shoes Hoes Pork Hams Harness Salt etc. etc., everything necessary for use on a Plantation. I am in hopes to reach Vicksburg by Tuesday morning and get to Plowing as soon as possible as the planting season begins the first of April. I have engaged a good Overseer, a Man who has planted Cotton all his life. I shall have to hire my hands from the government freed slaves. They are plenty and anxious to work, as they have been starving long enough. I shall work about 30 hands, Men & Women. Mrs Bolls has a few Mules and several servants that have never left her. These I shall hire. These freed men are classified by Government Agents. A No 1 man gets $25 per month, No 2 $20, etc. No 1 Woman $20 per month, No 2 $15, etc. I have to keep a store on my Plantation and sell to my hands. They have to pay for everything they eat or wear. I furnish [? all] these at cost and 15 per cent added for Transportation. [page torn] if I am successful in securing a Crop. As I am so near Vicksburg and surrounded by our Troops, I dont anticipate any danger from the Rebels. All the Plantations along the Big Black River from the Rail Road Bridge for twenty miles down are being worked by Northern Men, giving the owner a small share of the Crops. Cotton is worth in Vicksburg 65 cents per pound. An average yeald on my place would be 200 Bales of Cotton, 400 pounds in a Bale.

200	Bales
400	Pounds
80,000	
65	Cents
400,000	
4,800,000	
$52,000.00	
7,000	Expenses
$45,000	Profits

The probabilities are that Cotton will be worth one dollar a pound by January 1865. Of course there is some risk attending this Cotton raising, but the chances look favorable now. When I got back to St Louis I found Sam had been quite sick and been obliged to give up his situation at the Bank, so I concluded he had better go with me. Mr Sherman of New York who has leased a Plantation adjoining me wanted some one to go down with his goods and Sam left with them on the Steamer *J. C.*

Sevon one day ahead of me, but as the Boat I am on is much the fastest, I think I will get there first. We will reach Cairo about 4 Oclock this evening where I will mail my letters. Direct my letters to Care of Washington Hotel, Vicksburg. The Proprietor is an old Chicago acquaintance. I shall have to come to Vicksburg every few days. I have been so busy that I have had no time to write before. Frank, I wish you would copy this letter and send to John as I shall not have time between this and Cairo. I will try and keep you posted as to movements. Give my best love to all and write often.

Yours Affectionately
Willis E. Lauderdale

Direct Washington Hotel
V-g Miss
March 20 1864

My dear Mother:
...We had very pleasant passengers on board and a great many unpleasant ones—the 46th Ill Vol. They were on their way to join Sherman having enlisted & been home on furlough. A more ungovernable lot of fellows I never before met. Their officers had no control over them whatever and it was a continuous riot with them. At Cairo the *Pauline Carroll* arrived just before we left—had a few moments talk with Willis.... Willis assured me they would be in V-g before we were. We amused ourselves on the trip down by eating, reading, playing whist, dancing, talking, no walking—except with me. I used to go down aft and look at the mules—on account of the soldiers taking every bit of room outside of the Cabin and the Cabin was crowded so they had to fill it with Cots at night to accomodate the passengers, a perfect jam. We would watch with interest for all the points of Military interest, Columbus, Island No 10, Skippers Landing, Helena, etc. etc....
Between the morning service & dinner there was some excitement by one [of] the soldiers feigning to be crazy or having the delerium tremens and would not allow any one to come in his room—he had been given a room on account of his sickness—and cut his Captain very badly. Finally one of his Co having more courage than the rest took a gun & knocked the door in. When the door fell the fellow rushed & tried his best to kill the one that was trying to capture him & succeeded in stabbing him severely, though not dangerously. He was knocked down &'

ironed. In the evening a woman who claimed to be a medium addressed the Ladies. I happened to be present, and heard her remarks. When the doors between the Ladies and Gentlemens Cabins were closed she wished some one present would play the Guitar that she might be thrown into a trance. The Guitar was produced & played. In a very few minutes she was fully under the control of the spirits and went on with her nonsense. What she said did not amount to anything. So passed Sunday on the *J.C. Sevon* on the Mississippi.

... Reached Vicksburg Wednesday morning in a fearful rain storm, notwithstanding which the boat discharged her cargo, and the consequence was I had to fly around, find the man the goods were consigned to—Mr Burnham—get a permit to land there, find drays, & store room, and all that sort of thing. Sent for Burnham first. He finally came down and I found in a few moments conversation with him that he knew nothing at all, that is for business of this kind, he being a young New York lawyer. So I went at it, rec'd the goods, having first got permission to land them, checked them off & got drays to haul them to a store house and all this in the rain. If it had not rained, wouldn't have cared much about it. It took all that afternoon & the next morning until 12 o'clock.

The first person I saw as I was coming off the boat that morning about daylight was Willis, he having arrived in the night. So after all his talking he did not make the trip as quick as we did. After I got through with Burnhams goods, went & assisted Will with his which took until night. Next day his man, himself & myself took each of us four horses (Willis') & started forth for Bolls Plantation, which is by a very midling road thirteen miles but in an air line six or eight. Found everything as nice as he had pictured it (you no doubt rec'd an elaborate description), a very large fine house situated in a grove of stately trees from which hangs the long tufts of moss, a broad graveled road circuiting from the main road to the front gallery of the Mansion, from the rear of which a short walk down a gentle slope brings you to the broad Cotton fields, which extend for a mile or two to the east and are skirted by a forest to the east of which runs the Big Black. The fields contain one or two hundred acres. South from the house about a quarter of a mile the Negro Cabins are situated—they are very comfortable quarters in good condition, each cabin having a small piece of ground for a garden in which they (the nigs) can work saturday afternoons, which time they always want to themselves. The stables & out buildings are all in comparatively good condition, a fine door yard, the shrub'ry of which is kept very closely trimmed by a few goats, which I advised Mrs Bolls to kill for Mutton—completes the picture—external—of "Oakwoods." The House is very nicely furnished indeed and much to my gratification contains a fine Piano. Besides Mrs

Bolls and four children, the oldest about sixteen, youngest two or three. Mrs Bolls is a very nice lady & the children are the smartest & best natured I ever saw. They all understand every thing about raising Cotton. Mrs Bolls is a Methodist and always asks a blessing at the table....

There are four men boarding here who are working the adjoining plantation, the same farm that Willis first leased and they the persons he leased it to. All Maine men—Yanks. They will remain here until they get their house fixed & furnished, when they will keep house themselves.

My portion of the business is to attend to the afr's [affairs?], issue rations, run around after hands and go with the teams to town for supplies. There are quite a number of riding horses in the lot we brought down and I of course always have my horse to ride.

...We were a little late & afraid will be behind with the plowing, but everything is going off finely & we are getting along faster than any of our neighbors.

... [Willis] attends to the farming himself, prefering to have no overseer. We all get up very early & go to bed early, generally by ten o'clock, enjoy splendid health. I weigh about forty-five—that is, 145—pounds, got a good tan on our faces & hands....

I am sitting in our room with a nice fire, for it is quite cool—have not got far enough south for warm weather it seems. We have the best chamber in the House and live very nicely.

Love to you all your
affec. son
Sam
Oakwoods Mar 20th/64

Mrs Bolls Plantation
Near Vicksburg
Apr 3, [1864]²

My dear Sister Frances:

As your demand was so moderate I will do my best to comply with it. Will write once in two weeks with great pleasure. We were so glad to get such a fine lot of letters from home—Mothers, Bob's, & your own, all were truly welcome. I have not your letters with me now, Will has them, and if I fail to answer any of your numerous questions, just ask them again.

In the first place, then, our health is splendid. I never felt better in my life, think this out door business is just the thing exactly. The climate here is delightful, dont have the extreme heat as in St Louis & New York. The only objection to the place is, there are no churches nearer than Vicksburg which is twelve miles distant and they are not open. All the ministers have gone to the confederacy. There were two churches near here but the Federals very needlessly burned them when they came in from Grand Gulf to the seige of Vicksburg. Mrs Bolls has an elegant carriage and we brought down a perfectly splendid pair of horses which we would gladly take advantage of if there was any place of worship to attend. It will not probably be long before some of the churches in the city will open. There is a Scholl House on the grounds here & we may come to a "Nigger" preacher among some of the hands. If we do we will have him enlighten some of his "brevem" with his knowledge of the Gospel.

Have commenced on the second plowing, getting along much faster than we anticipated. Have employed twenty five hands, Men & Women, and Twenty Horses & Mules. The women make just as good field hands as the men, can plough equally as well, and the people say at picking cotton they are much better. Pay the first class hands $25. per month and so on down, sell them the rations at what they cost to get them here. In good many instances a hundred per cent cheaper than they can be got in Vicksburg. Deal them out every Saturday evening.

This Plantation is the very best on Black River, there is none equal to it, though the most of them are much larger. Will put in about three hundred acres to Cotton, nothing else unless a little corn for feed. The probable chances are, the planters on the Big Black will not be disturbed by the confederates, as they are interested very greatly that we should be successful, and in this way: The owners of the places are all widows or nearly all, very few exceptions, and they—the most of them—have sons or friends in the Southern army, and as the farms are leased of owners in such a way that if the crop is raised, they receive a certain per cent of the net proffits, and if the crop is destroyed or fails, they receive nothing... you see at once it is for their interest that the crop is raised. It is not so on the Mississippi, there the farms are what are called "Abandoned Plantations" and are leased from the Govt and it is quite natural that the owners should not like to see them worked by Yankees. I rather think most of them have been broken up by the rebels already—running off the mules & taking the supplies. Two I know of have been rented out twice, lost all their money & property and have gone north quite sick of southern life and planting cotton.

Willis was somewhat surprised to recv a letter yesterday from a friend in Western New York—not necessary to give name or place, at present—enquiring about Plantation Nigs etc. and if he could get a farm down here. He had heard we were in the business & as he had nothing to do would like to lease a plantation and try his hand at raising cotton. I wrote him he was at least two months too late & would be three before he could get to work.

What do people say about it? I little thought when I used to sing "Juno at the Gate" I should ever be living "In the Old Mississippi State" (oh! The letter referred to above was directed to Vicksburg Tenn & the grammar was decidedly rich. Excuse the digression) and so near to Pearl River. Haven't seen Juno yet but Nigs with almost any other name you could imagine. Each of them have two or three names. Owing to that, a joining planter issued over a hundred rations to sixty five hands. They would get a ration on one name & come right back & get another ration on another name. That was before the man knew his hands by sight.

There is any quantity of game about here—Wild Turkeys, Duck, Rabbits etc. and yesterday I brought out two shot guns & anticipated great sport hunting on leasure days. The only trouble now is we have no shot or powder & can get none in the city and unless we are fortunate enough to get some we may have some difficulty in shooting the afore-mentioned game.

Have just been to dinner. We had not a very great variety but first rate what there was. Ham potatoes Hominy corn bread, bisquit, tea & coffee, cabbage, & strawberries. Think that was the Bill. The last two Extras, the others Regulars. Am very fond of the corn-bread, it is made very coarse but it is very sweet & nice. You see our fair is perfectly substantial. Perhaps I should have mentioned before, the Strawberries were not of this years growth, though they tasted quite as good....

Give our united love to all our relatives & friends. Would be pleased to see any of them at Oakwoods.

... Do you correspond with Belle V. J. Smith? She was the best correspondent I ever had, but alas; alas, she is "done gone." It is so amusing to hear the Niggers talk, & the children talk just like them.

We are about half a mile outside of our Pickets—that is in the day. At night they are drawn in two or three miles. We are guarded from the Confed's by the Big Black, which is only fordable in one or two places.

Well my dear sister I have no more to tell you that I think would be interesting. If you should not get our letters as often as agreed upon, it will be on account of the delay at Vicksburg waiting a Boat.

We have rec'd but one letter from you & that two weeks ago today. Got a lot of papers from John a few days ago. They were very acceptable indeed.

Write often
Love to all
Affectionately Yours
Sam
3rd Apr Oakwoods

[*The appearance of Willis that evening with another batch of letters
from home occasions another page and a half from Sam, in which,
referring to their younger brother Robert, who is about sixteen at this
time, Sam writes: "Willis says tell Bob he must study and learn to write
well and it may be another year there will be some plantation he can
run and perhaps marry some young lady who owns one, plenty here."
The appearance of yet another letter, from his young sister Nettie,
sparks an additional two pages of response from Sam, mostly on family
matters, to which the following postscript is appended.*]

P.S. Wednesday. Sunday night there were six of our horses stolen &
for two days have been scouting with some cavalry for them. Found
where they crossed the river & gone over to "Dixie." Have no doubt but
a man by the name of Webb who lives not far from here hired some
Negros to steal them so he could trade them for cotton.
    Will write particulars next letter. Keep a guard generally but for few
nights have not had one. Will hereafter keep one on all the time.

[*Although it was written two months after the following two letters,
a letter to JVL from Walter Lauderdale, dated August 9, 1864, sheds
light on the events discussed below. "Those Planters who took abandoned places left by the Rebs," wrote his father, "soon found out that
they would not be allowed to work their plantations unmolested. They
were subjected to frequent Visits from the Raiders, their Mules were
taken away & their property destroyed.... The Planters of course were
obliged to abandon their places & lose all or nearly all their invest-
ments. Those who occupied plantations belonging to actual residents
fared some better.... Willis lost 6 Horses & had the Buildings of Mrs
Bolls set on fire, but after finding out that our boys came from Missouri
& that they were opposed to the Radical measures of the
Administration, the Raiders were more favorable to them.... The fact is
they are on the Confederate side of the Pickets & are obliged to act
wisely. Whilst they are perfectly Loyal they do not intend to do or say
anything to make themselves obnoxious to either side. If they should
have any trouble they would of course claim protection from the
Federals—but why do I say they, I have been so much in the habit of
talking about the boys that it is difficult to change and use the singular
number.... I cannot believe that an exchange of civilities between
opposing armies or civilians presupposes disloyalty in the least. I am
opposed to the barbarous custom of the Pickets of opposing armies firing at each other. If there is any intercourse at all it should be of a
friendly character especially when there is no fighting in progress....*]

*You can give [Willis] a long & interesting letter without saying a word
about the state of the country. The possibility that a letter from you to
him might fall into the hands of the Confeds makes it necessary that
you should be guarded...."]*

[Saml last letter][3]
June 8 1864

My dear Father
   Your good letter dated 22nd of May was duly rec'd. Was very glad
indeed to get it.
   You speak rather despondingly of Plantation affairs. I'm not surprised that you judge of things as you do. The information you receive,
particularly from the newspapers, would lead one to think that there
would not be the slightest chance for a person that exposed himself on
one of these plantations. Now let me tell you how it is. Some two or
three weeks ago Willis met Capt Montgomery[4] at Mrs Bolls and had a
very pleasant time with him. The Capt informed Willis there was not
the slightest personal danger to him and to go right along with the
work, that he would promise him he should not be raided or that any
danger would come to him at all. A few days after that Genl Slocum[5]
issued his order, which was that he would hold citizens within a circuit
of ten miles responsible for all raids or damage committed by the
Confeds i.e., Where one of the planters were raided the property of all
citizens within a circuit of ten miles from the farm raided would be
taken & sold to make good the planters loss, and where a life was
taken, $10,000 would be the remuneration, the money to be paid over
to the friends. On the strength of this order all the planters have
returned to their places or made other arrangements whereby their
places are being worked. A few days ago Genl Wirt Adams[6] issued an
order forbidding his men disturbing or in any way molesting planters
on the Big Black who were working the place with the consent of the
owners. Capt Montgomery rode right over & showed the order to
Willis. We stand very high in the Confederacy because we have always
treated the citizens as well as we knew how, doing a great many little
favors for them, and coming from St Louis and being so much opposed
to the Administration, but in fact talking very little about politics,
allowing them to have their own way about war matters. The truth is
the chance for raising a crop is so much better than when we first came
down that we feel quite encouraged in going ahead. The Cotton is looking perfectly beautiful. Never have had a better season for low-land
cotton than this — so they all say....
   Just learned this morning that the Republicans would nominate the

"Pathfinder."[7] Now would be the time for the Democrats to set up McClellan. He would run Freemont clear out of sight. Don't you think so?...

> Affectionately
> Your Son
> Sam
> June 8th 1864
> to W.E.L.

> Vicksburg June 17, 64
> W.E. Lauderdale M.D.

Dear Father

... It has rained constantly during this month which is rather unfavorable to our crops as the weeds and grass grow most as fast as the Cotton. I have about 250 acres of as fine Cotton as ever was seen. It has been worked over once and I am now busy trying to keep the grass and weeds down. I stay in the field most all the time as the blacks have to be watched very closely or they neglect their work. I like the occupation and hope to follow it for some years if successful this year. I am way out in the Confederacy and meet the Rebels often. So far I have found them very gentlemanly and agreeable. Capt Montgomery who has command of the Confederate Scouts near me is a relative of the Rochesters of Rochester, N Y. He is about twenty five years of age and very pleasant. He visits me quite often. He has two brothers in his company. One of their names is Rochester Montgomery. It was through the Captains influence that Genl Adams issued the order for the Rebels to allow us to cultivate our crops without disturbance. The hauling of supplies from Vicksburg is a great trouble and inconvenience as the roads are very rough and badly washed. I break down nearly every trip. I sent my team out the other afternoon and expect it will break down about four times before reaching its destination. Oakwood Plantation is beautifully situated. I wish you could visit us in our southern home. Sam has been stopping in the City since the stampede amongst the Planters, but I do not think it best for him to stay here during the hot months of summer. Country air is much more healthy. John is a long ways from home as well as Sam & I should like to hear from him. I wish I could visit home this summer but if I should leave, my crops would be lost. I have no Overseer but have the best stand of Cotton in this country. Franks letters are very interesting and we are always glad to get them. I was sorry to have been obliged to destroy yours the evening I received it but you spoke so unfavorably (though not unjustly) of the rebel depredations I did not want it to fall into their hands....

Your affectionate Son
Willis

Oakwood Plantation
Dr W. E. Lauderdale

Dear Father

So my dear Brothers body arrived safely at his native village and his relatives and friends have paid the last sad rites to his remains. How much I miss him.... Samuels health was never good while in St Louis and he had not got acclimated to a western climate, and then he neglected his disease for some time. I think had it not been for the bowel complaint the Doctor could have managed the fever. I am getting on very well with my cotton. It is the best crop in this section. I have increased my force considerable within the last few weeks and expect to commence picking cotton the last of this month. I have not much trouble from the confederate Scouts, occasionally have a horse or mule stolen by some one....

[Willis alarmed his parents when he began complaining of symptoms of poor health echoing Sam's recent decline. In a letter to JVL on April 27, 1865, Walter Lauderdale wrote: "We hear from Willis occasionally. He did not make any thing in Cotton last season. The Army worm destroyed almost the entire Crop.[8] He has taken another Plantation this summer in which he will not run any particular risk except his health— his Partners furnish all the Capital. Willis has been purchasing considerable Cotton & taking it to Vicksburg lately. In his last letter he says that on account of the rapid decline in Cotton he had been losing some money. He does not intend to make Cotton raising his business on the Plantation, but thinks of raising Corn which he thinks will be more profitable."

Willis never succeeded at the business of raising or selling plantation crops. In November 1865, he married Nellie Clark in St. Louis, where he went to work for an insurance company.]

Notes

Part I

1. The correspondence suggests that JVL may have worked for another druggist prior to this.
2. The organization and regulation of the pharmaceutical profession in the United States developed slowly over the course of the nineteenth century. With the exception of an 1832 New York State statute requiring a diploma or an examination for practicing pharmacy in New York City, which was effectively repealed in 1839, there was no Pharmacy Law in New York State until 1872.
3. More than ten years later, in March of 1864, JVL told Frank that the approaching World's Fair would be "one of the 'biggest' things since the good old days of the Crystal Palace. A pang of regret comes over me as I think of the destruction of that beautiful building. If we only had it, there would be no need of the light wooden structures they are putting up now." The gigantic iron and glass structure—nearly a full block in size—which was built for the 1853 New York Exhibition, burned in fifteen minutes on October 5, 1858.
4. JVL goes on to compare the character of Topsy to the Watsons' maid, Jinny, "who has been running around the streets this evening and when she came in Mrs Watson asked what she run away for. She said, 'dun no, dun no.' Mrs Watson said 'she would teach her,' she would see whether she was going to mind or not, and she took her up stairs, and gave her a good thrashing, and sent her to bed. Jin has been bawling so loud that I can hardly think of any thing to write to you." Nearly two and a half years later, still working for Mrs. Watson, Jinny vanished on her way home from school and was believed to have been kidnapped. "We miss her very much," JVL wrote, "but hope that she may turn up yet." He never mentions her again.
5. During his visit to New Providence, JVL traced the names of "some long deceased relations" in a churchyard there, including a Kennedy and Phebe Vance, whose son Samuel was shot at the Battle of Springfield during the Revolutionary War and died "June ye 8th In ye 20th year of his age 1780." Phebe Vance died in 1793 at the age of 63.

    JVL's mother, Mary Vance, was born in 1811 and died in 1882. His father was born in Cambridge, Washington County, New York, in 1806; attended

Geneva Medical College and became a physician and surgeon in 1828; and received an honorary degree from Buffalo Medical College in 1880. He died in 1893. JVL was born in North Sparta, in Livingston County, New York, not far from Geneseo, on November 13, 1832. Frances was born next, in 1834. Willis was probably born between Frank and Samuel, who was born in 1842. Their younger sister Nettie was born in 1844; Robert in 1847; and Walter E. Lauderdale, Jr., called Wat or Wattie, in 1850. Frank, who never married, died in 1903. JVL died in Brooklyn, New York, on January 22, 1931.

6. The pulpit was JVL's principal source of inspiration and entertainment. The relative merits of preachers was a subject of interest to him, and he chose his churches partly on that basis. While duly impressed with Beecher's talent for drawing a large congregation, JVL's evaluation fell short of Lincoln's remark that he was the best preacher since St. Paul. "He is a very good man, but he has some peculiar ways with him in his manner of delivery, and also in many of his remarks, especially his comparisons, which have a tendency to incite laughter, rather more than I think is proper." JVL saw Beecher again at Goupil's art gallery in New York City in December of 1863. see his letter of December 12, 1863, in Section 2: Bellevue.

Ironically, families were sometimes divided due to strong opinions on preaching. When, in 1855, JVL lived for a time in Cleveland with his Uncle Robert and Aunt Miranda, he placated their opposite preferences by going with each one to a different church on alternate Sundays.

During the time of his medical studies in New York City, JVL would sometimes attend as many as three sermons in one day, and he was willing to walk several miles to get to a church. Sermons affected him so strongly that during periods of constant attendance parts of his letters have the rhetorical ring of the pulpit.

7. More than ten years later, JVL's assessment of Barnum's Museum was unchanged. From Fort Bridger, Utah Territory, on August 12, 1865, JVL wrote to Frank: "In an Illustrated paper there is a frightful picture of the conflagration which resulted in the destruction of Barnum's Museum. Oh! What a pity! Where will you and I go when we visit the city together? The only place where we old people dare go burned to ashes! But Barnum like the fabled Phoenix will rise from his ashes, and in a short time he will have brot from the four corners of the earth many a thing rich rare and curious to delight wondering eyes; and when the new museum is ready we will be ready with our quarter to take a look at the long row of wax figures, or the fish or the happy family [Tom Thumb's]. Wont we? Dont forget your spectacles!"

8. In 1858, Dr. Spring's Brick Church moved to a new building uptown and became the New Brick Church at the corner of Fifth Avenue and 37th Street. The new site, a fashionable district known as Murray Hill, was the highest elevation in Manhattan at that time. In a rare show of religious humor, JVL punned on this detail in describing the church to his mother, who, like JVL, was a conservative Presbyterian and belonged to a rather sparse congregation in Geneseo. "So you see that Old Presbyterian," he wrote to her, "has the highest position of all others, at least in this city." He also told her that the interior of the church was furnished in a "beautiful but perfectly plain style," which he vastly preferred over the more lavish interiors of other Manhattan churches, which he felt detracted from the true meaning of worship.

During the war, Spring, a powerful Presbyterian figure, persuaded the Old
School Presbyterian Assembly to back the Union.

9. JVL had been to Cleveland as a boy, perhaps to visit his aunt and uncle.

10. The article first identifying the species credited Dr. Newberry alone with the
discovery, an error for which its author later apologized to JVL.

11. This passage is from "The Florida Expedition," by H.M. Lyman and S.E.
Elmore, *The Williams Quarterly* 4, no. 3 (March 1857): 293-329. Elmore contributed a section on a party that remained at Fernandina while the *Dew
Drop* explored the Keys. JVL's name appears in the list of participants at the
bottom of the first page of the article, which he kept among his papers. His
journal of the voyage is only a few pages of very faint writing, but, typically,
his letters to Geneseo provide a fairly extensive account of his activities.

William Walker, an adventurer from Nashville, Tennessee, had forcibly
established himself as president of Nicaragua on July 12, 1856. He and his
band of mercenaries, backed by Southern planters and Northern oppor-
tunists such as Cornelius Vanderbilt and U.S. Secretary of War Jefferson
Davis, were recognized as legitimate by the U.S. Government. Walker's vision
of ruling an ever-expanding Central American empire, which would depend
on slave labor and slave traffic, had its appeal to a South that was verging on
civil war. But as a result of Walker's intrigues with members of Vanderbilt's
Accessory Transit Company, Vanderbilt made it impossible for him to continue, and Walker consigned himself to the custody of the U.S. Navy in 1857.
He was welcomed as a hero wherever he went, and President Buchanan, who
did not indict him for neutrality violations, received him amiably at the White
House. Walker made two more attempts in Central America, the last of which
ended before a Honduran firing squad in 1860. The South mourned his loss.

In 1864, at Camp Conness, Utah Territory, JVL met one of the men who
served with Walker. On June 23, after an outing they took together on horseback, he wrote to Frank: "[Lieutenant James H. Stewart, 1st Nevada
Cavalry] told me that he was a nephew of Commodore Porter (of the Japan
Expedition), ran away to sea with his uncle when he was twelve years of age,
was with Walker in his Nicaragua Expedition, had lived in California a good
while, and at one time was a Pony Express rider for the overland mail Co.
and at times, chasing over the plains, armed to the teeth, with indians pursuing him in the distance. I had not such an experience and am not so well prepared for endurance as my friend."

12. The *New York Tribune*, edited by the provocative Horace Greeley, a
Republican who disliked and derided Buchanan, had the highest circulation
and the widest influence of any American newspaper. A New York daily, it
was distributed in condensed weekly and semiweekly formats throughout the
nation.

13. Ironically, this appears to have happened to JVL, whose views on black society underwent a long succession of sometimes contradictory permutations and
were always more simplistic than his behavior.

14. The Wide Awake was a well-organized Republican club. Lincoln spoke at
Cooper Union on February 26, 1860. As a result of its appearance in the New
York press, the speech was picked up nationally, and Lincoln later attributed
his election to that speech and to Mathew Brady, whose photos of Lincoln
were widely distributed.

15. Lincoln was known as Rail Splitter ever since a banner on two rails at the Illinois state convention introduced him as The Rail Candidate for President.

16. Election Day in 1860 was November 6.

    By the time of McLaren's letter, state elections in Vermont, Ohio, Maine, and Pennsylvania had proven so Republican that even Douglas knew he was going to lose. Although New York State was predominantly Republican, its urban districts were largely Democratic, none more so than New York City. Geneseo maintained a low Republican majority throughout the decade. A few nearby towns, such as Lauderdale's birthplace, North Sparta, had a slight Democratic majority, but there were no large Democratic majorities in Livingston County.

    On Election Day, Lincoln carried New York in electoral votes and all other free states but New Jersey, where he and Douglas tied.

17. George A. Otis and J.J. Woodward, eds., *The Medical and Surgical History of the War of the Rebellion* (Washington, DC: Government Printing Office, 1875-1888), Appendix to part I, 29.

18. Ulysses S. Grant, *Personal Memoirs of U. S. Grant* (New York: Charles L. Webster & Co., 1885), 355-56.

19. On March 18, 1862, Sherman reported to Grant that Pittsburgh Landing was "a magnificent plain for camping and drilling, and a military point of great strength" (General William T. Sherman, *Memoirs of General William T. Sherman* [New York: D. Appleton and Co., 1886], 260). As late as 1886, in his *Memoirs*, Sherman was still appraising its position between three bodies of water as "naturally strong" because it narrowed the locus of possible attack to within two miles. "We did not fortify our camps against an attack," he claimed, "because we had no orders to do so, and because such a course would have made our raw men tired" (Ibid., 257). A recently published letter written by Sherman from Camp Shiloh on April 4 clearly shows that he considered Johnston's advance forces to be strictly reconnaissance in nature (Joseph H. Ewing, "The New Sherman Letters," *Civil War Chronicles* 1, no. 2 [Winter 1992]: 25). On April 5 he wrote to Grant: "The enemy is saucy, but got the worst of it yesterday, and will not press our pickets far. I will not be drawn out far unless with certainty of advantage, and I do not apprehend anything like an attack on our position" (*The War of the Rebellion: A Compilation of the Official Records of the Union and Confederate Armies, Prepared Under the Direction of the Secretary of War* [Washington, DC: Government Printing Office, 1884], sers. 3, vol. 1, part 2, 93-94). It is interesting that the *New York Herald*, on April 2, predicted a major attack.

20. G.T. Beauregard, "The Campaign of Shiloh," *Battles and Leaders of the Civil War: From Sumter to Shiloh* (New York: Castle Books, 1956), 586.

21. In his postwar summary of the Federal position at Shiloh, Beauregard, despite his characteristically inflated prose, was probably closest to the truth in claiming that it gave Confederate forces "an opportunity for an almost fatal counterattack such as had rarely been afforded to the weaker of two belligerants in all the sinews and resources of war" (Beauregard, "Shiloh," 577).

22. Grant, *Personal Memoirs*, 349.

23. Ibid., 356.

24. Although it quickly fell apart, Beauregard's plan for Shiloh was modeled after Napoleon's plan of attack against Wellington at Waterloo. The day

before the battle, Halleck wrote from St. Louis to Secretary of War Stanton: "It is probable that the great battle of the war will be fought in Southwest Tennessee" (*War of the Rebellion*, sers 1, vol. 10, part 2, 93). His use of the singular here is significant. McClellan, the most influential proponent of this single-battle outlook, was, in this one respect, aptly known as the Young Napoleon. (JVL, like practically everyone else who had fallen under his spell, believed that McClellan deserved a freer hand in running the war. His encounters with McClellan in New York City are recounted in Part II: Bellevue.) Grant confessed to a similar outlook. "Up to the battle of Shiloh I, as well as thousands of other citizens, believed that the rebellion against the Government would collapse suddenly and soon, if a decisive victory could be gained over any one of its armies." (*Memoirs*, 368).

25. *War of the Rebellion*, sers. 1, vol. 10, part 2, 86.
26. *Medical and Surgical History*, Appendix to part 1, 32.
27. Ibid., 30.
28. Ibid., 38.
29. Ibid., 31.
30. Ibid., part 1, 299. A corroborative note is struck by Brinton in his official account of the battle. "The difficulty, at all events, as far as the army of the Tennessee was concerned, lay in the absence of supplies. This contingency had been foreseen, and strenuous efforts had been made by the medical directors to anticipate it. Requisition following requisition had been made for the very stores, medicines, and hospital tents, the want of which proved so disastrous upon the 6th and 7th of April. Unfortunately, at this time the medical department of the United States Army had not yet freed itself from that system of blind routine which, serving well the wants of a small army, in time of peace, yet failed to meet the necessities of a gigantic war" (*Medical and Surgical History*, Appendix to part 1, 31).
31. *War of the Rebellion*, ser. 1, vol. 10, part 1, 298.
32. Ibid.
33. *Medical and Surgical History*, vol. 6, 977.
34. Ibid., 972. A 60" model of the refitted *January* is on display at the National Museum of Health and Medicine in Washington, D.C.
35. In a letter to Frank written from Bellevue Hospital on August 1, 1863, JVL wrote: "One of my old steamboat friends called on me the other evening. He is now a surgeon in the field, Dr Hy Duane." A later note added by JVL reads: "Associate on Hosp Steamer *D.A. January*." JVL's index to the letters lists him as "Duane, Dr Henry."
36. JVL later changed his view. He wrote to Frank on April 11, 1864: "Since the days of photographs I have lost my affection for pencil sketches and have very little respect for wood engravings or any thing of the kind. No artist will, nor can, give as faithful picture of a thing. A photograph costs but little and you are sure of being correct. A pencil sketch costs a good deal of time to prepare it, and when done is never a perfect picture, as many things must necessarily be omitted. Still a rough sketch which you can prepare in fifteen minutes may convey an idea or two (like the one I enclose you) but is very far from being a good representation." JVL became an avid amateur photographer, using the camera to augment the chronicle his subsequent experience on the frontier, and there are many interesting photographs and lantern slides among his papers at Yale.

37. JVL was content without a uniform at this time, as he was again later when a contract surgeon in the West. Soon after he joined the Regular Army, Frank requested a picture of him in uniform. His reply from New York City on January 12, 1867, indicates that uniforms had become a sensitive issue among veterans.

> I have no doubt that the military dress will become me as well as any other suit but dont speak of my wearing that dress any more than I am obliged to. It is worn now by so many that have no right to it that Regulars are disgusted with their own uniform and never appear in the street in it unless they are on actual duty. Almost any day you can see some recently fledged lieutenant of the line parading the streets with all his military clothes on & his bright yellow buttons sparkling in the sun. He left his over coat at home and is willing to endure the cold that he may the better display his uniform. This is done by so many greenhorns that *old* Regulars are seldom if ever seen in the street with any thing that would indicate that they were connected with the service. Excuse me from sitting for my picture in that dress until I have been so long identified with the service that it may well become me.

JVL nevertheless does not seem to have taken his dress too seriously. In a letter to his father from New York City on June 8, 1867, he wrote:

> Yesterday I was at Shannons on Maiden Lane purchasing a sword and belt. In came an actor from one of the theatres who wanted to purchase a small short sword to use in the play of *Richard the Third*. I thought the real value of our several purchases in the line of swords was about equal in point of ability. But such articles are all in the play and whether one plays soldier in the army, or actor upon the stage, he must invest something for appropriate wardrobe. I have got my outfit nearly complete and could appear at inspection in full dress uniform to-morrow morning if so desired.

38. JVL never wrote anything carelessly. Writing to Frank from Utah Territory on April 13, 1866, he told her:

> I never sit down to write you a letter unless I spend at least two hours over it.... I don't take a pen and write down every random thought which courses through my brain. If I did I should fill my sheet in a few moments, and then I would have said nothing at all. You must practice culling out your thought, and when you write to your best friends select for them a few of your best thoughts. If you were going to get up a good dinner for a friend, you would not go to the pantry and take whatever comes first and tumble it into the basket indiscriminately, and then bring it forth, throwing the contents helter skelter at his feet. No! You would do nothing of the kind but every article of furniture and every article of food would come before your guest in its proper time and place....

39. One of the best Civil War diaries, George Templeton Strong's *Diary of the Civil War: 1860-1865* (edited by Allan Nevins [New York: Macmillan, 1962]), provides a vivid account of the activities of the United States Sanitary

Commission, of which Strong was treasurer and one of the most active members. Strong refers to five of JVL's teachers: Dr. John Draper; Dr. John T. Metcalfe; Dr. Alexander B. Mott; his father, Dr. Valentine Mott; and Dr. William H. Van Buren. Van Buren, director of the Commission, is mentioned frequently; and Strong repeats a good story told by Valentine Mott, whom he refers to as "old Dr. Mott," doubtless the sort of medical gem with which he regaled JVL's classes.

40. In November of 1862, Wadsworth, a Republican, lost the New York State gubernatorial race against Democrat Horatio Seymour. In a letter of November 7, 1862 (excerpted in Part Two), JVL calls Wadsworth "a good friend of mine," and after his death, he told Frank, on May 13, 1864: "The General was ever ready to do me a favor and I have more than one instance in mind, when he used his influence for me...." It is thus possible that Wadsworth helped secure Sam's position in his department. JVL refused to vote for him, however, because he was of the opposing party. Wadsworth was later at the battles of Chancellorsville, Gettysburg, Spotsylvania, and the Wilderness, where he received the wound of which he died in a Confederate hospital on May 6, 1864.

Toward the end of the eighteenth century, the Wadsworth family founded Geneseo.

41. The first two lines of this heading were added by JVL at a later date.

42. Avon was the main depot nearest Geneseo.

43. Flag Officer Andrew Hull Foote was naval commander on the upper Mississippi. See note 52 for his involvement in the taking of Fort Henry and Fort Donelson.

44. There is a small sketch here of a house with chimneys on two sides.

45. There is a small sketch here of the back and side of a three-story building with 15 windows.

46. There is a small sketch here of a keelboat being poled by a man standing atop a small cabin.

47. Attached to the top of this letter is a printed illustration of the *January*, which JVL completed by penciling in "US HOSPITAL" on the wheelhouse and a lightning rod configuration over the pilot house. Below it, he wrote: "*Our Boat*, The *D.A. January*." He also numbered the boat in five places: "1. My State Room. 2. Pilot House. 3. Texas dining room. 4. Cabins for the sick. 5. Yellow flag." The illustration of the *January* as it appears in *The Medical and Surgical History of the War of the Rebellion* differs materially both from this illustration and from the model at the National Museum of Health and Medicine, which also owns a sketch and plans of the *January*. The *Medical and Surgical History* contains four plans of the *January*

48. JVL used *Pittsburgh* and *Pittsburgh Landing* interchangeably to refer to the site of the battle, which in the South was better known as Shiloh, a usage which came to be favored in all parts of the country.

49. Newberry was the Western secretary of the United States Sanitary Commission, having been one of its founding members when it was first approved by Lincoln in June of 1861. During the war he wrote a number of reports, printed in Washington, D.C., on the activities of the commission in the West. In New York City after the war, 95 of the commission's publications were collected into two volumes, *Documents of the United States Sanitary*

Commission (New York: 1866), but it did not include Newberry's *The U.S. Sanitary Commission in the Valley of the Mississippi During the War of the Rebellion, 1861-1866*, document No. 96, which was published in Cleveland in 1871 by Fairbanks, Benedict & Co. Newberry died, at the age of 67, in 1889.

50. JVL's footnote: "Senator Harlans. Mother in law of Robert Lincoln."

51. The *Livingston Republican* was the principal newspaper for Geneseo and the other villages in Livingston County, New York.

52. The Federal victories at Fort Henry and Fort Donelson gave the North control of Kentucky and threatened much of Tennessee, effectively converting Johnston's defense lines in the West into corridors for moving the Federal initiative farther south both by water and by land.

    Fort Henry, a key Confederate stronghold on the Tennessee River, was under the command of Brigadier General Lloyd Tilghman when, on February 6, 1862, Grant attacked it in conjunction with a flotilla of Navy gunboats under Flag Officer Andrew H. Foote. Foote addressed the position with four ironclads—the *Essex*, the *Cincinnati*, the *Carondelet*, and the *St. Louis*—and three wooden gunboats: the *Conestoga*, and the two which were to aid grant at Shiloh, the *A.O. Tyler* and the *Lexington*. Although the horrible fate of the *Essex*, whose boiler was blown up, was a tragic loss for the Navy, Foote forced Tilghman to surrender in less than three hours of fighting, before Grant had even arrived. When he did, Grant discovered that on the morning of the battle, Tilghman, doubting the fort's defensibility, had evacuated all but 80 of his men to Fort Donelson.

    Fort Donelson, located on the Cumberland River not far from Fort Henry, was attacked on February 14-16 by the same Army and Navy combination. This time, however, Foote was forced to retreat under heavy firing after his flagship, the *St. Louis*, was struck 59 times and he himself was hit twice, leaving Grant to receive the surrender—the unconditional surrender which gave him his nickname—from Brigadier General Simon B. Buckner. Several thousand Confederate troops, under Brigadier General John B. Floyd, Major General Gideon J. Pillow, and Colonel Nathan B. Forrest, had managed to escape, but the victory was a turning point in the war and in Grant's professional life.

53. The *New York Observer* was one of JVL's favorite newspapers. Before leaving for California, in March of 1864, he wrote to Frank: "I think if I was going to the north pole I would in some way try and have that paper sent to me." Published by Sidney E. Morse & Co., it presented religious and other world news from a Protestant point of view.

54. General John Pope's chief engineer, Colonel Josiah W. Bissel, supervised 1,600 engineers in the digging of a 12-mile canal which enabled Pope safely to transport forces from the western to the eastern side of the Mississippi River. Dug through a forest between two bayous near the recently captured New Madrid, Missouri, at a point where the river bends sharply, the canal took 19 days to complete and was instrumental in the successful Army and Navy advance on Island No. 10, which gave the North control of eastern Tennessee and the waters above it.

55. JVL attached his own pencil sketch of Pittsburg Landing to the Shiloh portion of *Battles and Leaders of the Civil War* (New York; 1877-1888), which, on page 761, contains a photogravure illustration of Pittsburg Landing. See note 56.

56. *Frank Leslie's Illustrated Newspaper*, and *Harper's Weekly: A Journal of Civilization*, were the main sources for pictures of the war. They were printed from electrotyped metal copies of woodcuts, generally based on location sketches by men referred to as "Our Special Artist," including Winslow Homer, Alfred R. Waud, and Theodore Davis for *Harper's*; Henri Lovie, Arthur Lumly, and Edwin Forbes for *Frank Leslie's*. Most of the special artists were professionals, but now and then a sketch appeared by an officer who was involved in the battle depicted. The pictures varied in accuracy and in quality—some of the sketches were made from reporters' accounts, and some of the special artists had no special talent—but good or bad they nevertheless determined the look of the war for most Americans. Occasionally, an artist would also write a report on his experience. The best of the artists, working as eyewitnesses, produced evocative works of art of enduring power which, especially since there was no action photography during the war, have retained their vital importance and fascination, and favorably compare with the best verbal descriptions of the war.

At the start of the war, *Frank Leslie's* was of appreciably better quality than *Harper's* and, in the case of Shiloh, it was the journal's great fortune to have on the field its best artist, Frank Lovie, who arrived at the battle with Grant and was the only artist to sketch it from life. The *Frank Leslie's* for May 17, 1862 contained a two-page sketch of the battle by Lovie and a special sixteen-page War Supplement featured nine illustrations of the Great Battle of Pittsburgh Landing, at least eight of which are Lovie's. Illustrations such as "The Charge and Repulse of the Rebels at the Peach Orchard," "Desperate Defense of McClernand's Second Line by the National Troops," "Retreat of Dresser's Battery," "The Woods on Fire During the Engagement of Sunday, April 6," and, in a two-page spread, "The Last Line of the National Defense, from Which the Enemy was Repulsed, One Mile from Pittsburgh Landing, Sunday Evening, April 6," inspire more thanks than regret for the absence of action photography.

There are also evocative sketches by Lovie of "Gathering the Wounded after the Battle in Blankets," and "Burning the Dead Horses Near the Peach Orchard."

Portraits of major figures, however, were generally cut from photographs, as were occasional views of battle sites. A fine example of a photogravure shows five steamer transports, including Grant's *Tigress* and the gunboat *Tyler*, viewed from the bluffs of Pittsburgh Landing, a marvelous picture widely reproduced even today.

Illustrated newspapers had only begun to develop during the previous twenty years, and the enormous demand for pictures of the war, and for a sufficient number of artists to cover its wide geography, brought the practice into maturity. For JVL's comments on its replacement by photography, see note 36.

57. When William Henry Seward, Lincoln's Secretary of State, was a U.S. Senator from New York, he fought slave expansion into the West with an approach that became known as Higher Lawism, an appeal to a greater moral law beyond the Constitution. He later succumbed to political pressures and supported Douglas's notion of popular sovereignty, but his earlier agitations were not likely to fade in Confederate memory.

58. Typhoid was a highly contagious disease that was hard to treat. The bacillus, deriving in camps chiefly from human waste, was easily spread by human or insect carriers. An estimated one-quarter of all deaths from disease resulted from typhoid and similar "camp" fevers.

59. Kate Cumming, a volunteer nurse at Corinth Hospital, was, in a sense, JVL's Confederate counterpart, in that she kept a daily journal while attending both Federal and Confederate wounded from the battlefield of Shiloh. On April 23, eleven days prior to JVL's letter, she wrote: "Our men do not seem to stand half so much as the northerners. Many of the doctors are quite despondent about it, and think that our men will not be able to endure the hardships of camp-life, and that we may have to succomb on account of it; but I trust that they are mistaken." *(Kate: The Journal of A Confederate Nurse*, by Kate Cumming, ed. Richard Barksdale Harwell [Baton Rouge: Louisiana State University Press, 1959], 24-25). Her journal, which covers a varied itinerary over a three year period, contains many interesting parallels and polarities to JVL's opinions and experience.

    Corinth was so dense with Shiloh wounded from both armies that some had to be lain on the sidewalks.

60. Sunday was the 4th. Either the letter is misdated, or JVL dated it as the 5th because it was past midnight. As the previous midnight entry reveals, JVL used the word *evening* to mean night.

61. This is a reference to the fact that JVL was working for, but did not join, the Army and was not examined for his position. When he joined the Regular Army in 1866, he took the examination in New York City with a group that included his old boss, Dr. Hoff. Having helped Hoff with some of the answers, he was surprised when the published results showed that Hoff had scored higher.

62. In August of 1857, JVL attended a meeting of the American Association for the Advancement of Science, held in Montreal. Traveling by way of the St. Lawrence, he was impressed with the Thousand Islands and enjoyed the way his pilot, a Native American, negotiated the lower rapids, noting in his journal that it "was rather a dangerous passage" and that the pilot "dashed through the foaming waters in fine style." JVL had been hoping to see the naturalist Louis Agassiz, who was sitting on several committees, including the Committee to Memorialize the Legislature of Ohio on the Subject of A Geological Exploration of that State, a project of great interest to JVL's friend, Dr. Newberry. JVL missed Agassiz but was able to see him six years later at the Brooklyn Academy of Music (see Introduction to Part Two).

63. At the start of the war, General-in-Chief Winfield Scott proposed to isolate the Confederacy by blockading its southern ports, while advancing down and taking control of the Mississippi Valley. This noninvasive method of patiently choking the life out of Secession was unpopular, and the press derived the term from McClellan's alleged reference to Scott's Boa Constrictor. The plan was not tried.

64. At a later date, JVL added here the word *Tyler*, i.e., the gunboat *A.O. Tyler*.

65. After a journey on horseback at Camp Conness, Utah Territory, JVL wrote to Frank on May 19, 1864: "I remember the last time I rode a horse was over the battle field of Pittsburg Landing and it fairly used me up."

66. Hamilton Rowan Gamble, a Virginia lawyer, was provisional governor of
    Missouri during the war. He worked hard to keep his state in the Union, fos-
    tering moderation and compromise until his death in January of 1864. He was
    64 when JVL met him.
67. Andrew Jackson Downing (1815-1852) was a landscape architect.
68. No case is published under that name in the *American Digest* Table of Cases
    for 1658-1906.
69. Colonel Frank P. Blair, Jr., was a Missouri congressman whose pro-Union
    activities helped keep the state from seceding. He organized and led the
    Missouri Free-Soilers; the Wide Awakes; and the First Missouri Regiment
    when the Governor of Missouri defied Lincoln's call for militia. He became a
    major general in November 1862. His brother, Montgomery, was Dred Scott's
    attorney, and Francis Blair, Sr., with the help of Montgomery, was involved in
    trying to keep McClellan in command, believing him to be more politically use-
    ful leading an army than running against Lincoln. The senior Blair also con-
    ferred with Jefferson Davis on a proposal for both armies to join hands against
    Mexico.
      A week after this letter from JVL to Frank, Samuel wrote to her from
    Washington, D.C., depicting a different form of antiemancipationism. "The
    other evening," he told Frank, "one of those interesting objects 'An
    Abolitionist' was very freely expressing himself at Willard's, getting in conver-
    sation with quite a number of different ones until finally a young captain
    drawing his pistol told him to say no more or he was a dead man. The poor fool
    withdrew quite suddenly." Willard's Hotel, at 14th Street on Pennsylvania
    Avenue, hosted most of the city's VIPs, and its lounge and restaurant were
    teeming with congressmen, officers, and journalists—although not, according
    to Sam, with attractive women. "I have not seen half a dozen handsome ladies
    in Washington," he told Frank. "They are awfully scarce. Of all the borders at
    Willards there is not one really good looking. All in style, however." Sam
    roomed in a boardinghouse and took his dinners at Willard's.
      Congress had abolished slavery in the District of Columbia, with compensa-
    tion, as of April of that year. In a letter to Frank on June 15, Sam described a
    visit to an estate in Arlington Heights, Virginia, where there were four or five
    hundred "contrabands." Sam's companion gathered them into a room and
    asked them to talk and sing. "It was first rate," wrote Sam. "The real old
    Methodist style."
      Sam's letters from D.C. also reveal dissension within the military.
    "McClellan's stock is somewhat down just at present," he wrote on June 5,
    "Pope being the rising star. McDowell was "not much thought of. His own staff
    call him names such as Mickey, etc. He is not liked by the Corps, and the peo-
    ple generally think little of him." Two weeks later, he wrote: "All manner of
    rumors are afloat, in regard to the battle, at the White House. The first were
    very much to the injury of Gen. McClellan, principally coming from
    McDowell's friends. I was with some of his staff most of the day and I tell you
    what, they talked bitter enough. However before night they were quieted by
    the later reports."
70. The abbreviations are for Old School and New School Presbyterian.
71. This good sketch of the *January*'s flagstaff with three birds perched on it
    appears in the left margin beside the text.

72. To avoid being trounced by Halleck, whose troops doubled his own numbers, Beauregard sneaked out of Corinth during the night of May 29-30. He accomplished this with the simple blind of having the troops cheer at a coming and going of empty trains, deceiving the Federals into believing each huzzah was a reinforcement. On May 30, Halleck took the city and 2,000 prisoners, a disappointing return for a month's campaigning. The city was not the scene of a major battle until October.

    An extremely high percentage of sickness among his troops was one reason for Beauregard's withdrawal.

73. Dr. Charles McDougall, medical director of the Department of the Tennessee, was, technically speaking, the man with whom JVL signed his contract to work in the Western theatre, and when he later signed with McDougall again—this time bound for the Department of the Pacific—he noted the fact that McDougall's name was, literally, on both of his contracts. This did nothing, however, to correct JVL's spelling of his name.

74. Fowler's solution, formulated by British physician Thomas Fowler (1736-1801), contained arsenic trioxide as its principal active ingredient.

75. On June 13, Flag Officer Charles H. Davis, Foote's successor, led a flotilla up the White River, in Arkansas, to open a route for resupplying the troops of Major General Samuel Curtis, who were effectively cut off without provisions. In a bold advance against heavy Confederate firing at St. Charles, the Federal gunboat *Mound City* was struck in the boiler, its horrific explosion resulting in 125 casualties. As JVL suggests, the Federals "whipped them out after all," but to little purpose, for developments soon required Army and Navy withdrawal from the vicinity.

76. M.A.L. may be a reference to JVL's mother, Mary A. Lauderdale.

77. Island No. 10, located at a bend in the Mississippi 60 miles south of Columbus, Kentucky, resisted Foote's naval attack in March, but subsequent action by two of Foote's gunboats enabled Major General John Pope to land on its eastern shore with men from his Army of the Tennessee. On April 7, during the second day of Shiloh, Brigadier General William Mackall surrendered the Island.

78. In the Battle of Memphis, on June 6, Federal and Confederate ironclads clashed in front of Memphis and all Confederate vessels except one were captured or destroyed. Flag Officer Davis fought with five armored gunboats, in concert with two rams under U.S. Army Colonel Charles Ellet, who died five days after this letter due to complications resulting from a leg wound. Ellet, whose brother and son were also involved in the action, was the only Union casualty. The Confederate ram *General Beauregard* was destroyed when a shell from the gunboat *Benton*, under the command of Lieutenant S. Ledyard Phelps, blew up its boiler.

79. There is a 1" x 1" sketch here of a shack on stilts with a ladder in front of its door.

80. Major General Thomas Carmichael Hindman was commander of the Department of the Trans-Mississippi.

81. JVL gives this incorrectly as Wednesday the 19th, clearly a dating error, for the next page contains the end of this letter and the beginning of that of Friday the 18th.

82. Lauderdale Springs, Tennessee saw only a skirmish during the war, on February 16, 1864. JVL misdated the sketch accompanying this letter.

83. The day after this letter, Lincoln read to his cabinet the first draft of his preliminary Emancipation Proclamation, which issued September 22 and was effective January 1.

84. Between *together* and *to prevent* there is a sketch of the kit.

85. *A Rainy Day in Camp* begins:

> It's a cheerless lonesome evening,
>> When the soaking, sodden ground,
> Will not echo to the footfall
>> Of the sentinel's dull round.
>
> God's blue star-spangled banner
>> To-night is not unfurled:
> Surely *He* has not deserted
>> This weary, warring world.
>
> I peer into the darkness,
>> And the crowding fancies come;
> The night wind, blowing northward,
>> Carries all my heart toward home.
>
> For I 'listed in this army,
>> And have roughed it many ways,
> And Death has nearly had me;
>> Yet I think the service pays.
>
> It's a blessed sort of feeling,
>> Whether you live or die;
> You helped your country in her need,
>> And fought right loyally.

The poem continues for another thirteen verses, during which the soldier ponders that "big promotion," the day when God says "Come up higher."

86. See Part II, note 12.

87. On July 15, on the Yazoo River near Vicksburg, Mississippi, three Federal gunboats, the *A.O. Tyler*, the *Queen of the West*, and the *Carondelet*, were given chase by the *CSS Arkansas*, which, under the command of Captain Isaac Brown, was the most formidable Confederate vessel to date. The *Arkansas* emerged onto the Mississippi, where a large Federal flotilla, commanded by Captain Davis and Captain David G. Farragut (who became a rear admiral the following day), awaited the outcome of the mission on the Yazoo. In one of the most daring naval maneuvers of the war, the *Arkansas*, alone, attacked the entire Federal flotilla in an effort to make its way back to Vicksburg, where, after an hour of heavy firing on both sides, it arrived badly battered but still afloat.

88. There is a pencil sketch of this scene on a separate page, which reads: "The Hurricane Deck of Steamer *D.A. January* on the evening of July 30, 1862."

89. There is a small outline here of the fort's formation.

90. There is a pencil sketch of the hospital on a separate page. The verso reads: "U.S. Marine Hospital, Paducah, Ky. This building has been enclosed by

earthworks by the Union forces and put in a condition of defense. It is used at the present time for a general army hospital."

91. At the head of this sentence there is a small sketch of a mosquito.
92. The Second Confiscation Act of July 17, 1862, authorized seizure of property owned by Confederate sympathizers.
93. The *Victoria* became the *Abraham*.
94. There is a small diagram here, labeled: "1. Engine room. 2. Entrance and passage."
95. The sentry can be seen in JVL's pencil sketch, on a separate page, the verso of which reads: "The north end of the principal street in Columbus, Ky. The fort seen in the distance with the road leading up the hill thereto, also the foot path, hospital boat, etc etc. Aug 12, 1862." This one is signed *JVL*.
96. There is a pencil sketch of this church on a separate page, the verso of which reads: "A Church in Columbus, Ky. used as a place of worship by the 71st Rgt Ill. Vol, Aug 11th 1862."
97. JVL later made this notation because the page begins in mid-sentence, a previous page or more having been lost. The page begins: "....the town and looks up the river. We continued our way in that direction. All along our route...." See note 105.
98. Sketch.
99. Sketch.
100. Sketch.
101. Sketch.
102. Diagram labeled: "1. Perpendicular face. 2. Incline. 3. Mast. 4. Hill beyond."
103. Sketch of three tents, labeled: "Sibleys Tent," "Wall Tent," "Privates Tent."
104. Sketches of four types of ammunition, labeled 1-4.
105. On November 7, 1861, Grant steamed down from Cairo and captured Belmont, Kentucky, across the Mississippi from the extremely well-fortified Columbus, from which a Confederate force, under General Leonidas Polk, retaliated and caused him to abandon it. Pressure from both land and river forced Polk to evacuate Columbus in March of 1862.
106. Brigadier General Isaac F. Quinby was then in command of the District of Mississippi and of West Tennessee. Born in New Jersey, he had taught at the University of Rochester since 1852 and had raised the 13th New York Regiment at the outbreak of the war.
107. This sketch, on a separate page, is labeled "Gen. Quinbys Head Quarters, Columbus Ky 1862," and the verso reads: "Gen Quinby of Rochester N.Y. Headquarters at Columbus, Ky. Anchor taken from the *Merrimac*. [Word obscured] machines or mines seen in foreground near the rail road track. Aug 13, 1862." Despite, or perhaps because of, the fact that JVL has gotten the side of the house all wrong, and his figures, seldom more than sticks in clothing, are here almost ghostly, this is one of JVL's most interesting sketches.
108. Robert Lauderdale was about 15, Walter Jr., about 12. Walter Jr., also became a Geneseo physician and succeeded his father on the Board of Visitors of the Normal School, the two of them covering a span between 1871 and 1934. The Normal became a teacher's college that was the nucleus of the State University of New York at Geneseo where, on October 23, 1966, the Lauderdale Student Health Center was dedicated to commemorate the father and son contribution to Geneseo education.

109. There is a pencil sketch of the house on a separate page.
110. The *Rose Hambleton* may have been playing "The Star Spangled Banner" on her decks, but she was probably whistling "Dixie" in her storage. Six months later, during a Federal crackdown, the boat was seized for carrying contraband cotton.
111. This was at James Eads's Carondelet Marine Railway and Dry Dock Company.
112. Failed tests of the monitors *Osage* and *Neosho* required the redesign of both vessels. Besides the *Milwaukee*, Eads's produced the *Chickasaw*, the *Kickapoo*, and the *Winnebago*, names which may have been substituted later or which JVL may have misremembered, although it is possible that the *Choctaw* was the ironclad ram of that name being converted from the side-wheeler *Nebraska*. Farragut used the *Chickasaw* and the *Winnebago* in taking possession of Mobile Bay, Alabama, in August of 1864.
113. As English translations of Victor Hugo's novel began to appear, the Confederates came to be known as "Lee's Miserables."

Part II

1. JVL married a Brooklynite, Josephine Lane, on June 29, 1880. Their first daughter, Frances Helen—named after Frank—was born on August 15, 1885, but she lived only twenty-two days. Their second daughter, Marjorie, was born on September 30, 1886, and their son, John Vance, was born three years later. One of JVL's grandchildren is currently a physician.

   JVL's proximity to the making of hoop skirts apparently struck a chord in the Geneseo household, for JVL's mother and two sisters all placed orders for one. On November 27, he wrote to Frank: "Are not your ideas a little rather large in regard to the size you want? Just think of it, 50 hoops in a skirt. They dont make them with so many, unless it is for the Cuban trade, and they are not a shape that would suit this latitude. I trust you will be pleased with forty wires. I allowed Nettie thirty and Mother the same number.... The 700 women who manufacture these articles do not wear hoops themselves. They do not wear silks and satins, but are dressed in cotton ticking with the stripes running up and down. These letters are stamped on the back: 'WORK HOUSE,' so that if they should stray away, they will be known by the police."

   As recounted in Chapter 6 of his *American Notes*, Charles Dickens was rowed by a crew of convicts to Blackwell's Island during his first tour of the U.S. in 1842, although, unable to remember its name, he recalled it as "Long Island, or Rhode Island: I forget which." While it suffers from the book's fatal flaw, which is Dickens' determination to water down his negative observations, the description helps round out the picture provided by JVL, who, by contrast, appears never to even have noticed poor conditions in the institutions of Bellevue.

2. In October of 1863, JVL wrote to Frank: "We have such an army of students now you would think all the medical students in the country were assembled here. Bellevue College is running all the other schools under & all because it is attached to a hospital. Students know that hearing a lecture on pneumonia

is quite a different thing from seeing a case of it lieing on a bed before them."
In 1898, the medical colleges of Bellevue and N.Y.U. combined to make the
N.Y.U. School of Medicine.

3. Smith later defeated New York's most larcenous politicians in his crusade for
   municipal hygiene, instituting New York's first sanitary and health regula-
   tions and passing a bill creating its Vaccination Bureau. He was commissioner
   of the Metropolitan Board of Health between 1870 and 1874, and he was
   appointed by President Hayes to the National Board of Health. He also
   planned Roosevelt Hospital and was one of six planners of Johns Hopkins.
   Like JVL, he lived to the age of 99.

4. The Battle of Antietam was fought in Sharpsburg, Maryland on September
   17, 1862, the bloodiest day of the Civil War. The cornfield that saw some of
   the battle's thickest fighting is, like Gettysburg, still yielding a harvest of
   buried bullets every spring.

5. Mary Lincoln, shopping with Tad in New York City, was staying at the luxuri-
   ous Metropolitan Hotel at the corner of Broadway and Prince Street.

6. "Prince John" was the highly esteemed, much admired attorney John Van
   Buren, the son of President Martin Van Buren. A former New York attorney
   general, Van Buren was New York State chairman of the Democratic Party
   and a veteran of the New York political arena, which he enlivened with his
   acerbic wit. It was not, however, at its best in the speeches he made for the
   Democratic gubernatorial candidate, Horatio Seymour, and the *Tribune*, in
   castigating his shrill slander of certain Republicans, including Charles King
   (president of Columbia College), used Van Buren's nickname for some editorial wordplay. He had been known as Prince John ever since, at the age of 22,
   he had danced with Princess Victoria at a London ball. After a term of
   Seymour's antagonistic approach to the war effort, Van Buren denounced
   him as a destructive fool.
       Greeley aggressively supported the abolitionist James Wadsworth against
   Seymour, who, in his acceptance speech at the Democratic convention, made
   post-emancipation life sound even worse than the sack of Rome. *The Times*
   and the *Tribune* labeled his views treasonous. Attacks and counterattacks
   were fierce from both parties and in the highly partisan press, where the
   objective reporting of war news did not lighten the editorial hand until the
   later years of the war. See note 9 and part I, note 39.

7. The Long Island Sound.

8. The *New York Illustrated News*.

9. The *Herald* portrayed Wadsworth as a self-serving aristocrat, and speeches
   by the Democrats were casting nasty aspersions about the legitimacy of his
   lineage, etc. See note 7 and part I, note 39.

10. Either Dr. Isaac Wood, President of the Medical Board at Bellevue, or Dr.
    James R. Wood. See note 13.

11. The Democrats were already grooming McClellan for running against Lincoln.
    His elegant four-story house on West 31st Street was a present from his
    wealthier supporters, among whom was John Jacob Astor. Whether
    McClellan's visit among Bellevue's 300 wounded soldiers was partly an early
    campaign tactic is a matter for conjecture.

12. There is no modern equivalent to the Fairy Wedding of two of P.T.
    Barnum's star performers, the dwarfs General Tom Thumb (Charles S.

Stratton) and the Queen of Beauty, Lavinia Warren (Mercy Lavinia Warren Bump), with Tom Thumb's rival for Lavinia, Commodore Nutt (George Washington Nutt) acting as best man. Held on February 10 at Grace Church on Broadway and 11th Street, it was for ticket-holders only and was the hottest ticket in town. An event of intense national interest, it was attended by the highest of high society and by prominent figures from government and the Army. Even the Lincolns sent a gift, and entertained the pair at the White House during their international Bridal Tour of 60,000 miles.

JVL met one of Tom Thumb's entourage on the *January*. (See letter of July 26, 1862.)

13. Dr. James R. Wood, visiting surgeon at Bellevue, was an eminent and somewhat impetuous presence in the operating theatre.

14. See part I, note 57.

15. JVL's father was thinking along the same lines. His letter on the subject appears in Appendix A.

16. Around Chancellorsville, Virginia, during the first few days of May, Federal forces under General Joseph Hooker incurred extremely heavy casualties, and on May 4 they were forced to withdraw in defeat.

17. Grant's failed assaults on Vicksburg, Mississippi were initially cabled to Washington as victories and were subsequently reported as such in the Northern press, occasioning spirited celebrations.

18. The *Passaic* was one of several monitors in an armada of Union ships which, under the command of Admiral Samuel F. DuPont, attempted to retake Charleston Harbor on the afternoon of April 7, 1863. During the attack, which was a failure, the *Passaic* was badly damaged by thirty-five hits. "The turret of the *Passaic*," wrote *Harper's Weekly* on December 12, 1862, "is unquestionably the greatest engineering achievement of the time. The successful operation of this structure with its monster guns marks an era in the history of naval warfare."

19. James L. Jackson's iron works, at 167 East 28th Street.

20. This may have been the Washington Drove Yard Hotel at Madison Avenue and 43rd Street.

21. Although there were militia drills on the second floor, the Second Avenue Armory, not far from Bellevue, was essentially a rifle factory run by Mayor Opdyke's son-in-law, George Farlee. It was looted and burned in such chaos that eight of the rioters were burned in the fire, and two jumped to their death.

22. A house on Lexington Avenue was burned down due to rumors that it belonged to the provost marshal, to his chief-of-staff, and to Horace Greeley. None of the rumors were true.

23. The *New York Tribune* Building, in Printing House Square on Park Row, lower Manhattan, was set afire several times and was narrowly saved from destruction. It had to be fortified by barricades, howitzers, hoses, rifles, and hand grenades. The mob, eager to kill Horace Greeley, pulverized a man who resembled him, and burned his publisher's house, but Greeley escaped harm.

24. Located on Fifth Avenue between 43rd and 44th streets, the Colored Half-Orphan Asylum of the Association for the Benefit of Colored Orphans, a

four-story building that sheltered up to 800 children, was ransacked and burned, the children being evacuated moments before the rioters entered the building calling for murder.

25. In front of the burning Ninth District Draft Office on Third Avenue and 46th Street (a fire *started* by Volunteer Engine Company No. 33), a Virginia lawyer named John V. Andrews encouraged the rioters with a speech that excoriated the draft and the Lincoln administration. Later tried by a federal court for treason and conspiracy, he was sentenced to three years in prison. Although the *New York Daily News* opposed the Lincoln administration, Andrews had no connection with it. Former New York City Mayor Fernando Wood had held a rally a week earlier, denouncing the draft and calling for a cease-fire between the armies.

26. This may have been at the 18th Precinct Police Station on 22nd Street between First and Second Avenue, which was burned late Tuesday night.

27. Colonel Berens ran into serious trouble leading twenty-eight men and one howitzer from the 68th Regiment to guard Jackson's foundry on 28th Street. This may have been the fighting that JVL was watching.

28. Hiram Chandler, a policeman in the 21st Precinct, had been attacked at 34th Street and Second Avenue. His escort was from the 7th Regiment.

29. Concerning Herbert L. Johnson, a Geneseo friend of the Lauderdales, Sam wrote to Frank from St. Louis on August 13, 1863: "Herbert says that he dont propose to answer personally 'Father Abe['s]' invitation to Washington." The draft was not yet in Missouri, but anticipating it, Sam wrote: "The way we do here is to form ourselves in to a company—say ten—signing an agreement that each one will pay his equal share in buying the exemption of any one or more that have signed the agreement that may be drafted." The proportion will be one in ten, which would make the per cent to pay comparatively small for each of us." In this light, his statement that "I consider my self just as well off out of the Army as I would be in" loses its ambiguity.

30. This and the following letter were erroneously placed earlier in JVL's chronology. The Russian visit was in September-October, not in May-June where JVL placed it.

   The officers of Admiral Lessovski's Atlantic Fleet were lavishly feted throughout the city, and caused a tremendous commotion of interest wherever they went in the state. But what most New Yorkers viewed as a goodwill mission by a potential new ally against the Confederacy was, in fact, a shrewd Russian maneuver. Anticipating hostilities with the great nations of Europe over the czar's treatment of Poland, the Russians chose San Francisco and New York City to safely winter their warships without fear of attack by the British Navy.

31. In 1855, George Philip Cammann, a New Yorker, invented the binaural stethoscope, which enabled listening with both ears.

32. Mr. Neil was a preacher from Geneseo whom JVL liked although he was not at the very top of his list of favorites. Beecher was later accused of making himself too agreeable to his lady friends and was brought to trial on charges of adultery.

33. Stephen Foster, poor and alcoholic, suffered a serious fall at the American House, a flophouse on the Bowery, on January 10, 1864, and died at Bellevue Hospital on January 13.

One of JVL's uncles, also a physician, identified only as E. Lauderdale, wrote to JVL in a letter from Detroit on January 24, 1864 (misfiled and mislabeled by JVL as 1863): "That Mr. Foster you speak of I know well & his wife better. I have got their photographs. That Stephen Foster drank badly. That is to say he had bad sprees. He turned his wife out of the house after abusing [her] badly & then wrote 'Gentle Annie'. That was his wifes name. Mr Foster of Cleveland is a beautiful singer & quite a musician. I was invited to his house quite often."

JVL kept amongst his papers an unidentified clipping from a New York newspaper—possibly the *Brooklyn Eagle*—which reported on this century's first revival of Foster's songs, a performance tribute held at the Hanson Place Methodist Church. The mention of jazz in the piece suggests that it may have been written during the 1920s. After a description of the festivities, there is the following interesting paragraph:

> The meeting was remarkable for an incident which took place at the close of the service. An elderly man came forward and introduced himself as Dr. J.V. Lauderdale, a retired United States Army surgeon, of 241 84th st., Brooklyn, and said: "'I was the interne who received Stephen Foster at Bellevue Hospital when he was admitted to the charity ward. I remember that it was a bitter winter's day. He arrived in a carriage. I learned by accident that he was the famous song writer and I said: 'This man is a genius and should receive the best of care.' I turned him over to another physician and we did the best we could for him until he died."
>
> "Why was his body removed to the morgue to be with the unknown dead?" Dr. Lauderdale was asked.
>
> "Because there was nobody to claim him at that time," replied the doctor.

34. The 20th U.S. Colored Troops ferried over from Riker's Island to receive their colors at the Union League Club House in Union Square, where 100,000 New Yorkers witnessed the ceremony, after which the company marched down Broadway. George Templeton Strong, who was a member of the club, watched the procession from the office of the U.S. Sanitary Commission at 823 Broadway and gives an interesting account of it in his *Diary*.

A few months later, Lincoln received an unsigned letter from a soldier in this regiment (possibly Nimrod Rowley), complaining of numerous forms of unjust treatment, such as half pay, reduced rations and clothing, and debilitating work details. "Instead of the musket," he wrote, "it is the spad[e] and the Wheelbarrow and the Axe cuting in one of the most horable swamps in Louisiana stinking and misery." The letter concludes by asking Lincoln to "Remember we are men standing in Readiness to face thous vile traitors an Rebels who are trying to Bring your Peaceable homes to Destruction. And how can we stand them in A weak and starving Condition [?]" (Document #202: "New York Black Soldier to the President," *Freedom: A Documentary History of Emancipation 1861-1867, Selected from the Holdings of the National Archives of the United States, Series 2: The Black Military Experience* [Cambridge: Cambridge University Press, 1982], 501-2).

35. Since JVL seldom heard directly from Willis and Sam, he was often in the dark as to what they were doing. On April 11, 1863, for example, he wrote to Frank: "I received a letter from Willis. He tells me that Sammy is living down at Carondelet. That fact does not relieve me of a query which I once asked as to what he is doing? Is he in the Army? or Navy? Has he rented a farm down there? Or is he superintending the building of iron clads? or what is it? Please relieve me, by answering." At the time, Sam was keeping books for the St. Louis & Iron Mountain Railroad Company, living in Carondelet, Mississippi, during the week and spending his weekends with Willis in St. Louis. The "letters from the boys," in which they discuss plantation matters, appear in Appendix B.

36. There is no indication that JVL considered this prospect seriously. His views on the family interest in cotton fluctuated. In March of 1864, he wrote to Frank: "I am disposed to think that the boys have been well advised in regard to the enterprise which they are engaged in. If our army continues to hold the territory which they possess in the neighborhood of Vicksburg, and there is every reason to believe they will, I am sure that a crop of cotton may be raised and got off without any difficulty, and I know of no reason why the price of cotton should depreciate any during the coming year. There is some risk it is true from groups of rebels destroying the cotton, after it is picked, but of these dangers I cannot say anything advisedly.... Providence alone knows and can control the result of the enterprise and to him alone are we to look for the result." He felt much the same way the following month, but in June, after the area was disrupted by Confederate raids, he changed his tune. "I expected to hear bad news from our friends in Vicksburg," he wrote to Frank. "I have often thought they would have done as well to stay in St Louis. Raising cotton behind a line of bayonets is not a safe business...."

Part III

1. This letter, entirely devoted to politics, is one of JVL's longest, nearly twice the length of this excerpt.
2. In the left-hand margin of the first page of this letter, JVL sketched an American flag at half-mast, the stars and stripes rendered in colored ink.

Appendix B

1. Added by JVL.
2. This letter was written by Sam from Oakwoods Plantation, near Vicksburg, Mississippi, in April of 1864, but JVL mistakenly dated it 1863 and misplaced it in his chronology.
3. Added by JVL.
4. Willis discusses Montgomery in his letter of June 17, 1864.
5. Major General Henry W. Slocum, a native of northern New York, was Federal Commander for the District of Vicksburg. Later, during Sherman's march to the sea, he led the Army of Georgia.
6. Brigadier General William Wirt Adams, a Kentuckean, was serving in Major General Nathan B. Forest's Cavalry Corps, with whom he surrendered in Alabama the following year.

7. Frémont's early exploring career inspired this campaign nickname during his unsuccessful run as the first Republican candidate in 1856. He also ran as a third party candidate in 1864, for which he proved as poorly equipped as he was at commanding the Western Department in 1861 and the Mountain Department in 1862.

8. Writing in *Harper's Monthly* in 1854, a Louisianan named T. B. Thorpe conveyed something of what Willis must have experienced at the mercy of the army worm, the moth of which is described as having "a Quaker-like simplicity in its light, chocolate-colored body and wings":

> The little, and, at first, scarcely to be perceived caterpillars that follow the appearance of this moth, can absolutely be seen to grow and swell beneath your eyes as they crawl from leaf to leaf. Day by day you can see the vegetation of vast fields becoming thinner and thinner, while the worm, constantly increasing in size, assumes at last an unctuous appearance most disgusting to behold. Arrived at maturity, a few hours only are necessary for these modern locusts to eat up all living vegetation that comes in their way. Leaving the localities of their birth, they will move from place to place, spreading a desolation as consuming as fire in their path.
>
> All efforts to arrest their progress or annihilate them prove unavailing. They seem to spring out of the ground, and fall from the clouds, and the more they are tormented and destroyed, the more perceptible, seemingly, is their power. (T. B. Thorpe, "Cotton and its Cultivation," *Harper's New Monthly Magazine*, VIII, No. XLVI (March, 1854): 447-463.

Bibliography

Manuscripts

The John Vance Lauderdale Papers. Yale University, Beinecke Rare Books and Manuscripts Library, Yale Collection of Western Americana. The collection contains a helpful description of the papers by Bruce P. Stark.

Books, Journals, and Articles

Abbott, Martin. "The First Shot at Fort Sumter." *Civil War History* 3, No. 1 (March 1957): 41-45.

Adams, George Worthington. *Doctors in Blue: The Medical History of the Union Army in the Civil War*. Dayton, OH: Press of Morningside, 1985.

Alexander, DeAlva S. *A Political History of the State of the New York*. Vols. 2 and 3: 1833-1862. Port Washington, NY: Ira J. Friedman, Inc., 1969, (Reprint from 1909).

Andrews, J. Cutler. *The North Reports the War*. Pittsburgh, PA: University of Pittsburgh Press, 1985.

——. *The South Reports the War*. Princeton, NJ: Princeton University Press, 1970.

Angle, Paul M., ed. *The Lincoln Reader*. New York: Pocket Books, 1955.

Atlas to Accompany the Official Record of the Union & Confederate Armies, Published Under the Direction of the Hons. Redfield Proctor, Stephen B. Elkins, and Daniel S. Lamont, Secretaries of War. Compiled by Capt. Calvin D. Cowles, 23d U.S. Infantry. Washington, DC: Government Printing Office, 1891-1895. Reprinted by The Fairfax Press, New York, 1983.

Auchincloss, Louis, ed. *The Hone & Strong Diaries of Old Manhattan*. New York: Abeville Press, 1989.

Battles and Leaders of the Civil War, Being for the Most Part Contributions by Union and Confederate Officers, Based Upon "The Century War Series," edited by Robert Underwood Johnson and Clarence Clough Buel, of the Editorial Staff of "The Century Magazine." Part 1: From Sumter to Shiloh. New York: Castle Books, 1956. (Reprint of New York: The Century Magazine, 1887-1888.)

Berlin, Ira, ed. *Freedom: A Documentary History of Emancipation 1861-1867, Selected from the Holdings of the National Archives of the United Stated, Series 2: The Black Military Experience.* Cambridge, England: Cambridge University Press, 1982.

Boatner, Mark M., III. *The Civil War Dictionary.* New York: David McKay Company, Inc., 1959.

Bowman, John S., ed. *The Civil War Day by Day.* New York: Dorset Press, 1989.

Brooks, Stewart. *Civil War Medicine.* Springfield, Il: Charles C. Thomas, 1966.

Cadwallader, Sylvanus. *Three Years with Grant,* ed. Benjamin P. Thomas. New York: Alfred A. Knopf, 1961.

Carrison, Daniel J. *The Navy from Wood to Steel, 1860-1890.* New York: Franklin Watts Inc.,1965.

Catton, Bruce. *The Centennial History of the Civil War, Volume 1: The Coming Fury.* Garden City, NY: Doubleday & Co., Inc., 1961.

———. *Grant Moves South.* Boston, MA: Little Brown & Co., 1960.

Civil War Naval Chronology: 1861-1865. Compiled by the Navy History Division, Navy Department. Washington, DC: Government Printing Office, 1971.

Cook, Adrian. *The Armies of the Streets: The New York City Draft Riots of 1863.* Lexington, KY: The University Press of Kentucky, 1974.

Cumming, Kate. *Kate: The Journal of A Confederate Nurse,* ed. Richard Barksdale Harwall. Baton Rouge, LA: Louisiana State University Press, 1959.

Dammann, Gordon. *Pictorial Encyclopedia of Civil War Medical Instruments and Equipment,* 2 vols. Missoula, MO: Pictorial Histories Publishing Company, 1983, 1988.

Davidson, Marshall B. "A Royal Welcome for the Russian Navy." *American Heritage* 11, No.4 (June 1960): 38-44.

Davis, William C. *First Blood: Fort Sumter to Bull Run.* Alexandria, VA: Time-Life Books, 1983.

———, ed. *The Image of War 1861-1865,* 6 vols. Garden City, NY: Doubleday, 1981-1983.

———. *Memorabilia of the Civil War*. New York: Mallard Press, 1991.

Elmore, S.E., and H.M. Lyman. "The Florida Expedition," *Williams Quarterly* 4, No. 3 (March 1857): 293-329.

Faust, Patricia, ed. *Historical Times Illustrated Encyclopedia of the Civil War*. New York: Harper Perennial, 1991.

Foote, Shelby. *The Civil War, A Narrative: Fort Sumter to Perryville*. New York: Random House, 1958.

Fowler, William M., Jr. *Under Two Flags: The American Navy in the Civil War*. New York: W.W. Norton & Company, 1990.

Freedom: A Documentary History of Emancipation 1861-1867, Selected from the Holdings of the National Archives of the United States, Series 2: The Black Military Experience, ed. Ira Berlin. Cambridge: Cambridge University Press, 1982.

Gerson, Noel B. *Sad Swashbuckler: The Life of William Walker*. Nashville, TN: Thomas Nelson, Inc., 1976.

Gillett, Mary C. *The Army Medical Department 1818-1865*. Washington, DC: Center of Military History, United States Army, 1987.

Grant, Ulysses S. *The Papers of Ulysses S. Grant*, vol. 5: April 1-August 31, 1862, ed. John Y. Simon. Carbondale, IL: Southern Illinois University Press, 1973.

———. *Personal Memoirs of U.S. Grant*, 2 vols. New York: Charles L. Webster & Company, 1885.

Griffith, Paddy. *Battle Tactics of the Civil War*. New Haven, CT: Yale University Press, 1989.

Haller, John S. *American Medicine in Transition 1840-1910*. Champaign, IL: University of Illinois Press, 1981.

Harper's Weekly, A Journal of Civilization. 1861-1862.

Hay, John. *Lincoln and the Civil War in the Diaries and Letters of John Hay*, ed. Tyler Dennett. New York: Da Capo Press, 1988.

Hibben, Paxton. *Henry Ward Beecher: An American Portrait*. New York: The Press of the Readers Club, 1942.

Jenneson, Keith W., ed. *The Essential Lincoln*. New York: Franklin Watts, Inc., 1971.

Jones, Virgil C. *The Civil War at Sea: Vol 1: The Blockaders*. New York: Holt, Rinehart & Winston, 1960.

———. *The Civil War at Sea: Vol 2: The River War*. New York: Holt, Rinehart & Winston, 1961.

Kaplan, Justin. *Walt Whitman: A Life*. New York: Simon & Schuster, 1980.

Keegan, John. *The Face of Battle*. New York: The Viking Press, 1976.

Leckie, Robert. *None Died in Vain: The Saga of the American Civil War*. New York: Harper Collins, 1990.

Lightfoot, Frederick S., ed. *Nineteenth-Century New York in Rare Photographic Views*. New York: Dover Publications, Inc., 1981.

Lincoln, Abraham. *Speeches and Writings 1859-1865*, ed. Dan E. Fehrenbacher. New York: The Library of America, 1989.

Longstreet, Stephen. *City On Two Rivers: Profiles of New York— Yesterday and Today*. New York: Hawthorne Books, Inc., 1975.

McDonough, James L. *Shiloh—in Hell Before Night*. Knoxville: The University of Tennessee Press, 1977.

McKay, Ernest A. *The Civil War and New York City*. Syracuse, NY: Syracuse University Press, 1990.

Martin, David G. *The Shiloh Campaign: March-April, 1862*. New York: Fairfax Press, 1987.

Mearns, David, ed. *The Lincoln Papers: The Story of the Collection with Selections to July 4, 1861*, 2 vols. New York: Doubleday & Company, Inc., 1948.

Merrill, James M. *Battle Flags South: The Story of the Civil War Navies on Western Waters*. Madison, NJ: Fairleigh Dickinson University Press, 1970.

Miller, Francis T., ed. *The Photographic History of the Civil War*, 10 vols. New York: Castle Books, 1957. (Reprinted from 1911.)

Nevin, David. *The Road to Shiloh: Early Battles in the West*. Chicago: Time-Life Books, 1983.

Nevins, Allan. *The War for the Union. Vol. 2: War Becomes Revolution, 1862-1863*. New York: Charles Scribner's Sons, 1960.

The New York Times. 1861-1863.

Oates, Stephen B. *With Malice Toward None: The Life of Abraham Lincoln*. New York: Harper & Row, 1977.

Official Records of the Union and Confederate Navies in the War of the Rebellion, 31 vols. Washington, DC: Government Printing Office, 1894-1922.

Otis, George A., and J. J. Woodward, eds. *The Medical and Surgical History of the War of the Rebellion (1861-1865): Prepared in Accordance with Acts of Congress under the Direction of Surgeon General Joseph K. Barnes, United States Army*, 6 vols. Washington, DC: Government Printing Office, 1875-1888.

Pomeroy, Earl S. "The Visit of the Russian Fleet in 1863," *New York History* 24, No. 4 (October 1943): 512-17.

Pratt, Fletcher. *Civil War in Pictures*. Garden City, NY: Garden City Books, 1955.

Richards Atlas of New York State, ed. Edward Towle. Editor-in-chief: Robert J. Rayback. Phoenix and New York: Frank E. Richards, 1965.

Robertson, James A., Jr. *Tenting Tonight: The Soldier's Life*. New York: Time-Life, 1984.

Saxon, A.H. *P.T. Barnum: The Legend and the Man*. New York: Columbia University Press, 1989.

——, ed. *Selected Letters of P.T. Barnum*. New York: Columbia University Press, 1983.

Scharf, Thomas J. *History of the Confederate States Navy from its Organization to the Surrender of its Last Vessel*, vol. 2. Freeport, NY: Books for Libraries Press, 1969. (Reprinted from New York: Rogers & Sherwood, 1886.)

Sears, Stephen W. *George B. McClellan: The Young Napoleon*. New York: Ticknor & Fields, 1988.

Sherman, W.T. *Memoirs of General William T. Sherman*, 2 vols. New York: D. Appleton and Company, 1889.

Silver, Nathan. *Lost New York*. New York: American Legacy Press, 1967.

Simmons, Henry E. *A Concise Encyclopedia of the Civil War*. New York: Bonanza Books, 1965.

Steiner, Paul E. *Disease in the Civil War: Natural Biological Warfare in 1861-1865*. Springfield, IL: Charles C. Thomas, 1968.

Straubing, Harold E. ed. *The Fateful Lightning: Civil War Eyewitness Reports*. New York: Paragon House Publishers, 1985.

Strong, George Templeton. *Diary of the Civil War: 1860-1865*, ed. Allan Nevins. New York: The Macmillan Company, 1962.

Swanberg, W.A. *First Blood: The Story of Fort Sumter*. New York: Charles Scribner's Sons, 1957.

Sword, Wiley. *Shiloh: Bloody April*. New York: William Morrow & Company, 1974.

Thompson, Fletcher W., Jr. *The Image of War: The Pictorial Reporting of the American Civil War*. New York: Thomas Yoseloff, 1960.

Wagman, John, ed. *Civil War Front Pages*. New York: The Fairfax Press/American Ligature Press, 1989.

The War of the Rebellion: A Compilation of the Official Records of the Union and Confederate Armies, Prepared Under the Direction of the Secretary of War, by Bvt. Lieut. Col. Robert N. Scott. in 128 vols. Washington, DC: Government Printing Office, 1880-1901. Especially sers. 1, vol. 10, parts 1 and 2, 1884.

Web, Willard, ed. *Crucial Moments of the Civil War*. New York: Fountainhead Publishers, Inc., 1961.

The West Point Military History Series Atlas for the American Civil War. Series ed. Thomas E. Griess. Wayne, NJ: Avery Publishing Group, Inc., 1986.

Wheeler, Richard. *Voices of the Civil War.* New York: Thomas Y. Crowell Company, 1976.

Wiley, Bell Irvin. *The Life of Billy Yank: The Common Soldier of the Union.* Baton Rouge: Louisiana State University Press, 1990.

——. *The Life of Johnny Reb: The Common Soldier of the Confederacy.* Garden City, NY: Doubleday & Company, Inc., 1971.

Index

A

A.O. Tyler, USS, 86, 134, 215n.56;
 and Battle of Fort Henry, 86,
 214n.52; and Battle of Shiloh, 24,
 27, 86; and Battle of Vicksburgh,
 108, 113, 219n.87
Acacia, 137
Adams, William Wirt, 203, 204,
 226n.6
Agassiz, Louis, 37, 216n.62
Ambulances, confederate, *21*
Amputation: at Battle of Shiloh, 29;
 on *D.A. January*, 33, 60,133; John
 Vance Lauderdale performance of,
 170, 172; survival rate, 28
Andrews, John V., 162, 224n.25
Antietam, Battle of, 147, 222n.4
Arkansas, CSS, 113, 131, 219n.87
Ariel, SS, 146
Army Medical Department, inade-
 quacy of, 20, 24-26, 211n.30
Artillery: at Battle of Eddyville,
 108; at Battle of Island No. 10, 96,
 123; at Battle of Shiloh, 56, 68;
 demonstration of, 88; at Fort
 Columbus, 116, 117, 120, *120*,
 121, *121*, 122-23, 123; naval, 86,
 131, 159; at Paducah Marine
 Hospital, 111; shells, *123*
Artists, war, 215n.56
Atlanta, Union victory at, 184

B

Barnum, P. T., 10, 208n.7, 222n.12
Battles. *See* individual battles
Beauregard, G. T.: and Battle of
 Shiloh, 23-24, 210nn.21, 24; and
 evacuation of Corinth, 218n.72
Beecher, Henry Ward, 10, 171-72;
 Beecher's Bibles, 15; Beecher's
 Boats, 10
Bellevue Hospital, 144, 221n.1;
 Blackwell's Island facilities, 143,
 144; John Vance Lauderdale train-
 ing at, 3, 4, 34-36, 84, 132, 143,
 221-22n.2
Belmont, Battle of, 123
Benton, USS, 218n.78
Benton, Camp, 71
Bible Defense of Slavery, 103
Bissell, Josiah W., 53, 96, 214n.54
Black regiments, 173
Blair, Francis, Sr., 217n.69
Blair, Frank P., Jr., 217n.69
Brinton, John H., 21, 26, 27
Brooklyn Eagle, 224-25n.33
Brown, Isaac, 219 n.87
Brown, John, 16
Brooks, Preston, attack on Senator
 Sumner, 15-16
Buchanan, James, 16
Buckner, Simon B., 214n.52
Buell, Don Carlos, 22, 26, 52, 53

C

Cairo, Illinois, 46
Cammann, George Philip, 169,
    224n.31
Cannelton, Indiana, cotton factory at, 92
Cape Girardeau, fort at, 45-46
Carolina, 10
Carondelet, USS, 113, 214n.52,
    219n.87
Carondelet Marine Railway and Dry
    Dock Company, 221n.111; work
    at, 137-38
Chancellorsville, Battle of, 223n.16
Cherokee, 10
Chickasaw, USS, 221n.112
Chippewa, USS, 138
Choctaw, USS, 138, 221n.112
Cincinnati, Ohio, 64
Cincinnati, USS, 214n.52
City of Memphis, 26
Clarksville, Confederate occupation
    of, 136
Cleveland, Ohio, 12, 13
Collona, 114
Columbus, Ohio, 95
Columbus, Fort, 115, 116, *117*, 120-
    123, *120, 121, 122, 123*; artillery
    at, 116, 120-21, 122-23; Battle at,
    220n.105; church services at, 118-
    19; General Quinby's headquar-
    ters at, *125*, 220n.107; tents, *111*;
    water defenses at, *120*, 120-21
Conestoga, USS, 214n.52
Conrad, George, 38
Conness, Camp, *182*, 209n.11
Copperheads, 162, 179, 184, 186
Corinth: evacuation of, 76-77,
    218n.72; hospital at, 216n.59; as
    military objective, 22, 23; skir-
    mishes at, 3, 24, 74, 75, 83, 110,
    148; treatment of civilians in, 80;
    railroad lines to, 115, 116

Cotton, 99-100, 173; mills, 92; plan-
    tations, 194, 196, 204-5
Crescent City, 12, 22, 43,
Crystal Palace, 7, 207n.3
Cumming, Kate, 216n.59
Curtis, Samuel R.: army of, 98-99,
    105; headquarters at Helena,
    Arkansas, 99, 130

D

Davis, Charles H., 218nn.75, 78,
    219n.87
Davis, Jefferson, 100, 121, 177
    217n.69
Dead, burial of, 58, 59, 101
Democrats, 182, 210n.16;
    presidential candidates, 182-84,
    204, 222n.6
Dew-Drop, 13, 209n.11
Dickens, Charles: and *American
    Notes*, 221n.1
Disease: at Battle of Shiloh, 21, 48;
    wartime occurrence of, 20-22
Doctors, army, training of, 33
Donelson, Fort: battle at, 22, 38,
    214n.52; typhoid epidemic at, 21,
    25
Douglas, Stephen A., 19, 210n.16;
    Confederate opinion of, 59
Downing, Andrew Jackson, 71,
    217n.67
Draft riots, New York City, 145,
    161-65, 223-24nn.19-28
Dupont, Samuel F., 223n.18

E

Eddyville, Battle of, 108
Ellett, Charles, 98, 218n.78
Emancipation Proclamation,
    219n.83
Essex, USS, 214n.52
Exeter, 113

F

Farley, Henry S., 19-20
Farragut, David G., 219n.87
Floyd, John B., 214n.52
Foote, Andrew Hull, 123, 213n.43, 214n.52, 218n.77
Forrest, Nathan B., 214n.52, 226n.6
Fort. *See* individual fort
Foster, Stephen, 172, 224-25n.33
Fowler's Solution, 79, 218n.74
Fowler and Wells Phrenological Cabinet, 9
Frank Leslie's Illustrated Newspaper, 56, 149, 177, 215n.56
Frémont, John Charles: and 1856 presidential election, 16, 227n.7; and skirmishes at Corinth, 75

G

Gamble, Hamilton Rowan, 70, 104, 217n.66
General Beauregard, CSS, 98, 218n.78
Geneseo, 4, 18, 36, 38, 149, 158, 220n.108; regiments from, 70, 90
Geneseo Academy, 10, 14, 18, 19
Gladiator, 51, 86, 137
Grant, Ulysses S.: and Battle of Fort Columbus, 220n.105; and Battle of Fort Donelson, 21, 38, 214n.52; and Battle of Fort Henry, 53, 214n.52; and Battle of Shiloh, 22-24, 210n.19, 211n.24; treatment of sick and wounded, 25-26
Greeley, Horace, 17, 209n.12, 223nn.22-23

H

Halleck, Henry W.: and Battle of Shiloh, 22, 211n.24; and Confederate prisoners, 60, 64; and evacuation of Corinth, 76, 218n.72; treatment of sick and wounded, 26
Hamburg, 66, 67-68; hospital at, 56
Hampton Roads, Battle of, 38
Hannibal, 78, 81
Harper's Ferry, raid on, 16
Harper's Weekly, 215n.56, 223n.18
Harper's Monthly, 227n.8
Helena, Arkansas, 99, 130-31; General Curtis' headquarters at, *130*
Henry, Fort, 53; battle at, 22, 214n.52
Hewitt, Henry S., 26, 30
Hiawatha, 78
Hickman, 96
Higher Lawism, 156, 215n.57
Hindman, Thomas Carmichael, 130, 218n.80
Hoff, Alexander H.: and Army examination, 216n.61; and Confederate wounded, 64; and nurses, 31, 49; hiring of John Vance Lauderdale, 3; visit to Corinth, 77
Home Journal, 64
Hooker, Joseph, 158, 223n.16

I

Irish Brigade, 38
Iron boats, construction of, 138
Irwin, B.J.D., 29
Island No. 10, Battle of, 53, 96, 103, 123, 214n.54, 218n.77

J

Jackson Railroad, 195
James, George S., 19-20
January, D.A., 30-31, *31*, 47, 213n.47, 219n.88; cooking facilities of, 93; crew of, 51; entertainment on, *109*; flag of, 49, 75, *75*,

217n.71; meals for sick and
wounded on, 83; model of,
211n.34; renovation of, 73, 118,
132, 137
Jefferson Barracks, 81, 105; hospital
at, 104
Johnson, Fort, 19
Johnston, Albert Sidney, 23, 39,
210n.19

K

Kansas-Nebraska Act, The, 15
Keokuk, Iowa, 81, 82; hospital at,
48, 50; rebel attack on, 114
Kickapoo, USS, 221n.112

L

Lady Franklin, 135
Lancaster, U.S. Ram, 128, 136
Lauderdale, Frances (Frank), *6*, 7,
31, 208n.5
Lauderdale, Frances Helen (daughter), 221n.1
Lauderdale, John Vance, *ii*; as amateur scientist, 12-15; appointment
as contract surgeon, 3, 4; Army
career of, 179; Army dismissal of,
139; and assasination of Lincoln,
189; birth of, 208n.5; care of sick
and wounded, 33, 48, 49, 57-58,
60-61, 62, 79, 90, 133; church
attendance, 10-11, 37, 70, 85, 94,
107, 118-19, 150, 153-54, 156-57,
208n.6, 208n.8; and Confederate
wounded, 56-57, 59, 61-62, 64;
death of, 179, 208n.5; and death of
Samuel Lauderdale, 177-78; doc-
toral thesis, 37; on the draft, 161,
165-66; as druggist's clerk, 5, 8,
12; encounters with McClellan,
145, 152, 157; and end of war, 189;
on foreign intervention, 98; illness
of, 68, 73-76, 77, 79; marriage of,

221n.1; medical training of, 34-37,
143, 145, 155, 158, 170; and
Mormons, 178; and New York
social life, 7, 8-10; physical
description, 32; on photography,
211n.36; and politics, 16, 18, 149,
179, 181-84, 185-88; on secession,
4; on slave colonization of Africa,
148-49; on slavery, 4, 16, 73; on
tobacco, 112; on *Uncle Tom's
Cabin*, 9; uniform of, 212n.37; and
Vicksburg plantation, 226n.36, on
war, 4, 104, 114, 160-61
Lauderdale, John Vance, Jr. (son),
221n.1
Lauderdale, Josephine Lane, 221n.1
Lauderdale, Marjorie, 221n.1
Lauderdale, Mary Vance, *6*, 207n.5
Lauderdale, Nettie, *6*, 208n.5
Lauderdale (Clark), Nellie, *6*, 205
Lauderdale, Robert, 208n.5,
220n.108
Lauderdale, Samuel, 38, 203, 204-5,
217n.69, 226n.35; birth of,
208n.5; death of, 177, 205; on the
draft, 224n.29; and Vicksburg
plantation, 145
Lauderdale, Walter, Jr., 208n.5,
220n.108
Lauderdale, Walter E., Sr., 4, 5, *6*,
38, 207-8n.5, 205, 220n.108; on
the draft, 191-92; and politics, 17
Lauderdale, Willis, 31, 38, 139,
226n.35; birth of, 208n.5; and
death of Samuel Lauderdale, 205;
and the draft, 104-5; and John
Vance Lauderdale, 3, 43, 51, 71-
72, 79, 80, 84, 107; marriage of,
205; and Vicksburg plantation,
145, 193-96, 198-205
Lauderdale Springs, Tennessee, 102,
218n.82
Lessovski, Admiral, 224n.30

Lee, Robert E., 189
Lexington, USS: and Battle of Fort Henry, 214n.52; and Battle of Shiloh, 24, 27
Lincoln, Abraham: assassination of, 189; Confederate opinion of, 59; and declaration of war, 20; and 1860 presidential election, 19, 183,186-87, 209n.14, 210nn.15-16; and Emancipation Proclamation, 219n.83; and the Second Confiscation Act, 113
Lincoln, Mary Todd, 149, 222n.5
Livingston Republican, The, 153, 160, 214n.51
Louisiana, 59

M

McClellan, George B., 158-59: and Battle of Shiloh, 211n.24; and 1864 presidential election, 181-82, 183, 186-87, 222n.11; encounters with John Vance Lauderdale, 145, 150, 152, 157
McDougall, Charles, 126-27, 146, 218n.73
Mackall, William, 218n.77
Mann, Horace, 9
Memphis, 97-98; Battle of, 98, 218n.78; Union sentiment at, 129
Merchantile Society Library, 9
Merrimack, CSS, 38, 220n.107
Milwaukee, USS, 138, 221n.112
Minié balls, 27-28
Mississippi River, The, 30, 44-45, 73, 94, 95, 214n.54
Missouri Free-Soilers, The, 217n.69
Mobile and Ohio Railroad, 95, 124
Monitor, USS, 38
Monroe Democrat, The, 103
Mott, Valentine, 37, 212-13n.39
Mound City, hospital at, 127-28, 132, 133

Mound City, USS: attack on, 128; explosion of, 81, 218n.75
Mt. Morris Union, The, 114
Mulligan James A., 38
Murray, Robert, 26-27, 29-30

N

Neosho, USS, 138, 221n.112
New Albany, 62
Newberry, John Strong, 13-14, 47, 209n.10, 213-14n.49
New Madrid, 96-97
New Uncle Sam, 78
New York Central Rail Road, 124
New York Daily News, The, 162, 224n.25
New York Herald, The, 149, 166, 168, 169, 170
New York Illustrated News, The, 64, 149
New York Observer, The, 53, 56, 80, 84, 108, 173, 214n.53
New York Tribune, The, 17, 161, 209n.12, 222n.6, 223n.23,
New York World, 64
New York University Medical College, 3, 34, 222n.2

O

Ohio River, 30, 91, 94; falls of, 62, 65
Osage, USS, 138, 221n.112

P

Paducah, Kentucky, 52, 89, 108; church services in, 94; marine hospital at, 111, *111*, 220n.90; political sentiments in, 110-11, stemery at, 112
Passaic, USS, 159, 223n.18
Pauline Carroll, 194, 195-96, 197
Pea Ridge, Battle of, 38
Peresviet, 169

Petersburg, Virginia, evacuation of,
  188
Phelps, S. Ledyard, 218n.78
Pillow, Gideon J., 214n.52
Pillow, Fort, 100
Pittsburg, USS, 131
Pittsburg Landing, Tennessee, 3, 22-
  23, 54, 55-56, 57; Battle of. *See*
  Shiloh, Battle of
Platte Valley, 52
Plymouth Church, 10
Polk, Leonidas, 220n.105
Pope, John, 96, 214n.54, 218n.77
Pringle, J.S. 105
Prisoners, Union, treatment of, 132
Puritan, USS, 158
Putnam's, 185

                          Q

Queen of the West, U.S. Army Ram,
  137-38, 219n.87
Quinby, Isaac F., 220nn.106-7;
  headquarters at Fort Columbus,
  124, *125*

                          R

Railroads, 95, 115, 116, 124, 195;
  travel by, 41-43
Raymond, I., 108
Republicans, 149, 181-82, 183, 186,
  210n.16, 222,.6
Richmond, evacuation of, 76, 188
Rose Hambleton, 135, 221n.110
Russian fleet, 168, 169-70, 224n.30

                          S

St. Charles, Battle of, 218n.75
St. Louis, Missouri, 44, 69, 71-72,
  85-86, 87
St. Louis, USS, 129, 214n.52
Sanitary Commission, U.S., 25, 212-
  13n.39, 213n.49
Savannah, 54, 74

Scott's Anaconda, 66, 216n.63
Second Confiscation Act, The,
  220n.92
Sevon, J.C, 193, 198
Seward, William Henry, 59, 189,
  215n.57
Seymour, Horatio, 166, 213n.40,
  222n.6
Sharpsburg, Maryland, 222n.4
Sherman, William T., 22-23, 179,
  210n.19
Shiloh, Battle of, 3, 22-24, 210n.19,
  210n.21, 210-11n.24; artists at,
  215n.56; battlefield, 55-56, 57, 68;
  care of sick and wounded, 26-27,
  29; casualties, 24; disease at, 21
Shiloh Chapel, 22, 24
Silver Moon, 94
Skylark, 136
Slocum, Henry W., 203, 226n.5
Smith, Stephen, 145, 146, 153, 172,
  222n.3
Spring, Rev. Gardiner, 11, 148,
  208n.8
Soundings, depth, 101
Sovereign, 114
Stephen Decatur, 89
Sumner, Charles, 15-16
Sumter, Fort, Battle of, 19-20

                          T

Tennessee, CSS, 15
Tennessee River, 30, 52, 81, 94, 106;
  as drinking water, 21, 68, 73
Texas Rangers, 132
Thumb, Tom, 106, 155, 208n.7,
  222n.12
Tigress, 215n.56
Tilghman, Lloyd, 214n.52
Timekeeping, ship, 134-35
Tobacco, 112
Tyler, USS, *See A.O. Tyler*, USS
Typhoid fever: at Battle of Shiloh,

48; epidemic at Fort Donelson, 21, 25; on *D.A. January*, 50, 57, 61, 63; transmission of, 216n.58; wartime occurrence of, 20
Tycoon, 78

V

Van Buren, John, 149, 222n.6
Van Buren, William H., 37
Vicksburg: Battle of, 108, 131, 219n.87; plantation at, 193, 194-95, 198-99, 200; strategic importance of, 75
Victoria, 114, 220n.93

W

Wadsworth, James S., 38, 149, 213n.40, 222n.6, 222n.9
Walker, William, 15, 209n.11
Webster, Daniel: funeral of, 10
Whitman, Walt, 9
Wide Awakes, The, 19, 209n.14, 217n.69
Winnebago, USS, 221n.112
Wood, Fernando, 162, 224n.25
Wood, James R., 155-56, 223n.13
Wounded Knee, Battle of, 179

Y

Yankee Blade, 10